Praise for *Meet Me in Gaza*

'This book penetrates the surface, the dismal images that we have become all too familiar with from news coverage of the Strip, to reveal the more human face of the place, that few have been able to experience let alone describe. Unlike any other book about Gaza, this will please, educate and inspire. It is vividly written and is infused with a love of life that the author has exhibited in all her previous writing.'

Raja Shehadeh, author of *Palestinian Walks: Notes on A Vanishing Landscape*

'Not many of us would have the courage to lay ourselves on the line and go and live in the Gaza strip. Louisa Waugh shows her extraordinary credentials for this courageous undertaking: a deep wellspring of human warmth, a tenacious ability to find the tiny spark of joy in the most dismal surroundings, an incontrovertible honesty, and then the eloquence to tell us the story and make us understand. She treads a steady line of reason through all the absurdities and horrors she encounters, and comes up with a tender portrait of beleaguered humanity.'

Chris Stewart, author of *Driving over Lemons: An Optimist in Andalucia*

'Powerful and deeply heartfelt, Louisa Waugh has succeeded in showing us the true face of Gaza. We encounter Palestinians in their living rooms, at work, in cafés, and at parties and weddings ... I urge everyone to read this.'

Izzeldin Abuelaish, author of *I Shall Not Hate: A Gaza Doctor's Journey on the Road to Peace and Human Dignity*

MEET ME IN GAZA

Uncommon Stories
of Life inside the Strip

Louisa B. Waugh

The Westbourne Press

To all my friends in Gaza ... and to Ma

Published 2013 by The Westbourne Press

Copyright © Louisa B. Waugh 2013

The right of Louisa B. Waugh to be identified as the author
of this work has been asserted by her in accordance with
the Copyright, Designs and Patents Act 1988.

The Westbourne Press
26 Westbourne Grove, London W2 5RH
www.westbournepress.co.uk

A full CIP record for this book is available from the British Library.

ISBN 978-1-908906-20-5
eISBN 978-1-908906-21-2

Printed and bound by Bookwell, Finland

Louisa B. Waugh was supported by Creative Scotland during
the development of this book.

CREATIVE SCOTLAND
ALBA | CHRUTHACHAIL

Contents

Glossary

abid [sing. *abd*] – slaves
Ahlan wa sahlan! – Welcome!
ashira – extended Bedouin family or clan
baba ghanoush – smoked aubergines mashed with onions,
  tomatoes, garlic and tahini
beit shar – traditional Bedouin tent made of black wool
dabke – traditional folk dance, popular throughout the Middle East
dunam – a dunam is equal to about 900 square metres
Eid *Mubarak!* – Happy Eid!
fawdah – chaos
fil-fil – chilli paste in oil
fitnah – temptation, chaos, trial
habibti – my dear (f)
hafla – party
hammam – steam bath
haram – from the Arabic word for sanctuary, means something
  forbidden, but Arabs use it very casually, to express shame or pity
hijab – Islamic headscarf
Iftar – the breakfast meal eaten after sunset during Ramadan
Intifada – Palestinian uprising against the Israeli occupation
Inshallah – God willing
jawaal – mobile phone
jilbab – floor-length women's coat
kabsah – rice inlaid with fried almonds, onions, sultanas and herbs,
  and served with seasoned fried meat
Khalas! – Enough!
laziza – sweet, tasty, delicious (f)
mabrouk – congratulations
maftoul – couscous infused with herbs, olive oil, lemon and chillies
al-mahlab – 'the milking station'

mahshi – aubergines stuffed with rice, meat and vegetables

malfouf – steamed cabbage leaves stuffed with rice and meat

marhaba – hello

mata'm – restaurant

mathaf – museum

muhajaba – Muslim woman who covers her head and most of her body

munaqaba – Muslim woman who wears the veil

muqawamah – local armed Hamas fighters

Nakba – lit. 'Catastrophe' (used by Palestinians to refer to the loss of their land and the establishment of the state of Israel in 1948)

narghile/shisha – traditional Middle-Eastern water pipe

niqab – face veil worn by some Muslim women

sahlab – hot creamy drink made from dried wild orchid tubers, honey, cinnamon and nuts

salam – peace

shabab – youths

shahid – martyr (used for Palestinians killed in acts of resistance against the Israeli military occupation)

shukran – thank you

sijin – prison

souq – market

sumac – crimson spice powder

Taba'n! – Absolutely! (in the sense of 'Yes, of course')

taboun – traditional clay oven

tahdiya – 'period of calm'

taqiyah – traditional white lace cap worn by Muslims

Ummi – my mother

ustaz – teacher

Yallah! – Let's go! Come on! (depending on context)

Yehud [sing. Yehudi] – Jews (often used by Palestinians to mean 'Israelis')

za'atar – blend of crushed thyme, oregano and marjoram

zanana – lit. mosquito; also used for an Israeli drone

zebiba – callus on the forehead that some Muslims have from prostrating themselves to pray

zift – lit. black tarmac; also used for something that is really bad

'*Habibti* [my dear], this place Gaza is like an ancient rock star. He has all these scars from his many battles: his friends are bad, his enemies worse – he's always in trouble ... But the stories he can tell!'

Anonymous

Human beings travelling far and wide
have turned into the very monsters
they chased off the map

Judith Schalansky, novelist and cartographer

Introduction

The beach is quiet. Most of the tables and chairs have been packed away, the umbrellas folded. The carousel has just been turned off. The humid heatwave of summer has cooled a bit and now the air's soft and warm, tinged with salt. I pass a posse of kids shrieking with joy as they splash about in the shallows. A few young men stand waist-high in the waves, their shirts stripped off and wet skin slick, bathing their horses in the healing salt water. One of them catches my eye and winks. When I wink back, he raises his face to the sky and roars with laughter.

I am weary as an insomniac, but still need to walk. I've been in northern Gaza all day, interviewing parents. Some wept while telling us about their kids; others just stared blankly at the walls and spoke in dull monologues as if they were trapped in fog. After a day like this, the beach is my sanctuary. I don't have to talk or listen to anyone here, just to the waves. I stoop and unbuckle my sandals, looping my fingers through the straps so I can carry them in one hand, then straighten up, exhaling slowly. It feels so different standing on the beach in bare feet, the soft grit squeezing between my toes. Small pleasures matter.

There are no clouds, just clear sky and a blue sparkling tide. I can see a couple of small boats bouncing through the waves. Most fishing boats here are small; the local fishermen only scrape a living from the sea, but can't imagine doing anything else. If you stroll quietly around the old port, sometimes you hear them before you

see them, singing softly as they squat on the quayside stitching
their nets. Gazans are salty people – and not only the fishermen.

I wander away from the city, heading south, the roll of the waves
lulling me into a pleasant haze. I pass a young couple strolling close
together. His open-necked white shirt looks comfortably loose and
though she's completely swathed in black, including a black face
veil, she's walking barefoot like me – and they're holding hands.
Quite daring that, for a *munaqaba,* or veiled woman. She and I
both look back slyly and I can just see her brown eyes smiling. Up
ahead a family perch on plastic chairs round an empty café table
and a few solitary men are loitering, as usual. One stands erect as a
statue, staring out at sea. Another, with a thick beard and legs like
a spider, is cushioned in the sand, so lost in his thoughts or dreams
he doesn't even notice me walk past.

I have no watch and my mobile phone is switched off, so I guess
the time by the sun. When it is poised, molten, just above the
horizon, that's my cue to start heading home. Just about to turn
around, I notice two men right ahead of me, wading out of the sea.
The younger one is lean and athletic-looking, his shorts plastered
to his skin. The older guy has a full grey beard and he's wearing
a black-and-white striped costume that stretches from his broad
shoulders almost to his knees, like a Victorian bather. I realise that
I'm staring at them, so I turn on my heel and start walking away.
But they're laughing so playfully I can't help myself, and glance
back over my shoulder – just in time to see the older bearded guy
leap up into the air, arc into a graceful backward somersault and
land perfectly light and steady on his feet.

His younger friend cheers out loud, then casually flips forward,
somersaulting onto the wet sea edge light as a cat. I stand rapt, my
mouth open like a fish. The older guy wades back into the water,
carefully rinses his hands and pauses, gazing into the sunset flames.

His friend takes off, jogging loose-limbed along the shoreline. I take off too and grin all the way home. Another small pleasure.

❦

Back in the summer of 2007 I left my home in Scotland to work for a local non-governmental organisation (NGO) in Ramallah, on the Palestinian West Bank. Local Palestinians sometimes joked that they were living under two occupations – one by Israel, the other by international aid organisations. I could see their point. From north to south, the entire West Bank was besieged by Israeli checkpoints ... and expat human rights defenders, aid workers and journalists. Between us we documented everything that moved. When Hamas launched its bloody takeover of Gaza in mid-June that year, I watched it bug-eyed on TV. Four months later, in October, I was offered a job in Gaza City as a writer-cum-editor at a local human rights centre. I was ambivalent about staying on in Ramallah and excited but jittery at the prospect of moving to Gaza. So I decided to go as soon as possible, before I lost my nerve.

Gaza is a strip of the East Mediterranean coastline. Measuring approximately 25 miles by 6, the entire Strip is slightly longer than the Isle of Wight, though only half as wide, and home to approximately 1.7 million people. I wanted to see inside its tatty streets for myself, especially now that Hamas was settling down to rule its new roost. But first I had to secure an entry permit from the Israeli military, who control all traffic, human and otherwise, entering and leaving the Strip. They don't make it easy. After waiting more than six weeks and being screened by Shin Bet, the Israel security agency, I finally got my permit in mid-December of 2007. I drove down to the Erez border crossing that straddles southern Israel and northern Gaza and walked into the Strip.

My motives for coming to Gaza were simple: I wanted to see and experience it for myself, from the inside. The big political picture is infamous, but it wasn't (and still isn't) politicians or militants who interested me. I wanted to meet ordinary people living between the shadows of Israel and Hamas and listen to their stories of street life. I wanted to know, for instance, if Gazans ever have fun. What's the food like? Is the Strip beautiful? And do TV reports actually reflect ordinary life inside 'the world's largest open-air prison'?

I spent far longer in Gaza than I expected to because I enjoyed living there much more than I thought possible. Beneath the myths that have stoked this long, slow burn of a conflict, Gaza City is also one of the oldest continually inhabited cities on earth; an ancient citadel soaked in stories. While learning street Arabic and making friends, I also found myself literally stumbling over local histories – of pilgrims, pagans, madmen, sailors, purveyors of lingerie and Bedouin – that still resonate across the Strip. And I learned that water – both salty and sweet – has flowed through Gaza's torrid history, shaping the land, its peoples and now its very survival. This book is based on the time I spent in Gaza from the tail-end of 2007 until the autumn of 2010. But more than anything, it's the story of Gaza herself; a place we have all heard of, but one that most people will never see for themselves. This sun-drenched Mediterranean coastal strip is wracked with violence, grief and political self-destruction. But it is awash with extraordinary stories and histories, salty jokes ... and the odd acrobat.

PART ONE

these days you don't kid yourself
in these dodgy alleys
where a house stood one time
domestic like a crock on a shelf
for with neither dusk nor dawnscrake
the night's twice as dark –
its double darkness
is up to no good

Walid Khazendar, Gaza poet

Hammam al-Samara

December 2007

When I first walk into the Gaza Strip, a man called Hani picks me up at the Palestinian side of the Erez border crossing and drives me to Gaza City. Hani is the accountant at the local human rights centre where I am starting work tomorrow. He looks young and cheerful, and very well fed. Gaza, on the other hand, looks grubby and battered, full of rubble and bullet-smacked buildings, and scraggy donkeys dragging carts along broken streets. Just like I expected. There are green Hamas flags flapping on every corner, women in *hijabs*, or headscarves, and ankle-length black coats, men with thick dark beards, billboards of martyrs and overflowing bins. It's like I've been sucked inside a BBC news report on Gaza and in a bizarre way it feels almost familiar, because I have seen these images so often on TV.

The first surprise is my apartment, or rather the location. Hani turns left into a side street. Suddenly the buildings are not raw, grey, concrete tenements, but pristine white mansions with turrets and balconies, surrounded by wrought-iron gates. Bougainvillea is spilling over the walls like splashed paint and the palm trees have feathery fronds.

'Wow!' I say. 'This is ... different.'

Hani has just lit another cigarette. 'You are very lucky to be living here,' he says, smoke pouring from his nose and mouth.

'What's this area called?'

'This is al-Rimal and it is just five minutes from the sea.'

He helps me drag my suitcase and bags up four flights of stairs to my new apartment. It's huge and comfy-looking, with a balcony on either side – and best of all, a red light bulb in the spacious master bedroom. When Hani stops panting we go back downstairs and he takes me to a supermarket called Metro at the top of the street so I can buy some supplies. Most of the goods on sale are in packets, the majority from Israel. I buy coffee, longlife milk, pasta and, at Hani's suggestion, bottled water. Then we drive back to my apartment.

'We will see you at the Centre in the morning,' he says, escorting me to the gate. 'Put this number in your phone. They are called Lebanon Taxis. Call them when you are ready tomorrow; it is probably better not to walk alone, just to be on the safe side. Oh, and don't drink the tap water. Buy bottles at the supermarket.'

'OK,' I say, and he leaves.

The first evening in my new apartment, there's a long power cut. I sit shivering in cold candlelight, decide I'd better get used to it and go to bed early under all the blankets I can find in the wardrobe. When I wake up, there's still no electricity. I boil water for coffee on my gas stove, have a brief wash in cold water and call a Lebanon Taxi in my stilted Arabic. When the driver pulls up at the human rights centre a few minutes later, the Mediterranean Sea is glittering at the bottom of the street. I clamber out of the taxi, then hesitate at the front door, suddenly shy as a kid at the gates of her new school. But I can't just loiter out here, so I climb the stairs, push the front door open and am immediately greeted by a young woman with loose, shoulder-length black hair.

'Welcome to Gaza!' She holds out her hands to clasp mine. 'You are Louisa?'

Her name is Joumana and she is the Centre secretary. She shows me round with gliding efficiency, introducing me to dozens of people in various offices, as though she's done this many times before. After saying *marhaba* (hello) to dozens of people, we end up at my new office, at the front of the building, just next door to Joumana's.

'You will start work tomorrow,' she says, 'take your time today.' She checks I have the number for Lebanon Taxis, repeats what Hani said about not walking the streets alone and goes back to her desk.

Unsure of what to do now, I start checking my emails. As I'm typing messages home, a man sticks his head round the door. He has messy grey hair, big grey eyes set in a thin grey face and a wide crooked smile. 'I was out when you arrived,' he says, offering me a cigarette. His name is Shadi and he invites me to join him for coffee this evening at a hotel called the al-Deira. I have nowhere to be tonight, and appreciate the gesture, so we agree to meet up. After work, I take a taxi back to my apartment. Now there is electricity, so I cook myself a late lunch and have a snooze on the couch before I go to meet Shadi.

It's dark when the taxi drops me at the al-Deira. The hotel is a surprise too: it is arabesque, filled with graceful archways, lanterns, well-watered plants and tiled stone floors where footsteps echo like memories. Shadi is waiting for me in the café at the back of the hotel, which is huge and freezing. I can hear the sea hissing outside.

'Six thousand, six hundred and sixty-six welcomes to Gaza!' Shadi stands up, grins at me like an old friend. Welcoming guests is a big deal in Palestine, and his exaggeration makes me laugh, as does his first question, which is, 'Did you bring any whisky?'

I reassure him that I had so much booze stuffed inside my suitcase, I could hear myself clinking through the Erez crossing. Shadi laughs, exposing brown, smoke-stained teeth.

'You know alcohol isn't illegal here,' – he scans the few other busy tables – 'just prohibited. We used to buy it in shops like normal people, but the government closed the shops years ago, long before Hamas. Now because of this fucking siege we can't buy anything.'

In June 2006 a posse of Gaza fighters tunnelled into Israel and snatched teenage Israel Defense Forces (IDF) conscript, Gilad Shalit. In retaliation, the Israeli government sealed the crossings into Gaza and bombed the only power plant in the Strip. Since the Hamas takeover of Gaza, Israel has steadily tightened the blockade and now, says Shadi, everything, from industrial fuel to children's hearing aids, even orange juice, is restricted or outright banned. Local supermarkets mostly sell dry goods because they don't rot or need a refrigerator.[1]

We sit in the café with our coats on, drinking steaming black tea infused with sage leaves. As we talk, Shadi is constantly checking his phone or lighting another cigarette, shifting and restless like the sea outside. He tells me he is from southern Gaza and spent five years studying economics in Algeria, but he hasn't been out of the Strip since the summer of 2006.

'I have been a human rights activist more than fifteen years now, I never stop working. If there is even a whisper in the northern Strip, I still hear it.' He speaks English like a poet.

I drain my cup and huddle inside my coat, but I don't want to go back to my cold apartment yet. A man with hollow cheeks and deep-set eyes strides over to greet Shadi, then offers me his hand too. Khalil, his name is. As he is speaking to me, a loud dull blast booms close to us. For a few seconds everything in the café stops; customers freeze in their seats, cups in their hands, cigarettes half-way to their mouths. The waiters halt mid-step ... then, just two or three breaths later, they continue bearing trays across the café and conversations bubble up again. I've never heard a bomb explode before and look from Shadi to Khalil.

'That was an air strike,' says Shadi, his voice calm.

'We should be safe here,' says Khalil, 'but we shouldn't leave for a while.' He lights a cigarette and sits down.

Five minutes later, Shadi's phone bleeps with a message: Majid Harazin, senior commander of the militant group Palestinian Islamic Jihad, has just been blown up by an Israeli rocket while driving his car near the Gaza City beach front.[2]

'Hamas has warned people to stay away from the car as there might be more explosions,' says Khalil. His phone has also just bleeped. 'But Harazin was carrying $100,000 dollars in cash when Israel hit the car. There are dollar bills on fire all around it and people are out there, chasing the money.'

The two men exchange a glance. I look around, imagining the scene outside: $100 bills burning round a charred car, a hulk of roasted flesh still slumped in the driving seat.

I excuse myself and go to find the bathroom, then wander to the front of the café, where huge sliding windows open onto a terrace. I stand out there, breathing in cold salty air. The Mediterranean is glinting midnight blue like petrol and I can see small lights blinking on the horizon. They must be fishing boats. From here they look like a rope of small lanterns loosely strung together.

I don't feel frightened. I don't know what the hell to feel.

An hour or so later, Shadi offers to drive me back to my apartment. It'll be safe now, he says. His car is parked just outside the hotel. It looks like a square biscuit tin on wheels. When I squeeze inside, the dashboard is held together with brown tape and I can't shut the passenger door. 'Don't worry,' – Shadi chokes the engine into life – 'my car is the best-in-the-West!' He leans over and slams the door on my side shut. The whole vehicle shudders and my window slides wide open. I give him a look. We both start laughing and our laughter reassures me.

Over the next few days, Joumana keeps me busy at work at the Centre, editing documents and press releases that have been translated into English and writing official correspondence. Almost every afternoon there is a press release about one or more Gazans being blown up by the Israeli military, and every night I go to bed to the pounding of bombs striking northern and eastern Gaza. The bombs don't physically frighten me, they sound far enough away – more like resonant booms than the punching detonation I heard from the al-Deira Hotel. I sleep quite well. But a small knot of anxiety embeds itself inside my guts.

I think it's probably healthy to be slightly anxious here, like having my own early warning system. I just want to manage my fear, not the other way round.

Shortly before I left the West Bank, a friend of a friend, originally from Gaza, gave me some advice. 'Worry about your own safety, but not too much – there's no point,' he said. 'Just keep your eyes open, don't do anything really stupid – and laugh as much as you can.'

After work I either go to the Metro Supermarket or take a Lebanon Taxi straight back to my apartment. From my brief look around al-Rimal, I can see that my new neighbourhood is a posh corner of the city, maybe the only posh corner there is. I need to get out more, but don't know where to go; an hour after work, dusk is already thickening and the power cuts out every night. My landlord – his name is Abu Ali[3] – has given me a little electric bar heater, but even when there *is* electricity it makes little difference. Some evenings I just crawl into bed very early, longing for a hot-water bottle.

It's almost Christmas. Winter is going to last another two months. Feels like a long time.

Shadi, my colleague at the Centre, monitors the goods that Israel allows to enter into Gaza, including fuel, as part of his job. He tells me the power cuts are just going to get worse.

'Since October Israel has been reducing fuel supplies to us. Now they have cut 30 per cent of the gasoline [petrol] we need in Gaza every day, 42 per cent of the benzine [diesel] and 80 per cent of the gas [it comes in bottles; people use it for gas stoves].[4] If this continues, then the power plant will shut down suddenly. Gaza City will be in the dark, the towns and camps in the middle areas of the Strip too. Can you imagine?' He shakes his head and swallows a bitter laugh. The Israeli government claims these deliberate shortages are not collective punishment of the population of Gaza en masse, but aimed only at Israel's 'enemy entity': Hamas and its political supporters.

Shadi and I are sitting in his small office at the Centre, in our coats. I'm smoking because the heating is off and smoking distracts me from being so bloody cold.

'There is only one place to keep warm now, *habibti*,' he says, grey eyes glinting.

'Oh,' I say, thinking here we go …

'Hammam al-Samara!'

I sit up straight. 'What – a *hammam*, a steam bath, here in Gaza?'

'Yeesss …' He rolls the word inside his mouth like a wave about to crash. 'It is in the old quarter of the city. What is his name, ah, Abu Abdullah … he has been the keeper of the *hammam* for so many years. You should go and see it for yourself.'

Muhammad, one of the Lebanon Taxi drivers, pulls up in the narrow street outside Hammam al-Samara. It is hewn from oak-coloured sandstone bricks, now rounded like well-baked loaves. A small carved sign is mounted above an arched wooden door, left open just wide enough for a streak of winter sunlight to lead the way inside. I push the door and see a staircase descending into a passageway lit by coloured oil lamps. Irresistible.

Down I clamber, making my way along the passage to another slightly open door. Inside, a man with a thick silver moustache is sitting on a wooden chair. For a moment we look at each other, then he stands up, taking his time.

'Good afternoon. Is this your first visit?' As he speaks, his moustache twitches like a little silver fish.

'Yes. Are you Abu Abdullah?'

'Indeed I am ... Welcome to Hammam al-Samara.'

I am in a large domed chamber lit with a huge iron chandelier. There's a separate resting area set back into the thick walls, rugs and piles of crimson cushions draped across-wide stone ledges. The light is soft. It feels peaceful and very, very warm.

Ten minutes later, clad in nothing but a thin cotton wrap, I step into the inner sanctum of the steam chamber. I'm lucky: I brought my stuff with me and arrived at the hours set aside for women. As I enter the chamber, a wall of wet heat hits me full force. For a moment I can't see anything, then realise half a dozen women are either crouched on low stools, scrubbing themselves, or lying on towels on the hot stone floor as though they are sunbathing.

I find a stool beside a stone basin built into the walls of the steam chamber and begin washing my body. The basin is smooth as soapstone from aeons of bathers. I tip bowl after bowl of cold water over my soapy skin. Then, red and tingling, I lay my towel down on the stone floor too and surrender to the heat. Hot water pumps steadily through the old pipes lining the walls like the beat of the human heart. I chat to the woman lying closest to me, both of us dozy as cats. After she leaves, I lie there sweating until my skin feels newborn and my bones soft as oil.

When I finally stagger out of the steam chamber, the woman is still sitting in the changing room, fully dressed, stubbing out a cigarette. She offers me one and laughs as I collapse onto the bench.

'Come back next week, *habibti*,' she grins at me through a veil of smoke, 'this is the best thing we have in Gaza!'

When I eventually emerge, flushed and damp, Abu Abdullah is in his chair. He asks me if I've enjoyed my time. I say yes, and ask him how old this place is.

'Almost 1,000 years old. This is one of the oldest *hammams* in the whole Middle East, built in the Mamluk period. But never destroyed ...'

'How long have you been working here?'

'Forty years. But my family, we are the al-Wazirs, and we have been looking after this *hammam* for more than one century. It is part of our history.'

I pay him and thank him, then pause by the door, suddenly deeply curious about the histories and secrets soaked inside these old thick warm walls, and inside Gaza.

All I know of the Mamluks is that they were Turkish warriors, originally slaves, who once ruled this region, though I'm not even sure exactly when it was. But now that I think about it, the history of this place could be a key to understanding the violence festering here. I have plenty of time on my hands at the moment and I can spend some of it unravelling the story of this beguiling, broken place.

the *hafla*

The day before New Year's Eve one of my colleagues at the Centre takes me aside.

'We are having a *hafla* tomorrow night. Out of town. Someone will pick you up at your apartment at nine o'clock and we will drive somewhere away from the trouble. Don't tell anyone and don't bring anyone with you.'

A *hafla* is a ceilidh, or gathering. A party. This *hafla* is going to be out of town because violence is stewing between Hamas and Fatah again. New Year's Day is the anniversary of the founding of the Fatah movement, the de-facto government in the West Bank, and Hamas's political enemy. Hamas has banned all public Fatah celebrations in Gaza, claiming its activists are being harassed and detained by Fatah in the West Bank.[5]

I have been in Gaza just two weeks now, and don't know what to expect at this New Year *hafla*. At nine o'clock I am picked up just outside my apartment, as arranged, by a man called Samir and his wife. We drive north and park outside a large detached white villa. Inside, the villa is open-plan, with a sweeping staircase and a wood fire crackling smoky orange flames. There are a few other foreigners like me, and maybe thirty Gazans; most of them seem to be in couples. I'm introduced to everyone in turn – lawyers, businessmen, journalists, local UN staff, all of them elegant, wealthy-looking, confident. The host asks whether I would prefer wine, vodka or whisky. At first we sit around sipping our drinks and chatting, but soon people start getting up to dance. I hesitate, suddenly self-conscious among these strangers, until one of the men extends his hand. 'Dance with me,' he smiles.

We dance. And laugh, and get rowdy. At midnight we cheer as the men uncork bottles of champagne. There's lots of kissing – toasting the New Year and each other – before we descend on a vast spread of meats, salads, dips and warm flatbreads. Afterwards we carry on dancing for hours; a happy, sweaty rabble of men and women, laughing, occasionally stumbling, all of us enchanted. At some point I gaze around me, drunk and happy, mesmerised by the beautiful surprise of being here with these friendly, joyous people.

Despite its blighted history of being invaded and occupied over and again, there have been golden times too, when Gaza flourished and everything seemed possible. Perched at the edge of the eastern Sinai, the ancient crossroads between North Africa, the Middle East and Mediterranean Europe, Gaza was a lodestar of the medieval spice trade, once the most lucrative business on earth. For at least ten centuries Arabian merchants crossed the Rub' al-Khali, the fabled 'Empty Quarter', with fragrant cargoes of frankincense, myrrh and other spices, bound for the port of Gaza. This thriving port, and Gaza's proximity to Egypt, made the city a renowned spice emporium. It was also renowned for its beauty: back in the sixth century, a wandering Italian traveller, remembered only as the 'Piacenza pilgrim', found Gaza to be 'a lovely and renowned city, with noble people distinguished by every kind of liberal accomplishment [and] they are welcoming to strangers.'[6] The twentieth century also saw some good times in Gaza, squeezed in between half a dozen wars and military occupations. Even now, under the shadows of Israel and Hamas, my new friends are making life more than worth living.

Eventually I flop onto one of the couches for a breather, next to a
man whose name I can't remember. He offers me a cigarette and
leans forward to light it for me. We sit side by side, smoking and
watching the dancers. Stubbing out his dog end, he leans towards
me again.

'You see what a strange life we live here!' he says, with a sharp
laugh. He tells me he is a lawyer. Has been here most of his life.
Loves Gaza but hates the politics. 'We are not fighting the Israelis
any more,' he says sadly, 'just destroying each other. You're working
here – right? You will see how beautiful and terrible this place is. I
hope they are not killing each other out there again tonight.'

He's talking about Hamas and Fatah. Political adversaries since
Hamas was created in 1987 and now violent, bitter enemies, who
goad each other like punch-drunk boxers as the roaring crowd
flinches.[7]

I have no idea what time it is when the *hafla* starts to wind down.
But it is very late when we leave the villa. We move quietly, like
burglars or absconding inmates, no lingering or banter outside; we
just slide straight into the cars and start driving back to Gaza City
in small convoys. I'm in Samir's car again. His wife has already left
and a broad-shouldered Gazan called Tariq is on the back seat. The
three of us are great friends by now.

Just a couple of minutes after setting off, we see the car in front
being stopped by two masked gunmen. Samir curses. But we can't
do anything.

'Put your cigarette out,' he says to me, his voice terse. 'They are
al-Qassam.'[8]

Al-Qassam is the military wing of Hamas. These men launch
rockets and mortars against Israel and often have day jobs as
Hamas police officers. As the car in front slowly pulls away, one

of the gunmen motions us forward, gesturing for me to open my window so he can take a good look at us. Suddenly cold sober and dry-throated, I slowly wind down the window, staring straight ahead as he stoops and glares inside the car, his rifle clenched, his face a black balaclava with slits for eyes. He fires questions at Samir.

As he stares us down, I throw a glance at him and have a sudden terrible urge to laugh. It must be the booze. I know this is a bad situation. But the gunman is very short and is wearing small gold reading glasses.

We are being held up by a myopic masked midget.

I press my lips together hard and don't make a sound until the gunman nods and Samir pulls away as I wind the window back up. Samir swears all the way back, Tariq says we're lucky and I bray with nervous laughter.

At work the next morning, the colleague who invited me to the New Year *hafla* takes me aside again and reminds me not to mention the party to anyone. These things need to be kept quiet. People here talk too much. Then he tells me that violence has poisoned this New Year in Gaza.

While we were drinking champagne and dancing to Egyptian pop star Amr Diab, militants from both sides were out on the streets battering each other. Six people have been killed, including a man aged almost 80 – Ibrahim Abu Delakh – who lived with his family in Beit Lahiya, not far from the plush white villa where the *hafla* was held. Just before midnight, Hamas police officers raided the Abu Delakh home, beat the family up and ordered them to take down the yellow Fatah flags fluttering outside their house. Minutes after the police left, a masked gang swarmed into the house, murdered the old man in front of his terrified family and tore down the flags. The police stood by. Or joined in.

moles in damp tunnels

Early evening, a week or so after New Year. I am loitering outside my apartment. The street is dark and freezing. But above me something beautiful: a luminous full moon rising into the pitch-black sky. Peering across the street, I can make out the gated buildings opposite, palm trees lining the garden paths. I'm waiting for a taxi, but Muhammad the driver is late. I hope he won't be long. It is so cold, I am pacing like an animal in a cage. A dark cage. Tonight is a mother of a power cut.

When the electricity goes off, so does the heat and hot water, so I light candles and crawl underneath a pile of blankets. The candles are cheap and thin, and melt like lard, but the shops have nothing else. The white flames cast trembling shadows across my living-room walls as I huddle on the couch, lonely and haunted. When I move from the living room to the bathroom or bedroom, the freezing draught sometimes kills the candlelight. So I'm learning to feel my way around my apartment in the pitch dark, using the cold walls as my guide as though I were blind.

I'm not the only one; Gaza is full of families sharing waning supplies of these cheap candles and fumbling around their cold rooms at night, like moles in damp tunnels. Some people can afford to run generators, but Gaza is also rapidly running out of fuel. Israel has just shut the border crossing used for deliveries of industrial fuel to the Gaza power plant. Meanwhile, Palestinian fighters are launching rockets and mortars from Gaza towards southern Israel, dozens of them, every day.

Down in the moonlit street, I rummage round in my handbag for another cigarette. I've been giving up for years, but there's no hope for me here because every man seems to smoke, many of the women too. Maybe because they spend so much of their lives waiting. Cigarette in hand, I wrestle with my lighter. I don't really want to go out tonight. I'm dog-tired and it seems the whole city is under darkness. But Saida has already invited me to visit and she says they have electricity over on the east side tonight.

I've just finished my smoke when I hear the rumble of a car, and headlights glide towards me, picking up the gentle rise and fall of the street. The taxi skids slightly as it pulls over. A man leans across and opens the passenger door. Ah, it's Muhammad the driver.

'Hello, *ya* Louisa – sorry, very busy tonight.'

At least half the male population of Gaza is called Muhammad (or Mahmoud or Ahmad, derivatives of the same name), so to avoid getting utterly confused, I give each Muhammad that I meet his own nickname. Muhammad the driver – a gracious, foul-mouthed skinhead – is one of my favourite cabbies. Another is Yasser, who has a sad face and a twin brother called Arafat.

As he steers slowly down the street to the crossroads, Muhammad and I banter. He turns right onto Martyrs' Road and heads towards the city centre just a couple of minutes away. At the next right turn, a car with no lights pulls straight out in front of us. Muhammad brakes hard and I hit the dashboard – but only with my outstretched hands. I'm not wearing a seat belt. No one in Gaza does.

'Fuck you, man!' my driver shouts at the accelerating car.

'Your language is really terrible!' I berate him, rubbing my squished hands.

'And your Arabic is very bad!' he retorts.

We both chortle. It's our running joke. Muhammad the driver learnt good English, from years of watching American action movies. So he curses like Robert De Niro. And he's right about my Arabic.

As we drive through the city centre, thick clouds start to shroud the fat moon. There are no electric lights to be seen, just silhouettes from candles and lamps in upstairs windows. The street lights are dead, the traffic lights too. We pass weary donkeys pulling cargoes of vegetables, and weary vendors selling cigarettes, cakes, fruit, vegetables and kebabs from candle-lit, stationary carts. Muhammad and I fall silent.

A circle of men are huddled by an open fire. On the next street another group of men are sitting outside at a table, playing cards by the light of a small orange lantern. A little further on, a posse of young boys has gathered around what looks like a burning oil drum. There are no women or girls to be seen. We take another corner, the taxi rattling over potholes as we pass several large warehouses and the ragged shadow of a bombed-out shell of a building. This area is desolate, with just the odd shuffling figure or stray dog, and occasionally, another car. I have never seen a power cut across an entire city like this. Gaza looks different tonight. Older and even more haggard. It feels different too – stripped to its bare bones. It is as if Muhammad and I have slipped through a portal and suddenly found ourselves sucked back in time to Liverpool or London during the Blitz.

'I feel like we're driving back in time, Muhammad.'

'We are, *ya* Louisa.'

When we reach the district of al-Tuffah – Apple district – where Saida lives, the power has been cut here too. But even in the moonlight this doesn't look like al-Rimal, where I live. The streets are narrower and the buildings look dingy and squashed together. I call Saida on her *jawaal,* or mobile phone. She gives Muhammad directions and says her sister, Maha, will wait for me outside the front gate. This is the first time that I've visited her home. When we pull up, Maha is standing beside the gate, sheltering a candle in her cupped hands. She raises the candle to beckon me and I see her serious face. Waving to Muhammad, I follow her through the gate into a small courtyard, where dozens of ceramic pots are laid out in neat rows like pieces of chess. I used to live with a potter and instinctively stoop to examine them. They're delicately hand-painted, though I can't make out the motifs in this candlelight, which makes them appear old though I can still smell the varnish.

Some 4,000 years ago, when Gaza was part of vast ancient Egypt, its local craftsmen were already known for creating fine jewellery and delicate red-and-black ceramics. But the early populations of Gaza shifted like the Mediterranean sands; waves of immigrants arrived along this coastline by land and sea, all wanting to control this strategic crossroads between empires, cultures and continents.

Some time around 1200 BC the incoming 'Sea Peoples' included fleets of vicious warriors from Crete and Cyprus who wore tasselled kilts, built their own chariots and called themselves 'the Philistines'. The Pharaohs defeated them, but couldn't oust them – and over time the land became known as Philistia, 'Land of the Philistines', the genesis of the word 'Palestine'. When the Pharaohs established a Pentapolis of five city states within Philistia, Gaza emerged as the most powerful. But foreign invaders came thick and fast, galloping along the ancient Via Maris, or 'Way of the Sea', which ran parallel to the Mediterranean. These invaders – Assyrians, Babylonians, Persians and many others – battled, conquered, slaughtered, raped, enslaved, gouged, flayed and impaled each other, and the local populations. And amid these frenzied power struggles, including clashes between the Philistines and the Israelites, ordinary Gazans got on with their lives: the fishermen fished, the potters threw their clay and girls like Maha married young and raised their kids to be proud and tough.[9] All these millennia later, a handful of traditional potters still survive in Gaza. I imagine them as men with dull skin and dry hands who spend their lives in cramped workshops with crooked, stained walls inherited from their forefathers – like this one, tucked inside an unlit courtyard in the Apple district of east Gaza City.

Maha coughs, startling me. '*Yallah* (Let's go),' she says, impatiently. I stand up and follow her across the courtyard and through a doorway with no door. As we climb up bare concrete steps, I shiver and realise the big windowpanes set into the walls have no glass and the wind is knifing straight through.

Saida is standing at the top of the stairs. The first time I met her she was wearing a headscarf, but now her dark hair hangs thick and loose down to her shoulders. She pulls me towards her and embraces me like she has lost and found me again.

'*Habibti*, welcome! Come inside – my mother is waiting for you!'

Just a few months ago, Saida was living in Ramallah, on the West Bank, where I first met her through her elder sister, Alla', whom I worked with. Alla' and Saida are both from Gaza. Alla' introduced me to her younger sister because, after nine years in Ramallah, Saida had decided to come back to her family in Gaza, while Alla' was staying put in Ramallah with her husband and two young kids.

Saida and I stand in the doorway smiling at each other. I'm touched by the way she's greeted me, but I only met her a few times in Ramallah, on social occasions, so I don't quite know what to say now. She introduces me formally to Maha, who is standing watching us.

'My sister can speak English, but she does not like to,' says Saida. Maha shrugs.

'*Habibti*!' A fat woman pads down the corridor. It must be Saida's mother. She wraps me in a big soft hug, pulling me to her enormous bosom, and calls me Leeza.

'Are you hungry?' she asks. 'I have made dinner for you.'

'*Khalas*! (Enough!) Let her come through the door and meet everyone first,' Saida scolds her mother with stern affection. 'And then we'll eat!'

Her mother sweeps me into a kitchen with red walls, several pots steaming on the stove. As we scrape chairs around the table, Saida's father and brother come to greet me too. When her father, Nadim, places his right hand over the left side of his chest, just above his heart, I instinctively step forward with my right hand extended.

'No!' hisses Saida. 'My father, he does not shake hands with women!'

Oh, shit! I blush in the dark. I know some religious men and women don't shake hands with anyone of the opposite sex outside their immediate family, or even make direct eye contact, to guard against *fitnah*, or temptation. My cheeks are hot, but Saida, her mother and Maha laugh aloud and Nadim casts me a wry smile as he retreats from the kitchen. I don't see him again all evening. In fact, I never see very much of him even though Saida and her family become my sanctuary in Gaza. It's a long time before I find out about Nadim's former life as one of Palestine's legendary footballers, who refused to play for any other team, no matter what they offered him. Now retired from professional football, he spends much of his time with his son, Muhammad – who stands in the kitchen doorway, staring, until Saida tells him to come in and greet me too.

Muhammad beams, giggles and stares at the floor, his stubby fingers clasped together. He's in his early twenties and has Down's syndrome. Eyes still cast to the floor, he tells me that he loves Fatah and Yasser Arafat. And then, as though daring himself, throws up a brief, bashful smile.

Saida, Maha, Muhammad, their mother and I eat together by candlelight in the small cluttered kitchen, our dinner a feast of chicken in rich brown broth served with mounds of *maftoul,* home-made couscous infused with herbs, olive oil, lemon and fiery fresh chillies. The chopped salad is laced with parsley and drenched in lemon, salt and more olive oil. Saida's mother – her name is Hind – heaps more onto my plate with her spoon and her meaty hands until I resort to covering my plate with my hands in protest. But I love this food.

Sated, our hands washed, we move the candles into the family lounge, which is cold as a tomb. We wrap ourselves in blankets and huddle close together, slurping tiny cups of muddy Arabic coffee and nibbling at wedges of a thick semolina cake soaked with syrup.

Hind sits down with a heavy sigh and turns to me.

'Leeza, how is my daughter Alla' and her children? I didn't see them since four years.' Hind tells me she has seen her grandchildren just once or twice since they were born. 'My eldest son is outside Gaza too, in Chicago. He's a journalist.' She hasn't seen him for five years either. Though Ramallah, where Alla' and her family live, is ninety minutes' drive from Gaza in a fast car, it might as well be Chicago. I tell Hind that I saw Alla' and the kids just a few weeks ago. They are all doing well, but they miss her. She pulls a tissue out of a box and turns her head away.

After a moment she says, her voice thick, 'You like Ramallah, Leeza?'

'Yes.'

'Life is so easy over there – why you came here?'

'Because I have a job here and I want to see Gaza for myself.'

'You think the people in Ramallah like us?'

'Some of them. Not all.'

The animosity is ingrained. When I took Arabic lessons in Ramallah, from a Gazan university student, some of my liberal West Bank Palestinian friends mocked my 'village' accent. I've heard West Bankers describe Gazans as primitive villagers and as crazies who cannot be trusted – and heard Gazans complain bitterly about West Bankers despising them and doing nothing to break this choking siege. Israel's divide-and-rule policy has helped turn Gaza and the West Bank into bitter divorcees, to Israel's own short-term advantage.[10]

Because my Arabic is basic and stilted, Saida translates most of my conversation with her mother. When Hind goes to pray in her bedroom, Saida and I sit and face each other on the couch.

'What is it like, being back here?' I ask her.

'I am happy to see my family again,' she says. 'I was away from Gaza for a long time and I really missed them. I like being close to my mother and my father – you see, they are simple people, but they are good. When I was in the West Bank, I was lonely without my family. I am not like my sister, you know.'

I can see this already. Her sister, Alla', never wears the *hijab,* has untamed curls – and a temper like the sea at high tide. Saida, on the other hand, has almost straight hair, scraped off her face and restrained with a large grip. Her face is brown and serious. She has big, dark eyes and a small scar raked above her left brow. Her voice is even and strong.

'You see our life in Gaza, *habibti*. We suffer because of the Israelis and there is nothing to do but to work and to hope our situation improves,' she says. 'I want to be happy here, but – who can be happy in Gaza? I tell you, things are worse now than before I left nine years ago. We did not have to sit at home like this before, eating our food in the dark. I don't know if coming back was the right decision for me. But I am here now.'

She tells me she trained as an economist in the West Bank. Now she's job hunting, and volunteering at another local human rights organisation, hoping they will offer her paid work. She excuses herself to pray.

While she's gone I look round the room, at the crimson couches, embroidered cushions and gold curtain drapes, and rub life back into my cold hands. Saida returns within minutes with a tray of hot sweet tea and a plate of local oranges. We share the cold, sweet segments between us and compare notes on Ramallah, which already feels like a far-away country to both of us. In Ramallah we went to different venues and mixed with very different crowds; our paths rarely crossed. She is serious and sober, with brief flashes of warm humour. I really like her.

But it is getting late, so I call Lebanon Taxis for a ride home, though I don't feel like leaving. I am comfortable here and hope they'll invite me back again soon.

The taxi beeps from the street. I stand to go and Saida stands up too. She takes my hands and says to me, almost fiercely, 'This is your home in Gaza – come here whenever you like, you are always welcome.' She hugs me again and calls her mother and sister.

'Next time I will cook *malfuf*,' says Hind, referring to another local favourite of steamed cabbage leaves stuffed with rice and meat. This lady really likes her food.

Maha escorts me back to the taxi, holding a candle stub above our heads so we don't stumble down the steps. Outside the moon glows above the still dark and silent streets.

After that evening, Saida calls me most days, 'just to know you're OK, *habibti*.' Often we meet up after work, in the al-Deira Hotel café, just down the street from my office. We sit in our coats, drinking thick strawberry juice from the glut of Gaza's winter strawberry harvest, or *sahlab*, a hot creamy drink traditionally made from dried wild orchid tubers, sweetened with honey, cinnamon and nuts. Sometimes Saida smokes a narghile water pipe that bubbles and perfumes the air around us with apple-scented smoke. She is as stern with me as she's protective, but occasionally lets herself go for a moment, throws her hands up into the air and bursts into laughter.

Outside, just beyond the hotel terrace, the Mediterranean sparkles and rolls. We can see the decrepit, picturesque port, a modern version of the ancient port that stood just north of the city, where pagans once worshipped their god of fertility, Dagon.

Every day is clear, cold sunshine, only a rare cloud in the sky. No one told me Gaza could be so beautiful.

When we get fed up sitting around the al-Deira, Saida takes me shopping. We stand at the roadside, she flags down an ancient yellow six-door Mercedes and we squeeze inside with the other women on the back seats. It is a public taxi, ferrying people around the city for 2 shekels a ride, about 30 pence.[11] This is my first ride in a public taxi, and the only thing that happens is that lots of people smile and say *marhaba* to me. Ten minutes later we climb out. Saida takes my hand in hers, guiding me like a child amid the crowds in a busy local shopping street and through the mouth of an unlit alley that spits us out into a long, narrow food market.

'This is Souq al-Zawiya, and it is a good place for fresh fruit and vegetables, *habibti*,' she says as we step over and around thick wires from small diesel generators roaring all around us, like angry beasts illuminating the *souq*. We wade through the crowd, Saida still firmly clasping my hand. When she stops to buy vegetables, I browse nearby. The swarthy traders are selling beef tomatoes and strong onions, trays of black olives slicked in oil, aubergines, red and green peppers, sheaves of parsley, dried herbs, herbs in oil – and pyramids of local strawberries so perfectly ripe I can still smell them through the heavy odours of sweat, piss, meat, mint, sage and rotting vegetables.

I buy a bag of silver-green sage leaves to drink with my tea, and a dollop of *fil-fil*, a red chilli paste in oil that comes in a little plastic sac. Saida says it will flavour fried vegetables and chicken, 'but only use a little, *habibti*,' she warns me, 'you are not Gazan and it tastes like fire!'

When we emerge from the *souq*, the sudden darkness startles me. It looks so late, I check my mobile for the time. It's only 6.30 in the evening, but it looks and feels like midnight. Saida and I are on a long street, lined on both sides with small stores selling clothes and scarves, and black, floor-length *jilbab* coats for women. Again I feel a visceral sense of being sucked back in time. As we start walking, I see these stores are all candlelit, each filled with shadows like those that haunt my living room.

❧

An evening or two later, I am in my apartment finishing my dinner, wishing I had listened to Saida and gone easier on the *fil-fil*. My mouth is on fire and I'm gulping bottled water like a thirsty crow, letting it trickle straight down my chin and neck. Wiping my mouth, I go into the kitchen, turn on the tap and let the water run, to see if it might be OK for boiling. But it smells slightly dank, as usual, so I use more bottled water to make a brew, then settle down in front of the television. We have electricity right now, so I can watch the news on Al Jazeera International.

The news fascinates me because Gaza is always in it, and for the first time I can judge for myself how it reflects day-to-day realities inside a 'war zone'. So far it reminds me, more than anything, of a trailer for the kind of action movies that Muhammad the driver watches – brief clips of drama, violence and tragedy, all strung together by a narrator with a deep, grave voice.

'The only power plant in the Gaza Strip is scheduled to shut down in one hour.'

As the TV camera slowly pans across the brightly lit news studio and settles on the Al Jazeera newsreader – he's dapper as a game show host – I remember my colleague Shadi warning me that Israel has now stopped all deliveries of industrial fuel to Gaza, and the power plant is spent. The newsreader opens his mouth, but just as he's about to speak to camera, there is a soft *pop* and the screen blinks shut like an eye.

I am in a dark apartment on a dark street in a city with no power. The blackness is thick as sauce. The small knot of anxiety pebbles in my guts. Why the fuck did I choose to come and live here? But there's nothing to do right now, except reach for my matches.

Someone knocks at my door.

'It's open.'

I am four floors up and don't bother locking my front door, except at night, and even then I sometimes forget. It's bombs that worry me here, not burglars.

'They shut the power station and I want to see if you are OK.'

It's my landlord's son, Ali, who lives with his wife just across the landing. Sometimes he and I sit and smoke a cigarette or two together.

'I'm fine. Come on in.'

Ali is carrying a candle. The tip of his cigarette glows red.

'Come – look out of your kitchen window at our city,' he says.

I follow him into my kitchen, touching the walls to make sure they're still there. We stand at the window together, gazing across the city, where a sea of tiny candles are flickering, as though we are in a ship slowly sinking beneath the waves.

sun and moon letters

At work the next morning I am asked to draft an appeal to the 'international community', urging them to pressurise Israel into immediately resuming fuel supplies to Gaza. Seven hundred thousand people are now without mains electricity. Gaza City's biggest hospital – al-Shifa – has patients on kidney dialysis, and premature babies in incubators, whose lives depend on generators for which the hospital has no spare parts and barely any fuel. Bakeries have shut down because there's no fuel for the ovens. The Gaza Ministry of Religious Affairs is appealing for emergency supplies of concrete for a new cemetery, saying it is running short of space to bury the dead.

I spend an hour at my desk, drafting the appeal. Whoever this amorphous international community actually *is* – and I'm really not sure – it has boycotted Gaza and the Gazans ever since Hamas won the legislative elections in January 2006. So I don't feel too hopeful. It's a bit like writing an appeal to God.

When I look up from my screen, Shadi is standing in the doorway, smoking.

'I came to see if you are OK,' he says.

'Thanks – but I'm fine. You OK too?'

'We are used to this in Gaza.' He offers me his grey, mocking-the-situation smile.

Shadi is always looking out for me, always inviting me for coffee with him and his friends at the al-Deira Hotel, and giving me a lift

home in his 'best-in-the-West' old banger afterwards. I've been to
his home too, and shared supper with his wife and three children.
His eldest son is a teenage rapper, his wife is a therapist. Among
his family, Shadi seems somewhat mellower; he sprawls on the
couch and slows down for a little while – until his phone rings
and he immediately fumbles for his car keys. Wherever I see him,
he's always deliberately and defiantly cheerful. But this morning
his face is drained.

We publish the appeal that afternoon. Then we all go home.
Twenty-four hours later Israel allows limited shipments of fuel to
enter Gaza and the power plant partially reopens. But the acute
sense of uncertainty still grips the city. I can almost feel Gaza
holding its breath, like a bolshy teenager with a broken face, hoping
his father's mood will be better tonight.

When the electricity has come back on, I decide to make more use
of my time off work and take Arabic lessons. Joumana, the secretary at the Centre, offered me Arabic lessons when I first arrived,
but I didn't take her up on it. But now my lack of Arabic is really
starting to cramp my style. I want to hold my own with my new
friends and their families – like Saida's mother, Hind – and to meet
Gazans who don't speak English. So I ask Joumana if I can arrange
these lessons and she gives me the number for Mounir, the *ustaz*, or
teacher, that the Centre employs to tutor its foreign staff. I'm the
only foreigner at the Centre right now, but there have been a string
of others before me. I call *Ustaz* Mounir and we arrange a lesson at
my apartment after work on Sunday.

Mounir arrives bang on time. I buzz him through the gate, but
it's a good few minutes before he knocks at my fourth-floor front
door. When I open the door, he's outside, breathing heavily.

'Eighty-eight stairs. You live at the top of your building.'

He doesn't look, or sound, very happy to be here. I invite him inside, offer him an armchair and ask if he'd like some tea. 'Yes, please,' he replies without smiling.

His blue suit is slightly too big for him, his eyes are very dark and his gaze hard. I serve us both tea infused with sage and watch him spoon three heaped sugars into his glass mug. Resting the mug on the coffee table, Mounir unpacks sheets of exercise papers and a large notebook from his briefcase.

'I have been teaching Arabic to foreigners for more than fifteen years.' He sounds righteous as a judge. 'Have you studied our language at all?'

'I had some lessons while I was living in Ramallah.'

'So what can you say?'

Clearing my throat, I start speaking. But I'm immediately self-conscious, stumbling over words and phrases that I'm familiar with, because this feels like an exam. I pause, lose my train of thought, then pick up the thread again. I feel myself blushing. Oh, shit.

Mounir holds his pen poised but writes nothing, merely watches and listens intently, asking me to repeat some words. Then he is silent. I look down at the carpet, which is red and brown and swirly, total 1970s kitsch. I'm not sure I really want these lessons.

'Your problem is that your first Arabic teacher was an amateur,' he states. 'So we are going to have to start right back at the beginning.'

My first Arabic teacher – Sharif – was from Gaza. He is Saida's cousin, but I met him while I was in Ramallah. He was studying journalism at Beir Zeit University, just outside Ramallah, and teaching Arabic to foreigners like me to support himself. Sharif left Gaza in 2005, after securing a permit from the Israeli authorities to travel to Ramallah for just twenty-four hours. By the time I met him, he had been in the West Bank for two years without a permit. This left him in the surreal, and lousy, predicament of effectively being an illegal immigrant in his own country; at constant risk of being stopped at an Israeli checkpoint in the West Bank and sent straight back to Gaza.[12] He travelled the few miles between Ramallah and Beir Zeit University every day, but never any further.

'I escaped from one prison, and here I am inside another!' he laughed bitterly during one of our lessons.[13] He was 22 years old – though he looked about 16 – and missed his family badly, but couldn't risk visiting them because he was afraid Israel would not allow him to leave Gaza again, and then the education his parents had saved for would be ruined. Sharif didn't want me to go to Gaza. He said it was a prison filled with broken people and shattered dreams.

Mounir is pulling no punches about his opinion of my first teacher. But he's right. Sharif was an amateur. Glancing at his wristwatch, Mounir puts down his pen.

'Excuse me, I have to pray now,' he says.

I nod and sit back on the couch as he unlaces his shoes, places them neatly beside the chair, kneels, then prostrates himself on the carpet, softly praying aloud. He appears completely at ease, worshipping in front of me as the muezzins' call echoes through the streets. There is literally a mosque on every corner of Gaza and I often see men unfurling prayer mats and kneeling to pray on street corners.

A few minutes later, his prayers finished and shoes re-laced, Mounir sits back down and for the first time he smiles at me.

'Your colleagues at the Centre tell me they call you *Louisa Laziza*,' he says. 'Do you know what it means?'

I do. My nickname at work is a gentle play on words. *Laziza* means sweet in Arabic and rhymes with my name, so it's stuck. I like it. Compared with most of my previous nicknames, it's a gem.

Now we are both smiling and the atmosphere between us feels easier. Mounir asks me again, more gently this time, to speak in Arabic. At first I still stumble, searching for the correct words in the right order, but with him prompting me I slowly describe a recent evening in a nearby café with some friends, and walking home afterwards just as the power went off for the night. With no light pollution and no moon, the stars shimmered like a mirror shattered across the black sky.

He is a good listener, my new teacher. I relax, and then of course the words begin to flow a little. But soon, glancing at his wrist-watch again, he says he has to go. Gathering his things, he pauses by the door for a moment and offers me his hand – a formal but friendly gesture. We shake briefly, standing well apart. But we have scheduled our next lesson. I've even asked for homework.

'I think you are interested in learning something about our life here,' he says, looking me in the eye for the first time. 'If you study well, I will open the doors of our beautiful language to you. And you will hear stories that will amaze you.'

Palestinians speak Levantine Arabic, a dialect of modern standard Arabic. The Levant, 'country of the sunrise', is a wide strip of the eastern Mediterranean coast, now divided between Palestine, Israel, Lebanon, Syria and Jordan.

In Ramallah, local West Bank Palestinians crack jokes about Gazan peasants with rough accents (and about men from Nablus in the northern West Bank being closet gays and those half-wits from Hebron [in Arabic, al-Khalil] down in the southern West Bank). Gaza lies just 25 miles from the southern West Bank as the crow flies, but the local accent here is tinged with inflections from neighbouring Egypt.

Ustaz Mounir tells me what he thinks. 'We Gazans do have a slight accent from our Egyptian neighbour,' he says during one of our lessons. 'But our Arabic is softer than the Egyptians', more like the language of the Lebanese and the Syrians.'

Arabs are Semitic people, originally from the Arabian peninsula and its surrounding area. In some ancient Semitic languages, 'Arab' can mean the desert, a raven, a nomad or the verb to mingle. Arabic, the language of the Arabs, is the most widely spoken living Semitic language, its history pre-dating Islam by centuries. Inscriptions of Arabic texts from at least 200 BC have been unearthed in Saudi Arabia. The earliest known Arabic literature was poetry, and the pre-Islamic poets included the Su'luk – rebellious, ragged vagabonds who wandered the deserts of northern Arabia reciting verses in praise of solitude and railing against the conservative confines of tribal life. Some Su'luk began their recitals with a mournful 'standing at the ruins' prelude, evoking a beloved's scorched desert home. Many of the ancient Semitic languages eventually died out or became merely ceremonial. But from the mid-seventh century AD onwards, Arabic flourished alongside the dramatic rise of Islam.

The different histories of Gaza have been laid one over the other, like layers of rich sediment. It's easily forgotten, but before the Muslims swept in, most Gazans were actually Christian. And before Christianity they were pagans, with domed temples across the city dedicated to deities like Dagon, whom they worshipped first as a symbol of fertility, later as the god of rain, grain and fishing. Christianity arrived in Gaza in the first century AD – after all, Jerusalem was just up the road, so to speak. But it wasn't until the end of the fourth century that Gazans began taking the religion seriously, following the arrival of a zealous, middle-aged Orthodox Greek bishop called Porphyry,[14] who obtained an imperial decree to destroy Gaza's eight major pagan sites.

When the Christians torched the main Pagan temple with pitch, sulphur and fat, it blazed for days. Afterwards, beating back the pagans with clubs and staves, they used the blackened temple stones to pave the city streets and built a church over the heathen ruins – where, to this day, Gaza's small Eastern Orthodox community congregates every Sunday. Though some Gazans were converted by these violent tactics (or faked it to save their own skins), many Gazans despised this pious new religion being forced down their throats. Pagans rioted inside the city, slaughtered groups of priests and nuns and fed parts of the bloated, stinking corpses to the local pigs. The surviving Christians were undeterred; persecution was part of their mission. How do you defeat men for whom death is an act of faith?

Mark the Deacon, a thin-lipped monk who arrived in Gaza with the Greek bishop, came upon local pagans who doggedly refused to accept Christianity. He described them boldly worshipping a life-size marble idol in one of the city squares. It was, he said, the 'image of a nude woman, with her pudenda exposed – [and] held in high esteem by all the citizens, especially the women who kindled lights and burned incense in its honour.'[15] This voluptuous beauty, with her rope of golden hair, was Venus Anadyomene, 'Venus Rising from the Sea', the pagan goddess of love and sexuality, who shared her devotees' dreams and inspired women to find good men as husbands. Mark the deacon was having none of it. He stoutly declared that when a holy crucifix was held in front of the naked idol, she shattered to smithereens.

Back in the present, Mounir has suggested two Arabic lessons a
week. And he does indeed take me right back to the beginning,
guiding me through the three vowels and twenty-eight consonants
of the modern standard Arabic alphabet. The consonants are divided into two groups of fourteen, known as sun and moon letters. Basically, sun letters assimilate with the preceding article and
moon letters do not. Mounir is a grammar fanatic. When I groan,
he shakes his head.

'If you do not understand the grammar, Louisa, you will never
grasp this language. You think it is hard but it is not. Arabic is pure
logic. Learn the logic.'

But he sometimes smiles now during our lessons. And I do my
homework because I like the challenge and am determined, damn it,
to crack the grammar. I enjoy Arabic because I love the way it sounds
and the way that Arabs feast on words the same way they feast on
their food. Arabic is poetry; how else do you describe a language
which has a word – *m'nowrah* – to describe a woman who is shining;
and a name like Bassem, meaning 'he who is so often smiling'?

But Gazan Arabic is salty too; tinged, like every aspect of life here,
by the Mediterranean. Mounir surprises me one lesson by asking
whether I know any local insults.

'If you ever have trouble on the streets with *shabab*, you might
need a few strong words,' he says with the merest spark of a twinkle
in his hard eyes. *Shabab* are youths, and in Gaza, like everywhere
else in the world, they loiter, spit and curse on street corners.
There are a lot of Gazan *shabab* (the median age here is just 17
and three-quarters of the population are aged under 25), but they
rarely bother me. I know some filthy Arabic words by now, but
censure myself, telling Mounir I'm familiar with just one or two of
the classic insults, such as '*Ishrab min al-bahr*' – Go drink from the

sea – which basically means, 'Go to hell!'[16]

He nods. 'Yes, we've been saying this in Gaza for so many years. But my advice, if any of the *shabab* are bothering you, is to tell them "*Igliboh*" and I'm sure then they will leave you alone.'

'What does it mean?'

'Capsize!'

My twice-weekly lessons with Mounir are a mixture of grammar and conversation. Despite being almost the same age, we are in many ways polar opposites. He is a conservative, religious, married Muslim in his early forties, and father to five children. I'm in my late thirties, unmarried and nomadic, with no children and no orthodox religion. But we are both curious people who ask a lot of questions and we always find lots to talk about.

Mounir is proud of the differences between Arab and Western culture.

'We Arabs are not Westerners and I don't think we should imitate Western culture or be expected to imitate it,' he says. He is passionate about the communality of Arab culture, and traditional male respect for modesty among women, and believes all Muslim women should cover their hair. His wife is a *muhajaba* (a Muslim woman who covers her head and most of her body) and he says she sometimes chooses to wear the *niqab*, or face veil, too.

'Before I was engaged to my wife, I told her parents that I could not marry a woman who didn't cover her head in public,' he tells me during one of our lessons. 'Her parents told me they could not allow their daughter to marry a man who doesn't go to the mosque regularly to pray. We were all in agreement, including my wife. I attend the mosque and she never goes outside without her head covered, out of respect for herself and her religion.

'You know, I have visited your country, Louisa. I was in London about five years ago – and I was not impressed with the way that men treat women in Great Britain. I think many of the British men do not respect women. The freedoms that you have in England and Europe are the freedoms that men want you to have for their own benefit – and what kind of freedom is that, really?'

'I know that men do not always respect women in Britain, *Ustaz*. But I still feel free there. I don't think women here in Gaza have much freedom. Men tell them how to live.'

'Yes, women have less freedom here. But we treat them with more respect.'

'So why can't women have freedom *and* respect, *Ustaz*?'

'I told you, our culture is different.'

We both stand our ground in these discussions about sexual politics that we never call sexual politics. Sometimes I get frustrated, and occasionally really pissed off, with Mounir, for his conservative patriarchy and traditional views of women. He gets frustrated and pissed off with me too. Sometimes we both raise our voices, insisting on being heard. But we carry on talking and listening to each other. One of the reasons I enjoy his company is because he's *not* a liberal, and very often we don't agree with each other. I like the challenge and I'm learning a lot about Gaza from him. Many of our debates, which flow from Arabic to English and back again like the local tides, take place in candlelight. Often there is no electricity when Mounir arrives, or else it cuts out within the first few minutes of our lesson. He tells me how lucky I am to have electricity when I come home from work. In his home, near Jabalya refugee camp, they get their ration of electricity late at night, after his family have all gone to bed – and he can't afford to buy a generator.

'We Gazans used to dream of freedom,' he says. 'Now we dream of having electricity and enough fuel to make dinner on our kitchen stoves.'

Almost 70 per cent of Gazan families are refugees who were expelled from other parts of Palestine by the Zionists in the years leading up to the 1948 establishment of the state of Israel. Registered Palestinian refugees receive assistance, protection and advocacy from the United Nations Relief and Works Agency (UNRWA). There are eight refugee camps across the Gaza Strip.[17] Jabalya camp, where Mounir comes from, is up in northern Gaza. After he was married, Mounir taught in a local Jabalya camp school and he and his wife saved to build their own home outside the camp, the ambition of many young couples from refugee families.

'You cannot imagine how hard life was in Jabalya camp,' he says. 'Really we lived in fear, especially during the second intifada. So many times I was frightened that my wife and children would be killed in front of me.'

I've been to Jabalya camp, a sprawling ghetto of more than 108,000 people crammed into just over half a square mile – and a traditional Hamas stronghold, where militants use open areas around the camp to launch rockets and mortars towards southern Israel, and where the Israeli military strikes with an iron fist. It is a concrete jungle with no trees, where children grow up with fearful parents inside anxious walls.

'I worked hard and saved hard,' Mounir continues, 'and finally a few years ago I was able to build my own house and we moved out of the camp. We have to stay near Jabalya camp because the rest of my family is there – and in our culture families stay together, or near to each other. I do not want to live on the other side of Gaza from my family. But now we are in Beit Lahiya and it's a better place to live. But I have been kept awake so many nights in Beit Lahiya too.

'I have five children now, and there have been times at night when the situation with Israel was so bad I thought we would be killed in our beds. Some of those times I told my wife to dress the children, and we left the house and got into my little car and we drove away from the north in the middle of the night. Because my family is all in Jabalya, and my wife's family is from Egypt, there is nowhere else for us to go – nowhere safe to protect my wife and children from what might happen. We have slept some nights in my car on the street in Gaza City, in these streets near your apartment – because this is the safest place in Gaza. Can you imagine the feeling of knowing you can't even protect your own children? It is like being eaten by fear.'

That evening, after Mounir has gone, holding onto the banister so he doesn't topple down the dark stairs, I sit alone on my couch as the candle burns down, picturing a man spending a night in a car with five cold children, his wife too scared to cry as explosions rock the streets around them. I stub out my cigarette, thinking how darkness takes many different forms.

Towards the end of winter, a Palestinian blows himself up in a shopping centre in the Israeli city of Dimona, dismembering an elderly woman as she is making her way to her local bank. This is the first Palestinian suicide attack inside Israel for more than a year and it really rattles me because I do not hear a word of pity for the dead woman from anyone. I do not hear people rejoicing at her killing or celebrating the death of a Palestinian *shahid*, or 'martyr'; I just hear them hoping the suicide bomber is not from Gaza. Because if he is, then God help us, they say: Israel will make everyone here inside Gaza pay for it. During our next lesson, I blurt out my agitated confusion to *Ustaz* Mounir.

'All killing is wrong,' he says, 'including killing Israelis. This was not a good Muslim.'

He is the only person I hear condemn the suicide bombing.

With three hours tuition a week, and so many lessons devoted to conversation, my Arabic does really start to improve. And so does my confidence about walking the streets and interacting with people I meet along the way. I greet people easily and get to know many of the local shopkeepers by name. At the Centre my colleagues notice the difference too. I can banter with them in Arabic a little – and even answer them back. Every day I learn a few new words. It is like having another sense begin to fully awaken.

On my way back home from work one afternoon, carrying a bag of fresh warm pitta breads from the bakery just down the street, I pass by a posse of *shabab*. I've seen this lot before, but this time I can hear them egging each other on until one shouts, 'Nice arse!' The others start braying like the local donkeys and soon they join in too: 'Nice-arse-nice-arse-nice-arse ...!'

I stop dead in the street. Turning on my heels, I remove my sunglasses and stare them down. Then I launch into a slow, loud tirade of Arabic.

'Is this how you speak to women in Gaza – with no respect at all? *Haram*! Shame on you! If only your mothers – and your fathers – could hear you now ...'

I'm really quite enjoying myself. But the posse are staring at me, bug-eyed, their feet glued to the pavement. I take a slow, deliberate step towards them.

'Now listen to me – don't you ever dare speak to a woman like this again. *Igliboh*!'

Their jaws hit the ground. And to a boy they all apologise for being so rude.

even the foreigners are escaping!

One morning at the end of January, Hamas blows up the southern Gaza border with Egypt. The operation is well planned, brilliantly executed. Sections of the 12-metre-high fence are detonated one after another until it lies in a concertina stretching for more than three and a half miles. By the time I get to work, just after 8.30 in the morning, thousands of Gazans have already poured across the border into northern Egypt. My colleagues are hanging out in reception, smirking like teenage joyriders.

Shadi struts across reception, beaming about the busted border.

'You heard the news? Six thousand, six hundred and sixty-six *mabrouk* (congratulations) to Gaza! Hamas has suddenly broken the prison walls!' His smile is radiant as a sunrise.

We try to work. But everyone is too gleeful and we can't settle at our desks. The impossible has been done and the air is charged with possibilities. We are all nervous, restless and excited. I keep imagining what the atmosphere must be like down at the border – the elated crowds spilling over into Egypt, seizing the day. Gazans are always saying they live in a *sijin,* a prison, and local resentment against Hamas is slowly gathering because for all their firebrand rhetoric, nothing is changing inside this siege. Now, for once, they have delivered.

In the early afternoon, I get a call from Tariq, who I met at the New Year's Eve *hafla,* when we encountered the masked midget. Sometimes he and I have coffee together in the evening at the al-Deira Hotel. Tariq is a chain-smoker with the body of a rugby player; he works for one of the local UN departments and this evening he too is crossing to Egypt.

'You want to come with me, *habibti*?' he asks.

'I can't,' I tell him, catching the reluctance in my own voice. But my colleagues have warned me not to go to Rafah. The Egyptians could start re-sealing the border at any moment, the Israeli military might get involved and the whole thing could burst like a piece of overripe fruit into a bloody clash. I have a job here and am expected at my desk first thing tomorrow morning. I really cannot join him.

❧

Late that evening: a white ear of moon suspended in the black sky. We walk slowly forward, keeping the pace of the crowd. Thousands of us are clambering over the concertinaed fence; the atmosphere is like a huge carnival, the air charged not with anxiety, but laughter and shouting. Round-shouldered old men and women hobble, clutching the arms of youngsters who lead them tenderly, like lambs. Whole families have come out to share the joy of tonight's walk into another country.

I clamber down from the fence with a little jump and Tariq and I make our way over the wasted no-man's-land between Gaza and Egypt, past lines of Egyptian soldiers brandishing riot shields, yet passive as waxworks. For the first, and almost certainly the only time in our lives, we walk across a fortified international border without papers. And congratulate each other with tears in our eyes. I had to see this for myself, I just had to.

The city of Rafah is divided between Gaza and Egypt in more or less the same way that Berlin (where I was born) used to be divided between East and West Germany, with houses on each side of the fortified border lying within sight of each other.[18] On the Gaza side, the houses are so bullet- and mortar-spattered they look pebble-dashed. Some look half-eaten. The Egyptian side of Rafah is smaller, and between the two is the 12-metre-high border fence that imprisons Gazans inside the Strip. But now most of the fence is lying on the ground, buckled and useless as a crashed car.

At the end of no-man's-land we enter Egyptian Rafah. I have never seen so many people swarming in a single street, so many trucks bulging like obese men, as flocks of worried sheep and goats on rope leads are being driven back into Gaza (Israel has also banned imports of livestock). Cars, motorbikes and donkey carts are stranded in the melee as the crowds push all ways at once. For a moment the sheer volume looks like a mob and really frightens me. But then I see that amid the chaos is some kind of calm; people are helping each other, and often waiting for their turn to move. This is an exodus, not a riot.

'You all right?' asks Tariq.

'Yes, I'm good, thanks. Glad I'm here.'

We want to reach the next Egyptian town, al-Arish, because Tariq has Palestinian friends living there, so we press on down the street. Because Rafah was only divided back in 1978, most of the locals in this Egyptian half of the city are Gazans too.

I haven't seen anyone who resembles a Westerner – this story has only just 'broken' and I guess the foreign press hasn't arrived on the scene yet. With my short hair and white fake-fur coat, I feel utterly conspicuous. As we attempt to wade across the street – which right now feels like trying to part the sea – one man in all these thousands suddenly stands still, points straight at me and roars something at the top of his lungs. The crowd surrounding him all appear to turn their eyes on me at once and then erupt into guffaws of laughter that bounce across the street towards us.

What the ...?

Like a confused child to a parent, I turn to Tariq for an answer – but he's laughing so much that he is almost bent over double.

When he straightens up, he says, wiping his streaming eyes, 'That man over there, he shouted: "Look! Even the foreigners are escaping from Gaza!"'

I start laughing too. Tonight I'm a jailbreaker!

Eventually we find a minibus we can squeeze into and start the tortuous crawl south out of Rafah towards al-Arish. Our elation saps as we stare at the crowds and vehicles bottle-necked at the town entrance. My head is throbbing and my lungs sting from diesel fumes leaching out of hundreds of vehicles going nowhere.

Tariq slumps in his seat, which is too small for his big, square body.

'I'm glad we are here, to see this – but it's crazy. You know, we Palestinians used to dream of real freedom, our own independent state. And look at us now – blowing up our border to escape for a few days shopping. Pathetic.'

He pushes drooping hair out of his eyes. Tariq came back to Gaza just seven months ago. He was studying at university in the US, and returned here the week before Hamas took over the Strip. He cracks jokes about his own terrible timing. His father is Gazan, his mother comes from the Balkans. I met her once and she told me in her still-strong Slavic accent that she could live with war; people from the Balkans and Gaza, they know how to live with war. It was the imprisonment that was slowly killing everyone, she said; this siege is like sentencing people to a long, slow death.

Tariq has told me that on his way to work, he sometimes has

the overwhelming urge to keep driving his car until he reaches the border fence, then crash straight through it and just go out in flames. He lights a cigarette and offers me one, and we smoke because there is nothing else to do. I've been too caught up in the thrill of this night for any kind of reflection, but for all its audacity there is something pathetic about this crush; it's like a mass breakout of prisoners or refugees with nowhere to flee to because nobody wants them. Many are already on their way back inside. Tariq asks a man squashed beside us in the bus why *he* crossed the border this evening.

'To breathe some fresh air outside our *sijin*,' he says.

He's a Hamas policeman. His friend, sitting beside him, is a po-liceman too – but a Fatah supporter, so he is out of work.[19] The two of them say they are best friends and have just come along for the ride. They're going to al-Arish too, then back to Gaza before dawn, because the Hamas guy has to be at work in the morning. Come to think of it, so do I.

The minibus barely moves and eventually the four of us desert it. We start walking out of town and eventually find a Bedouin man with bad breath and a bashed Mercedes-Benz who agrees to take us to al-Arish for a price. Everything has its price.

Al-Arish is a small Mediterranean seaside resort 28 miles south of the Gaza border, on the road towards Cairo – but we all know that checkpoints have been erected just outside al-Arish, to make sure Gazans don't stray beyond the town. The Egyptian authorities don't have the resources to rebuild the wall for at least the next few days, but offering sanctuary to Gazans would jeopardise Egypt's brittle rapprochement with Israel – and the authorities there fear Hamas's relationship with the radical Muslim Brotherhood movement.

As he tears along rough roads with no headlights on, the Bedouin's Mercedes bucks like a horse. When we eventually reach al-Arish it's very late and Tariq and I are exhausted. But the Bedouin has mentioned a hotel with a bar in town and Tariq's thirst is now almost as great as mine. We easily find the hotel – a square monstrosity on the main street – and invite our two new policemen friends along for a drink in the bar. Which turns out to be a plush red circular salon with long drapes, frilly pouffes and two uniformed waiters who both look about 12 years old. But there is beer and gin behind the bar – and they even have ice! I ask for a gin and tonic, and when the boys look at me blankly, I just slip behind the bar and mix it myself. Tariq has a beer. The policemen both drink Egyptian-style Coca-Cola. We raise our four glasses and drink a toast to freedom, giggling about this ridiculous luxury just down the road from our *sijin*.

It is much too late to talk politics, but I can't resist asking our police escort how they became such good friends, given that one of them works for Hamas and the other for Fatah.

'We are from the same village,' says one of them. 'We have always been friends and we never talk about politics.'

'Palestinian politics is poison,' says the other. 'They want us to fear and hate each other – just like the Israelis want us to hate and fear each other. But I think for myself. That is the only freedom we've got in Gaza.'

When we leave the bar, the policemen bid us goodnight. They've seen what they came here for and are going back home now.

Hours later I wake up in the pink bedroom of a young girl who has been shunted to another bed so that I can sleep in hers. For a few seconds, I forget about arriving here after the bar and being welcomed by Tariq's friends. Instead I look around, bleary-eyed, trying to recall where the hell I am. Then remember that this is Egypt, not Gaza, and I should be at work now. I call the Centre and whine about having a bad upset stomach, saying hopefully I will be well enough to come to work tomorrow.

'It is probably the drinking water,' says Joumana, who is so sympathetic and concerned – even offering to pop round to see me on her way home – that I feel slightly queasy afterwards for lying to her.

Our hosts are Gazans who settled in al-Arish before 1978 and they like life here. It's busy in summer, quiet in winter – and not occupied by Israel. They are delighted to see Tariq, who's one of the extended family. He's in good spirits this morning, teasing me about calling in sick at work and joking that Gaza is so small, one or both of us is bound to see someone we know here. We share a late breakfast, then all stroll down to the beach for some Egyptian sea air. The beach – the main attraction here – is a long stretch of clean, pale sand, washed by clear shallows that gift good bathing and fresh seafood. We wander slowly along the sand towards a local café.

I pull off my shoes and paddle just for the pleasure of it. The water is cold and my toes tingle. I feel like I'm on holiday; last night seems an unreal, and surreal, experience. Right now I don't have the words to describe it, even to myself.

Cities are besieged when belligerent forces want to beat the local population and their overlords into submission. After more than 3,000 years of invasions and occupations, Gaza is a veteran of sieges. When Alexander the Great, King of Macedonia, arrived in Gaza in 332 BC during his conquest of the Persian Empire, he expected the city to fall quickly or else to send advance notice of its surrender, as other cities en route to Egypt had done. But Gaza had a secret weapon: a charismatic, statuesque eunuch called Batis, who was a daring and resourceful military commander. Batis defiantly hired Arab mercenaries, rallied local Philistines, Persians and Arabs to gather weapons, food and water and prepared the city for siege. Its slightly elevated hillside position gave the Gaza stronghold a great advantage, and the city was also protected by a high wall that Alexander's troops found impossible to penetrate.

The siege lasted more than two months, during the height of summer. Alexander was wounded twice as his troops tried over and again to breach the Gaza City walls. Reeking, rancid and half-crazed with thirst as the local wadis (riverbeds) ran dry, his troops became murderous. Finally, on their fourth major assault, they broke through the walls into Gaza and unleashed bloody carnage, slashing and slaughtering some 10,000 of the men inside until the walls were crusted with their black gore, raping and enslaving women and children, and sacking the city of its treasures, including its troves of perfumes and spices.

But even in defeat, Batis refused to bow to Alexander. The conqueror's henchmen forced through a rope between Batis's ankle bones and his Achilles tendons, bound the rope to Alexander's own chariot and dragged the eunuch alive around the city until his body was nothing but eviscerated meat.[20]

With Gaza crushed, Alexander continued south towards the Nile Delta, where he 'liberated' the Egyptian Empire, founded the city of Alexandria and was pronounced the new 'Master of the Universe', at the grand old age of 24. His men would have stormed down the ancient 'Way of the Sea', right along this coastline where I am standing now, barefoot in the placid Mediterranean.

Tariq and his friends are slightly ahead of me, but someone else is waving at me from the beach. Not another joker, please. He comes loping towards me, a man with a shaved head, smiling like he recognises me. Ah – now I know who it is.

'*Marhaba, ya* Louisa – how you like al-Arish?'

'It's beautiful!' I exclaim as Muhammad the driver and I shake hands, laughing.

'Fucking *helwa* (great)!' He almost sings the words, his face alight with joy. This is the first time I've actually seen him outside his taxi.

'Did you bring your family with you, Muhammad?'

'No. We don't know how long the border will be open and you know my wife is pregnant. I will go back to Gaza tonight – I just came to see this with my own eyes.'

He doesn't say anything else. Just stands there with a blissed-out smile.

'Look, Muhammad, I'm supposed to be at work today – so, er, don't tell anyone you saw me, OK?'

'Loueeza!' His expression is pure wicked triumph. He has caught me out and is delighted to have done so. But I'm sure he won't tell on me. A few minutes later I have to go, to catch up with Tariq and his relatives. When I reach them and glance back over my shoulder, Muhammad is still standing at the gentle lip of the sea.

Tariq, who did tell his boss he was crossing to Egypt, wants to stay here another day or so. Fair enough, I say, this is a nice place to linger. But I must be on my way. We easily find a crowded minibus heading back to Rafah and I set off alone, just after lunch. A few hours later I stroll back past the waxwork Egyptians with their riot shields. As I clamber over the crumpled fence, this time in sunlight, the man in front of me is guiding a herd of goats into Gaza. And the TV cameras have arrived.

Why did Hamas do it? Did they blow up the border to boost their popularity with Gazans? Or to thumb their noses at Israel, or at their neighbour and gate-keeper, Egypt, the first Arab nation to sign a peace treaty with Israel, back in 1978? Many Gazans despise the Egyptian authorities for allowing Israel to control the crossing at Rafah and effectively seal it – they did this in June 2006, after the kidnapping of Gilad Shalit (thereby cutting off the only route out of Gaza that bypasses Israel).

The Egyptians also cooperate with Israel over the network of Gazan smugglers' tunnels snaking under the Rafah border. My colleague Shadi is from Rafah and has told me about the Egyptians pouring concrete down the tunnels and pumping gas into them, forcing the smugglers – men and boys – to escape from 15 metres underground, like foxes fleeing from hounds. Not all of them make it. Several have already suffocated this year.[21]

Twelve days after Hamas has blown up the border, the Egyptian authorities begin rebuilding it. They give Gazans still inside Egypt a few days' grace to return before the border is completely re-sealed, but don't allow anyone else to leave Gaza except Egyptians who crossed into the Strip to see family and friends. By now around half the population of Gaza has crossed back and forth over the broken border into Egypt and Gazans have spent millions of US dollars in northern Egypt (one estimate is $250 million in al-Arish alone), giving a massive boost to the local economy. I half-expect, half-hope, that thousands of Gazans will refuse to be corralled back inside the Strip and instead just sit it out at the border, demanding that Egypt keep the Rafah crossing open and maybe even shaming the 'international community' into confronting the Israeli siege.

But like songbirds allowed out of their cage for a brief stretch of their clipped wings, or jailbirds recalled from parole, the Gazans obediently cross back over before the wall is rebuilt around them. For a couple of days, I still see the odd wagon with an Egyptian flag and passengers in white headdresses who don't quite look Gazan. But the party is almost over.

What with one thing and another, I haven't seen Saida for a little while. The next time we meet, back at her home, we eat with the family, then retreat to the bedroom she shares with her sister, Maha, to talk among ourselves. Saida has some news: the human rights centre where she has been volunteering has offered her a full-time job, researching human rights in Gaza. In her serious, steady voice, she tells me that she's very happy about this.

'But already they are giving me a lot of work, *habibti*. I know I am going to be very busy. *Khalas*! (Enough!) – it's better to be busy in Gaza and not think about our situation too much.'

I raise a toast to her new job. We clink our coffee cups.

'Did you cross the border this week?' I ask her afterwards, curious as to whether she would have done so or not.

'And go where?'

'To Egypt.'

'No. Did you?'

'Yes, just for one night. With Tariq. We climbed over the fence, with thousands of other people, and we ended up going to al-Arish with a Bedouin ...'

I want to share the whole escapade with her, but falter under her penetrating gaze and fall silent. When I've finished speaking, Saida is silent for a moment. Then she says: 'That is your choice. But I will not cross the border like this, climbing over a broken wall like a prisoner escaping from jail. No, *habibti*. When the Egyptians really open that border, then I will walk across it with my family and we will visit Egypt like normal people visit other countries. But not like this.'

I see the steel flash of her eyes and know that she means every word.

Gaza from the air

When the Egyptians re-seal the southern border, life returns to, if not normal, then what it was before this brief interlude of freedom. One of the most striking things about life in Gaza for me is the daily semblance of normal street life. Gazans get on with their day-to-day lives because what is the alternative? As Mediterranean people, most of them are early risers. After breakfast, the lucky ones go to work (unemployment is running at 40 per cent right now, one of the highest rates in the world), women cook and clean for their families, and children go to school – frequently in shifts because there are chronic shortages of classrooms and no available materials to build new schools. The Muslim working week is Sunday to Thursday; Friday is for prayers and Saturday is traditional family time.

During the week I'm usually at work by 8.30 in the morning, and back home again around half past three in the afternoon, for a late lunch. By then I'm usually ravenous. But often I just have a snack of bread, tomatoes and hummus because I receive so many invitations to dinner. Gazans I've never met before, friends of my Palestinian friends over in the West Bank, keep calling to invite me to eat in their homes and meet their families. I have dinner with Saida and her family too, at least once a week. When I first arrived here, almost two months ago, I presumed I would be spending most evenings home alone. But my mobile keeps ringing and now I rarely spend an evening in my own company. I wonder how many people in Scotland or England invite virtual strangers to their houses for meals that last half the evening.

One night I have dinner with the family of Sharif, my first Arabic teacher, who I met in Ramallah. After we've eaten a fine meal, Sharif's mother takes me to one side. She tells me Sharif has been in touch: he's very homesick and wants to visit them. She takes my hands and begs me to see her son next time I'm in Ramallah and to persuade him, for his own sake, not to come back.

When I go out at night, it's usually Muhammad the driver who drops me off and then brings me home again later, when I'm sleepy and full of good food. I always enjoy his company as we drive around town. Most of the time we just banter, making bad jokes about the life here, distracting ourselves from the realities festering around us – like the mounds of rubbish stinking in the streets because there is no fuel for the municipal trucks or enough power for the plants to crush the rotting debris.

Occasionally, though, Muhammad talks to me about what's really going on in his life; he speaks about his wife, Lina (Tender One), who is pregnant with their fourth child, and his worries for his three young children and their future here, with all these bombs, the endless political troubles and the lack of money. Like hundreds of thousands of other Gazan men, Muhammad used to work in southern Israel. He spent ten years as a textile worker in an Israeli factory.

'They spoke Arabic, we spoke Hebrew, we all ate the same food. I used to go to work in Israel, then come home to Gaza to my family. *Ya Allah* (By God), life was better then,' he tells me as we drive, his voice suddenly dreamy and nostalgic.

The first Palestinian intifada began in Jabalya refugee camp in December 1987. Years of Israeli–Palestinian tensions, exacerbated by the brutish 'Iron Fist' policy of the Israeli military, erupted when an Israeli tank driver knocked down a group of men from Jabalya, killing four of them. Palestinians united against the Israeli occupation in seven years of mass, mainly non-violent, demonstrations and civil strikes that tainted Israel's image, yet utterly failed to deliver independence for the Palestinians. The second intifada, which started in September 2000, saw blood on both sides' hands.[22] The Israeli military launched tanks, helicopters and live ammunition against unarmed Palestinian demonstrators and stone-throwing youths. Impotent against Israel's military might, Palestinian militants launched suicide missions, deliberately blowing themselves to pieces in crowded Israeli discos, cafés and public buses crowded with civilians. Hamas, and others, unleashed forty-seven suicide attacks inside Israel in 2002. Overall, it is Palestinian civilians who have borne the brunt of these clashes. Three and a half times more Palestinians than Israelis were killed between December 2000 and February 2005, thousands of Palestinians still languish inside Israeli jails – and a whole generation of Gazan men like Muhammad the driver lost their jobs in Israel and started scrabbling for work inside the Strip.

This evening Muhammad drops me off in Nasser district, just north of the city centre, where another friend of a friend has invited me for dinner. Her name is Niveen. When she opens the door, I see a small, middle-aged woman, with striking cheekbones and shoulder-length, thick mahogany hair. She lives with her plump teenage son, Fadil, who comes into the kitchen, says *marhaba* and promptly disappears straight back into his bedroom.

Niveen has invited three other people for dinner. She

introduces me to a woman called Sousi and two men, Muhammad
and Wissam. We all stand around the large kitchen-cum-dining-
room, watching as Niveen scoops fried fish from a pan and lashes it
with fresh lemon juice. When she called to invite me over, Niveen
warned me she was a lousy cook. But soon we sit down to the fresh
crispy fish, accompanied by bowls of clear broth with barley, rice
inlaid with baked root vegetables, sultanas and almonds, various
salads, and *baba ghanoush* – smoked aubergines mashed with
onions, tomatoes, garlic and tahini. With all these hearty dinners,
I'm starting to look very well fed myself! Niveen's son doesn't
join us at the table. He's hanging out on the roof terrace, smoking
narghile.

I sit opposite Muhammad. He's a class act, this guy – with his
black winkle-pickers and his shiny, two-tone purple shirt. A real
smoothie. His dark hair is shiny too, slicked back, gleaming with
oil. He looks me up, then down, taking his time. Sousi, on the
other hand, is pale-skinned, modestly dressed and seems quiet as a
dove. It is Wissam – who works as a TV news director for a foreign
broadcasting company – who completely dominates the dinner-
table conversation.

'We will be having more armed clashes soon – and I love
clashes!' He beams around the table. 'I do not care if it is the
Israelis, or Hamas and Fatah – if there's a clash, I'm *always* the first
on the scene! We're lucky – we can see everything from my studio
because it's on the fifteenth floor of the media tower, downtown.
Louisa, *habibti* – come on up with Niveen and see the view! I'll
send a driver over to collect you.'

As we savour the feast in front of us, Wissam rolls out stories
of weaving through Gaza's refugee camps and border buffer zones,
shooting clashes. I watch him, gesturing like a ringmaster whipping
up the crowd, gleefully complaining about the lack of clashes at

the southern border last week, when the Egyptians were re-sealing the blown-apart fence. We all know he's performing, and he knows that we know. But we are enjoying these tall stories because he does it so well, mocking the mainstream media, war voyeurs and Gaza's livid streak of self-destruction. All in the same take.

After dinner Wissam swans back to his studio to work late, Sousi and Muhammad the Smoothie sit discussing something like the old friends they obviously are, and I finally get a chance to talk to Niveen. She tells me about her work as a gender researcher, specialising in the social and economic conditions facing women and girls in Gaza. She prefixes many of her sentences with the words: 'Speaking as a Gazan woman ...' And she laughs a lot – a great dirty laugh, full of smoke and mischief, a cigarette constantly clasped between her fingers. She strikes me as an unusual woman here – economically independent, free-spirited and alone. She does not wear the *hijab* because she doesn't feel the need, and insists on exercising her free choice. I've seen other women out in the streets without a *hijab*, but not many. Niveen must sense my curiosity about her seeming alone-ness, because at one point she looks straight at me and says, 'I'm a widow, *habibti*. My husband, he died five years ago.'

'Ah – I see. I'm really sorry.'

'Gaza is the city of death!' She enjoys a dark chuckle. 'Most welcome to our seaside prison camp!'

I start laughing, and so do Sousi and the Smoothie. It's different for me, I can leave the Strip but they can't, and this gallows humour is something like local medicine, to relieve the anxiety that constantly charges the air, like low-level static.

Sousi stands up. She has to go now, though it's still early. She reaches for the black *hijab* lying on the shoulder of the couch and starts wrapping it round her black hair.

'She has to be home before dark,' says the Smoothie. 'The *muqawamah* are always on the street outside her house. If they see her, they'll want to know why a married woman is out after dark without her husband.' He sneers.

The *muqawamah* are the local armed resistance, the masked Hamas fighters who prowl the eastern outskirts of the city at night as its self-proclaimed sentinels and protectors. There are a dozen militant factions in Gaza, and some of them hate each other as much as they despise Israel.

Sousi looks over at me and nods.

'They're on the road outside my house every night, so I must leave early.'

She kisses each of us goodbye and closes the door quietly behind her.

The Smoothie sits back and lights another cigarette, clearly settling in for the evening. Niveen touches my arm.

'*Habibti*, why don't you and I visit Wissam in his TV studio this week and see what the city of death looks like from the sky?'

❧

The view is astounding.

Today's sky is cloudless, perfect, vast as the sea. Gaza is spread around us like a giant open book. We are standing fifteen storeys above Umar al-Mukhtar Street, smack in the city centre, high enough to see across the entire city over to the shining Mediterranean, yet low enough to appreciate the details. Niveen and I gaze in all directions, like we are drinking Gaza in, or searching for someone who is lost. The streets look ordered and peaceful from here, built in cross-sections with squares in between. Umar al-Mukhtar Street – named after the Libyan 'Lion of the Desert' who fought the Italian colonialists until they hanged him in 1931 – appears as wide and tree-lined as a European boulevard.

We look down over the pale, elegant Parliament building in its fine courtyard, and the main city hospital, al-Shifa, sprawling behind it. As our eyes adjust to the panorama, Niveen and I can make out individual cars and donkey carts trafficking through the streets, diminutive figures walking – and, out to sea, a wink of fishing vessels pitching through foaming waves as the sunlight sparkles like summer rain. Beyond our gaze, Israeli warships are out at sea too, patrolling Gaza's waters day and night. As my eyes move back towards the shore, I can see the modern port, lying slightly south of the city.

The ancient Gaza port was built slightly north of the city, at a site called Anthedon – City of Flowers – where the remnants of Roman columns, villas and a pagan temple can still be found today. Gaza's coast road stretches from one end of the Strip to the other, bypassing towns, villages, refugee camps and fishermen's huts dotted along the Strip. Niveen and I try to pinpoint our individual apartment buildings, but get lost in the sunny seaside metropolis planted below.

'I cannot believe it!' She shakes her head, pushing her hair out of her eyes. 'I thought I knew my city so well, but I never saw it like this before, so beautiful ...!'

Travellers, scholars, pilgrims and kings have all been beguiled by Gaza over the centuries. During the Hellenic era that followed Alexander the Great's conquest of Gaza, the city was rebuilt and repopulated. It became a citadel to protect the ancient 'Way of the Sea' towards Egypt and communities of Arabs and Bedouin tribes settled in and around the city. A great library is said to have attracted scholars and scientists from across the region, including the city of Alexandria. Once again, Gaza prospered.

How I would love to have seen Gaza in these medieval times and wandered its spice- and incense-decked streets, relishing the unwashed, perfumed chaos! Imagine the sites and stories ... But now, millennia later, I have an acute sense that I could be looking down on some old-fashioned holiday resort; a rambling, sunny seaside city with a popular beach, arcades, restaurants and bars – the kind of place that families return to faithfully, year after year, like an affectionate old friend.

I wander over to the other side of the large roof terrace, stepping around a wired-up satellite dish. Now my perspective shifts. I see green fields in the distance, stretching to the northern border with Israel, and the barriers that surround Gaza – barriers with watchtowers, like photographs of the Berlin Wall before it was torn apart. I can't see them from here, but I know there are also large white spheres suspended over the northern and eastern borders with Israel. They look like big white balloons, but they are actually Israeli listening devices, sucking up every sound we make inside Gaza. And on a day as clear as this, you can sometimes see white unmanned aerial vehicles – drones – circling the sky above us, audibly buzzing as they take constant video and stills images. Gazans call them *zananas* (mosquitoes). But they make people here flinch, because some carry lethal missiles.[23]

Gaza – one of the oldest, most isolated and most closely surveilled cities on earth – has always lived under foreign occupation ... never been free to choose its own fate. But every single one of its occupiers has, sooner or later, been ousted by the next.

Wissam steps out onto the roof terrace. 'You like my view?' He takes off his gold-rimmed aviator shades and blinks in the early afternoon sun. He's beaming, but the skin beneath his eyes is a shade darker, like he hasn't had much sleep lately. His office is just a few steps below the terrace and he invites us to come back inside and drink coffee.

As Niveen and I move towards the steps, Wissam says to me, 'We often film up here, you know. Sometimes we are shooting live footage, panning across the city – and my foreign colleagues are on the phone shouting, "Hey, man, c'mon – where the hell are you?" Because they don't actually believe this could be Gaza.'

coffee and cigarettes

When we leave the TV tower, Niveen and I stand outside on Umar al-Mukhtar Street, not quite sure what to do next, both of us a bit dazed after seeing Gaza from the air. After a few moments she says, 'Let's go and drink coffee somewhere and sit for a while. I know a quiet café down by the beach.'

The café she takes me to is at the southern edge of the city, just beyond the modern port. It's a truly ugly building, the outside walls pasted in cracked seashells, but it is right next to the beach, with an unbroken view of the Mediterranean. Niveen knows the owner, a portly man also called Muhammad, who greets us both like friends. We choose a corner of the café terrace, a little sun-trap, and he goes off to make the coffee. We seem to be the only customers.

Niveen and I sit gazing out to sea. We both light up cigarettes and neither of us exchanges a word until Muhammad returns with our coffees, two glasses of water and an ashtray. He leaves us to it and we sit in silence again. But it's a nice, easy silence and I feel no need to break it. I just rest in the sun, enjoying the view, the salt-tinged air on my face and the strong, cardamom-scented coffee. I suddenly feel very relaxed.

'My husband loved the sea,' says Niveen.

I look over at her after a while. She is gazing ahead, with a soft, sad expression on her face. I don't reply because I am not sure who she's talking to right now.

'When I was young, I wanted to marry an ex-prisoner and give myself to my country. My husband was eleven years older than me, and when I met him he had just been released after seventeen years in jail in Israel. Sarah, my daughter, was born in 1987, the year after we married – and my son Fadil was born the year after that. Fadil was just a few months old when the Israelis came back for my husband. He was still an activist in the PFLP (the Popular Front for the Liberation of Palestine) and they kept him in Israeli administrative detention for six months.[24] And for that half a year I did not know if he was dead or alive. Afterwards, they sentenced him to five years, and I visited him in jail every month for those five years. So hard, so humiliating! We women would get up at 2 AM and hope to be at the Israeli jail by 10 AM for the visit. Yes ... those years were hard, and the visits were hard, and when he came out of jail it was hard too. I had dedicated myself to working and studying, so that I could provide for our children while he could not. When he was released, I had my own identity and agency as a Gazan woman, and we were both different people.'

She shakes her head and lights another cigarette, still gazing ahead, and her voice picks up again:

'Other Gazan women, you know, they blamed me for being ambitious and not giving my attention to my husband. When I was accepted to study my Masters in the UK, I took Sarah to live with me, and Fadil stayed here with his father. Afterwards, when we came back to Gaza, my husband treated me very badly. I asked for a divorce, but he threatened to take the children away and eventually I gave in, because I wanted to keep my children. So we stayed married and I learned to manage the situation because I had to – and then he *was* ashamed. He bought me a small piece of land outside the city and planted yellow roses there for me because I love yellow roses.'

She sighs. Traffic rumbles along the street behind us. The waves break.

'Four years ago, a university in Wales offered me a place to study my PhD. I took Sarah with me again. My husband understood this time. But while we were in Wales he had a heart attack. He was on our land and he died right there, next to the yellow roses. But we couldn't reach Gaza in time to bury him because Erez was shut. And that's why my daughter hates Gaza and why she will never come back here. Because she loved her father, and the Israelis prevented her from burying him.'

'So where is she now?'

'In Cairo. Studying. My dream is to go back to Wales and finish my PhD and take my children with me, so we can live together as a family again.'

We look at each other. Niveen smiles, but her face looks weary and a little haggard.

'But at least I could visit my husband when he was in jail,' she says, 'not like our women now. You know, the Israelis have prevented them from visiting their men in jail since Hamas took over.'

Every Monday morning, a crowd of some 200 women gather in a courtyard just outside the Gaza City office of the International Committee of the Red Cross (ICRC). The women clasp photographs of their husbands, sons, brothers and a few daughters, all of them prisoners inside jails in Israel. More than 900 Gazan men, and 4 women, are in Israeli jails, and since the Hamas takeover, Gazan families have been denied all rights to visit them.[25] I went to the vigil recently with one of my colleagues, and one of the women there told me she has not laid eyes on her son for six years now. But like the rest of this silent flock, she returns to the courtyard every Monday morning to take her place, clasp the photograph of her son and wait.

zift

Early spring arrives, the days get longer and more foreign visitors start arriving; most of them are journalists, aid workers, or foreign delegates on fleeting two-day visits. My landlord, Abu Ali, has a few small apartments in our building that he rents out to the handful of foreign visitors who are free to roam the city like me. The majority of expats inside Gaza work for the local United Nations Relief and Works Agency (UNRWA) and are confined to their offices and compounds and a few security-vetted venues like the al-Deira Hotel.

On the streets, people stare at me and I stare back. Women and children stop me on my way to and from work and ask me to take off my sunglasses, just so that they can gaze up at my blue-grey eyes. When I got here, I presumed most Gazans would have dark skin, dark hair and brown eyes. Many do, but others are blond and pale, there are blacks too, a smattering of redheads with blue-green eyes, and I've even seen one or two albinos. Gazan people reflect roots extending back to so many different places – the Middle East, Europe and Africa; they are Arabs and Christians, Bedouin, refugees and immigrants. Just a quarter of the local population can trace their families' origins to within the modern Gaza Strip.

On my way to work one morning, I bump into a white-haired gentleman on the stairs. He's a foreigner wearing a faded denim cap studded with a dozen silver badges and his brown face is creased as a paper bag. He looks like an old sea dog. Coming down the stairs just behind him is a young man, a Gazan. We step outside into the sunshine and introduce ourselves. The white-haired guy is an American photographer called Skip. The young man beside him is Mahmoud, his interpreter. Mahmoud has short, tight black curls and a goatee beard and is dressed as though on his way to a business meeting.

Skip suddenly snaps his fingers; he's left something in his room. He turns around and trudges back upstairs.

'Do you speak Arabic?' Mahmoud asks me, in Arabic.

'Yes, I'm learning.' We converse in Arabic for a few minutes. I tell him about my recent 'capsize' triumph with the local posse of *shabab* and he laughs out loud.

'You should come and talk to the *shabab* in Jabalya camp, where I live!' he says. 'Have you been to Jabalya?'

'Yes, but just for work.'

'Here's my mobile number. Call me when you are free and come up for lunch.'

'*Shukran* (Thank you),' I say. 'That would be nice.'

Jabalya, up in northern Gaza, consists of a town and a refugee camp that lie side by side, like a lumpy old married couple. The town is considered the better place to live, though it's hard to tell where one ends and the other begins. Like everywhere else in Gaza, Jabalya has an epic history of shifting populations who between them have shaped the contours of this land. Jabalya used to be famous for its fertile fields and vast orchards of fruit trees; these days the refugee camp is one of the most densely populated places on earth.

I call Mahmoud a few days later and we arrange to meet at the gas station next to the main *souq* in Jabalya camp. When

Muhammad the driver and I reach the gas station, the streets surrounding the *souq* are heaving with traders, pedestrians, taxis and knackered-looking donkeys. The streets are narrower here and the houses smaller; the traffic flows in all directions, and noise ricochets off every surface. People shout, engines backfire and donkeys bray. Muhammad the driver tells me to wait inside the car until Mahmoud arrives. I take my cigarettes out of my bag; whenever I'm waiting for something, or someone, I reach for them now, like a reflex.

'Louisa, don't smoke here,' he says. 'We are not in the city now. The camp is different.'

'Oh, OK.'

'Shit, man, this place is crowded. We Gazans have too many children – like cats!'

'Or rabbits.'

'Yes, but we eat all the rabbits!' Muhammad quips.

I have to laugh. Rabbits are popular in Gaza; families keep battery cages of them in their gardens and courtyards, for the pot. A store at the bottom of my street sells them alongside cages of squawking, stinking hens.

I see Mahmoud approaching and he spots me getting out of the taxi. He's dressed in sharp black and white again, his hair gleaming and his goatee freshly razored. Most Gazans are well turned out, but there's something polished about Mahmoud. I wave goodbye to Muhammad and shake hands with Mahmoud.

'You look good,' I say.

'I am a Jabalya dandy!' he grins.

Mahmoud and I walk through the camp towards his house. When we turn off the main street, the wall of noise falls away. Now we're on a sandy side street, the walls either side daubed in red graffiti. Small dark kids streak ahead of us in bare feet, shouting

'Hello, hello!' A few shout, '*Shalom, shalom!*'

'Too many visits from the Israeli soldiers!' grins Mahmoud. I tell him I get this in the city too sometimes, from kids who think any foreigner in Gaza must be an Israeli. The only foreigners many Gazan children have ever met are Israeli soldiers and settlers.

Mahmoud lives with his family in the south-eastern stretch of the camp. We enter their building via a small courtyard.

'My family is lucky,' he says, as we climb the stairs up to their second-floor apartment. 'We have space in my house. Many families in the camp are sharing one or two rooms between all of them.'

The living room has thin patterned mattresses to sit on. Mahmoud tells me to make myself comfortable and goes off into the kitchen. I can hear him laughing with someone, and clattering in the kitchen, as the smell of meat and herbs wafts under the door. I would much rather hang out in the kitchen, like I do with Saida and her family, but as a first-time guest here, this is my designated place. It's different with Saida's family now. I spend time in the kitchen with her mother, Hind, watching as she makes her soups, her *malfouf* and *maftoul*. I love the way that Hind cooks, sniffing the ingredients to make sure they are fresh, flinging them into pots, tasting the dishes with her fingers at every stage, adding more *filfil*, lemon juice or handfuls of olive oil. She is a sensuous cook and an affectionate matriarch. Sometimes when I arrive at their home, Hind calls me into her bedroom where she often rests and I sprawl next to her, laying my head on her bosom like a young child as she strokes my hair.

After a while Mahmoud appears, brandishing a large metal dish in both hands.

'*Kabsah*!' He lays the dish on the low table with a flourish. *Kabsah* is not fiery, but a delicacy of rice inlaid with fried almonds, onions, sultanas and herbs, served with seasoned fried meat. We tuck in and as soon as the rice cools a little, we abandon our spoons and just use our fingers, scooping the rice up with warm flatbread, too happy eating to talk.

Finally, stuffed, we slump against the cushions and grin at each other. A young woman comes into the room to take away our plates, then brings us coffee. Mahmoud thanks her and she smiles at my Arabic as she disappears back into the kitchen.

'Let's go; we can drink our coffee outside,' he says.

We carry our cups down to the courtyard, now lying in half-shade, and settle ourselves on white plastic chairs. Out on the streets I hear rasping car engines, people shouting to each other and an ambulance siren wailing like a lost child. Mahmoud has a narghile water pipe and starts filling it with the molasses-coated, apple-flavoured tobacco I smell wafting from café doorways across the city.

'Are there many dandies in Jabalya?' I ask him.

He looks up from his tobacco stuffing, throws back his head and laughs.

'We have dandies *and* dancers here in our *zift* refugee camp, *habibti*!'

Mahmoud is 24 years old. He used to work with the Palestinian Authority (PA) Presidential Guards, aligned with the Fatah movement, Hamas's political opponent and enemy. After its takeover of Gaza, Hamas sacked all Gazan policemen and security personnel in the pay of the PA. Like thousands of other PA employees, Mahmoud still receives his salary, but cannot go back to his old job. The PA still pays thousands of salaries in Gaza; it wants to keep its redundant staff on side, fears them drifting towards the arms of Hamas, especially in the camps, where the movement is strongest. But Gazans are, by necessity, innovators and these days Mahmoud has several different jobs. He works as an interpreter and also at a local youth centre; he makes short films about life for young people inside Gaza; and he helps out with a local dance troupe based at the youth centre.

'The work at the youth centre is the best,' he says. 'We make sure all the boys and girls spend time together, and they dance together too. You know, we always remind them that there is nothing wrong with boys and girls mixing for fun. The day Hamas stops us working like this, then I will leave the centre for good.' He exhales a thick ribbon of white smoke, wipes the mouth of his pipe with a tissue, then offers me the pipe. 'I can't always speak my mind about these things here in the camp because I have to live here too,' he says, his voice dropping. 'But I want to tell you something, and I want to ask you something. OK?'

'OK.' I coil the narghile pipe on my lap, like a striped serpent.

'We get a lot of foreign visitors here, especially delegations who come to Gaza just for one or two days. Often they come to Jabalya camp – because it has a very bad reputation, so of course they want to see it. And I meet with them because I live here and I speak English. But they always want to see the worst things here. They are like this' – he mimes someone shooting photos, one after the other, his index finger pressing an imaginary shutter button – '"Look! Look! See over there: something terrible or broken or ugly. Snap, Snap, Snap, Snap!" So tell me, Louisa, why do these foreigners always concentrate on what is *zift*? They always want me to tell them how *zift* things are here. And if they send me an email after they leave, they just want to know about the *zift* situation. Only what is *zift*. What about us and our dreams?'

'What *are* your dreams?' I raise the striped pipe to my lips and inhale.

'My dreams? To be free to walk along the beach with my girlfriend and hold her hand without people watching and talking; and to get married for love, and live in a house with soft lights from lamps – not these strips of bright white lights we all have in our houses, like prison lights. I dream of living in a place where I can really relax and not always have to talk or even think about the fucking *zift* situation.'

He sits upright, his eyes bright with smoke and righteous anger.

'Other people's *zift* situations are always fascinating,' I say.

Before I came to Gaza, I watched a lot of TV footage about the Strip – it was mostly presented as bombed-out ruins filled with masked *jihadis*, veiled women, scowling mullahs and weeping children. I never expected to be living in a neighbourhood like al-Rimal – which has an elegant local French Cultural Centre – or to be drinking coffee in an arabesque seafront hotel like the al-Deira. These places are exceptions, but they are not mirages. The Gaza streets are dirty, sometimes filthy, but they feel reasonably safe to walk. Hamas is cracking down on its political opponents – literally – but has also made the streets much more secure and popular new cafés are opening up across the city centre. There are chronic shortages, overcrowding and poverty. But Gazans are not starving and there are pockets of family wealth here too. Last week, for instance, I paid a visit to the Gaza Equestrian Centre, where well-heeled parents pay $200 a month for their children to learn the pleasures of horse riding and show jumping.

Many of the Gazans I meet – and not just the wealthy and privileged – expend most of their energy on making their own lives worth living. On the face of it, Gaza is not quite as *zift* as I expected.

But just beneath the surface I can feel livid strains of anxiety and fatigue, from years of chronic uncertainty and fear. Compared to many conflict zones, the death toll here is low. But I have never met such weary people in my life. I say all this to Mahmoud.

'We are not animals or victims; we are ordinary people who want to be allowed to live and breathe,' he says in response. And we leave it at that.

I wander over to the other side of the small courtyard in my bare feet, to a small bush of red roses, and squat down to smell their tentative perfume.

'Do you have to go back to the city now or can you stay here for the afternoon?' asks Mahmoud.

'I'm free all afternoon.'

'Shall we go to the youth centre and watch them dancing *dabke*?'[26]

We wander back though the sandy streets, where the dark-skinned, barefoot kids are still running around, and then cut through the crowded *souq*. Above the boisterous din I can hear another ambulance wailing. More women are veiled here and more people stare at my uncovered short hair. Some scowl at me and my shoulders tense. It's the first time I have felt any personal hostility here. Mahmoud leads me out of the *souq* into a narrow alley, then into a two- or three-storey whitewashed building. As we climb the stairs, we can hear pulsing music and feet thumping the floor. We reach a wide landing. Mahmoud walks to the far side, pushes open a door and gestures for me to follow him.

Inside, a long line of teenagers, boys and girls, are flowing across the floor, laughing and clapping as they buck into the air, like unbroken young horses. The boys kneel, the girls sweep forward, then dart away, looking back over their shoulders at the flushed boys looking back at them. They whoop and cheer and stamp and blaze with life. Mahmoud and I stand just inside the door, grinning at the dancers, and each other.

'See!' he shouts over the pulsing music. 'Boys and girls having fun together in a *zift* Gaza refugee camp!'

scents of history

A Saturday afternoon towards the end of February. I have just finished work for the week and am in a taxi, on my way to the vegetable market at Souq al-Zawiya to stock up on fresh food. Saida and I were going to do our shopping together, but she called to say she was working at home because finally they had electricity and so she could finish off a report for work. I decided to shop alone. But Muhammad the driver seems reluctant to drop me off in the old quarter.

'Why you want to go shopping here?' He frowns as we pull up at the busy crossroads beside the *souq*. 'I can take you to a good fruit store in al-Rimal and drive you back home afterwards.'

'I like this *souq*.'

'But how you will get home?'

'I'll take a public taxi.' I am referring to the yellow, six-door Mercedes taxis that Saida and I take all over the city together.

Muhammad gives me a reluctant nod. As I open the door, he adds, 'Be careful. You know you can call us for a car if you have *any* problems.'

Muhammad is reminding me to be careful because of the recent threats to kidnap foreigners inside Gaza. The Army of Islam – a militia of pumped-up thugs, led by the Doghmush clan, who kidnapped BBC journalist Alan Johnston last summer – were rumoured to be on the look-out for another hostage.[27] When the first threat was issued, a few weeks ago, staff at the Centre insisted I take a taxi everywhere and did not walk outside alone at all – just to be on the safe side. On the first day, I felt a brief thrill of fear. But it dissolved into tedium as I went from my apartment into a taxi to the Centre, then into a taxi back to my apartment, for more than two weeks. Until the threat was dropped from 'high' to 'moderate' in the daily UN security bulletin, my colleagues even accompanied me to the Metro Supermarket on the corner of my street whenever I went shopping.

Clans, each made up of hundreds of interrelated local families, used effectively to rule Gaza. Before the Hamas takeover, the previous Fatah-dominated government – the Palestinian Authority (PA) – courted the clans because they wanted to use their local power bases to police the Strip. PA officials hired clan members and as these unaccountable, armed-to-the-teeth local militias prowled the streets, they fed on Gaza's civilians like vultures on carrion. The clans became Gaza's kings of *fawdah*, or chaos, extorting, murdering, kidnapping and bullying until they were rich and feared and despised, because in the money-changers' eyes of the clan leaders, *they* were the law inside Gaza.

Now Hamas has struck back hard, warning the Doghmush, the Hellis and the Abu Hassanein clans, and others, that their days of lording it over the Strip are over. Hamas police stand on every corner of the city, and though many locals despise their ideology, they have welcomed the new law and order that has secured the streets. Even the Doghmush, always the most hard-faced of the clans, have a whiff of desperation about them these days. The police have already torched half a dozen Doghmush apartments, and if the Army of Islam does carry out its threat to snatch a foreigner, Hamas will no doubt butcher them.

But even though this latest kidnap threat is probably grandstanding, I know I am vulnerable going out on my own like this. I always wear long sleeves and trousers and a modest neckline, though I don't cover my hair. But I have yet to see another Westerner walking the streets here. I've only seen them sitting inside white UN four-wheel drives. That knot in my guts twinges whenever I set off alone. But I have to wander around, otherwise I won't see anything.

Pushing through a narrow side street into Souq al-Zawiya, I immediately see and smell the fruits, meat and spices on display. This stretch of the *souq* is dominated by fruit traders, now flogging left-over crates of oranges and strawberries – the season for both is nearly over – but further along, the men are mainly selling vegetables. The meat section, with its stinking cages of half-bald hens, is somewhere in the middle. Herb and spice stalls are dotted in between, along with stalls selling pots, pans and other household bits and pieces.

I'm always drawn to the spice stalls and their opulence of seeds, powders, dried flakes and leaves. I stop at one now, to buy another bag of sage leaves to infuse my tea, plus a stub of ginger, a crimson spice powder called *sumac* (which Saida tells me has a delicate lemony taste and is especially good with chicken) and, as an afterthought, some black peppercorns. The stallholder scoops them loose from the tub with a wooden ladle, pours them into a small plastic sac and seals it with a quick knot. He asks where I come from.

'Scotland,' I say.

'Ahhh, Scotlanda – Braveheart!'

We laugh. Every country needs its heroes, real or imaginary, usually an amalgam of both. Braveheart is very popular here (though I doubt many people know that his real name was William Wallace). But Che Guevara is beloved, his name and profile plastered in red all across the city, his hooded eyes staring down at the Strip as though he can save Gaza from the Israeli occupation and from itself.

The stallholder wants to know if I like Gaza. I say that I do – the people are friendly and the food is good. He gives me an indulgent smile. Then, like the businessman he is, he asks if I would also like to buy some *za'atar*, a blend of crushed thyme, oregano and marjoram, to eat with bread and olive oil. Gazans do love their spices.

❦

One of the reasons that Alexander the Great laid siege to Gaza back in the fourth century BC was his desire to control the lucrative international spice trade, of which Gaza was a key hub. Spices were being traded across the Arab world before history was recorded, and as an ancient crossroads spanning three continents, Gaza became a vast international spice market and caravanserai. The peppercorns I have just bought are an everyday household item here, though not a great favourite with Gazans. But pepper – by far the most popular spice in the history of the trade – and other spices, like cinnamon, cloves and nutmeg, were branded as decadent 'must-haves' of the ancient world. And from the early days of the trade, raconteurs wove incredible stories about the perils of harvesting spices. Most of the tales were sheer colourful nonsense – but they thrilled customers and knocked up the price, and the kudos, of exotic spices.

It was from the brimming warehouses and heaving ports of Alexandria and Gaza that vast quantities of spices, perfumes and incense were shipped across the Mediterranean to Western Europe. Incense was considered a sacred spice, as it soothed angry gods of all persuasions. From at least the third century BC, Arabs rode camel caravans from the south-eastern tip of the Arabian peninsula to Gazan *souqs* like the one I'm browsing right now – along the legendary Frankincense Trail.

Frankincense and myrrh are both gum resins. They are harvested from shrub-like trees that still thrive in the Dhofar region of southern Oman, the world's richest frankincense garden – and in the mountains of neighbouring Yemen, where these precious shrubs are so grasping, they have been known to grow straight out of solid rock. Omani and Yemeni farmers still harvest frankincense the old way – gouging deep, thin 'wounds' into the bark and peeling away narrow strips that bleed a milky liquid, which solidifies on contact with the air, forming resin 'tears' that are slowly dried out in the sun.

Back in the third century BC, merchants would descend on Dhofar and southern Yemen in the spring and autumn, when the frankincense harvest was ready. These merchants were Minaeans, one of the ancient Yemenite peoples who transported incense across Arabia by camel. When they had bartered hard, the Minaeans loaded up their beasts and set out north-west along the Frankincense Trail. Avoiding high mountain passes that harboured feuding tribes and throat-slitting bandits, they followed an inland trail roughly parallel to the Red Sea coastline, which then led them through the Rub' al-Khali, 'Empty Quarter', an ocean of sand and shifting, orange-red dunes stretching for some 250,000 square miles across the southern Arabian peninsula. The Minaeans also passed by pre-Islamic cities like Ma'rib and Timna, where they were obliged to pay hefty local 'spice taxes'.

The ancient Roman philosopher, Pliny the Elder, recorded the distance between Timna and Gaza as sixty-two days by camel. The entire Frankincense Trail – from Dhofar to the port at Gaza – was some 2,100 miles, more than two and a half times the length of Great Britain. But for the Minaeans, men as dry and unyielding as the Empty Quarter, it was well worth their while. Myrrh, and especially frankincense, were literally worth their weight in gold; every temple and wealthy home across Babylon, Egypt, Greece, Jerusalem and Rome required these precious resins to please their gods.

The vast majority of spices, apart from gum resins, originated far east of the Arabian peninsula; but frankincense was so cherished that poets wrote that all Arabia exuded 'a most delicate fragrance', and sailors on the Red Sea were rumoured to be able to catch its astringent scent from offshore breezes. It was not only spices that the Arabs traded; merchants made fortunes from selling olive oil, wheat, fish, wine – and Gaza traded heavily in slaves as well. But the majority of Gaza's international trade was over land, not by sea, and the overland incense trade was still going strong when Gaza was conquered by the Romans in 63 BC. At that time, some 1,000 camels were arriving here every month, each weighed down with sacred spices. Frankincense was so plentiful in Gaza that these ancient, narrow streets must have been awash with the stuff. Maybe even pungent old Souq al-Zawiya was fragrant, back in those days.

❧

I walk on through the *souq*, passing a crippled old Bedouin lady selling small bunches of fresh mint for a shekel (15 pence) each, and buy one from her. Just ahead of me is the al-Umari Mosque, the largest and oldest mosque in Gaza. As a non-Muslim, I cannot go inside, but an open side door offers me a glimpse of a spacious, light sanctuary, with a vast wall-to-wall carpet – smooth, flat and emerald as a bowling green. Running along one side of the mosque is the local gold market: just one narrow passage of bare-bulb-lit stalls, where fat men with bloodhound jowls and eyes like coal sell gaudy Jordanian gold to hard-bargaining mothers for their daughters' dowries. The gold market has an atmosphere all its own, like the Hammam al-Samara Turkish baths, which are literally just across the street. This old quarter of the city is built, like Gaza itself, on an ancient crossroads.

Half an hour later, my arms are weighed down from bulging plastic bags and my shopping is done. I emerge back onto the main street, turn right and walk along a short pedestrian lane to the corner where the yellow Mercedes public taxis stop to pick up and drop off passengers. Men are selling vegetables and fruit out here on the street too – but also shawarma, baked sweets dripping with honey and rolled in pistachios, and hot, sweet coffee. Women browse arm-in-arm with their friends as smoke rises like incense from food stalls. Men, women and children smile at me and I smile back.

I know there are extremists in Gaza, and not just the Doghmush clan. Pockets of Salafists in the southern Strip espouse ancient Islam, Shari'a law and *jihad*, and some of them have a violent hatred of Westerners.[28] One of the first times I walked alone in a quiet street in the city centre, a man hissed at me so that I would see him openly masturbating; and when I flinched, he laughed and bared his teeth like a dog. Since that bad start, though, I have experienced very little harassment on these streets. I feel fine about taking one of the yellow public taxis because all that I've encountered here today has been friendliness. But tensions are tightening. The rumours that Israel is about to launch another military operation are circling, like the *zanana* drones in the skies.

great night for a party!

The bombing starts a few days later, on a Wednesday afternoon. Israeli spokesmen in suits and narrow ties appear on television, claiming that Palestinian terrorists have smuggled long-range rockets, like Katyushas and Grads, into Gaza through the tunnels and that Israel is 'responding' to the situation with a military operation in order to disrupt terrorist infrastructure inside the Strip. The prime minister of Gaza, Ismail Haniyeh, states that Hamas will respond to any Israeli attack. Israel has bombed Gaza almost every day since I arrived here nearly three months ago.

I spend that Wednesday evening alone in my flat and try to watch TV. But the reception is garbled. *Zananas* are patrolling the skies and they disrupt transmission, so the newsreaders look warped on the screen and they sound like staggering drunks. I turn the television off and attempt to start reading. But then the electricity cuts out. Cursing, I reach for the matches and candles that I keep within reach on the table. Now I can hear bombs pounding. Three missiles strike somewhere close to my apartment, each one a stomach-clenching thump. I hear a helicopter in the sky. I can't help myself – I want to see what's going on out there, so I step out onto my living-room balcony, my back pressed hard against the wall. There is smoke everywhere, a helicopter hovering above. It emits a brief flare of red lights and what sounds like machine-gun fire. I feel an electric surge of pure fear and reverse back inside, my heart pounding out of control. This calls for emergency measures.

Feeling my way along the walls into the dark kitchen, I open the fridge and fumble inside the melting freezer, where I keep a bottle of vodka. I twist off the cap, take a good swig, then another one. I don't want to feel anything right now.

Saida calls me: '*Habibti*, are you OK? The situation is terrible. Listen, open your windows a little. If there's a big explosion near you, the pressure can break all the glass and I don't want you to get hurt.'

Her voice, usually so calm and measured, is faintly shrill. She's truly scared, and so am I. But we both pretend we are feeling all right, and this will soon be over. When we've finished talking on the phone, I take a candle into my bedroom, pull the curtains apart and open the windows a little. In between explosions all I can hear is *zananas* buzzing in the sky like giant wasps.

At work the next morning we sit at our desks because we have jobs to do and because there is nothing else to do but work. We're safe enough here, in the centre of Gaza City. The Israeli military have been targeting Hamas government installations around the city centre, but in this assault – branded as Operation Winter Heat – they are pounding a district called Izbat Abed Rabbo, east of Jabalya camp in northern Gaza. No one knows exactly how many people have been killed, but the death toll is rising slowly like a sea-tide, amid rumours of a full-scale Israeli invasion of the Strip.

By early afternoon we are all loitering around reception, most of us smoking. I'd presumed my colleagues would all be used to these attacks, battle-hardened and emotionally numb by now. But it's quite the opposite. The atmosphere is tense and sad and very quiet. Only Shadi breaks rank, mocking the Apache helicopters that swarmed around the city last night.

'That was nothing, *habibti*!' He waggles his cigarette at me. 'You wait till they bring out the F-16s! When we hear them whistling above us, then by sudden we are in six thousand, six hundred and sixty-six tons of *BIG* trouble!' Everyone within earshot laughs, including me.

The office doesn't close early. We leave at the normal time. As we are getting our jackets on, ready to leave, Joumana says to me, 'If you want to buy anything for the weekend, go now, *habibti*. The shops will close soon. They always close early at times like this.'

I thank her and say that I hope she has a good weekend though I feel slightly ridiculous saying so. My colleagues keep repeating these mantras to each other: Take care; Enjoy your weekend; See you on Sunday; *Salam*; Life goes on …

Shadi offers me a lift home in his 'best-in-the-West' car, but I tell him I prefer to walk. I need to buy some things on the way home because I am supposed to be having friends over for a small *hafla* tonight.

I'm having a *hafla* at my apartment this evening because I have to leave Gaza in a few days, to make a visa run. I will cross back into Israel, then leave Israel for Egypt and then re-enter Israel a couple of weeks later, hopefully with a brand-new, three-month Israeli tourist visa, which is issued at the border. I will need a new entry permit for Gaza, which is also issued by Israel. The Israeli authorities may refuse to issue me with a new tourist visa, a new entry permit or both … in which case I am screwed because I don't have a permit to work in Gaza either. I would love a work permit, but there's absolutely no point in applying for one because permits for foreigners to work in Gaza are issued by the Israeli Social Affairs Ministry, and I work for a Gazan human rights organisation which monitors Israeli abuses in Gaza, so the Israelis will not issue me a permit. In light of all this uncertainty, I've decided to throw this *hafla* to say a temporary goodbye to my friends. My landlord, Abu Ali, has agreed (which is kind of him, as Hamas are not mad keen on parties). In spite of the situation, Shadi insists we should go ahead tonight.

'We can dance and enjoy ourselves, and that is better than sitting at home listening to reports about how many Gazans the Israelis are killing tonight,' he says as we leave the Centre. 'I will collect Saida from her home and we will come to you about seven o'clock. I will bring the salads.'

I don't think he realises how heavy his smile is.

On the way home I can hear reverberations of bombs in the distance, yet the streets look and feel quiet. Some shops are already closing, battening down the hatches for the weekend ahead. But the Metro Supermarket is open. Inside, a small crowd of men are gathered around a television, shaking their heads. I stand behind them and look at the screen. Footage of local ambulance crews dragging blood-spattered people – I can't tell if they are women or men – onto stretchers, while other people flee inside buildings, clutching small children howling in their arms. The TV report says that the Israeli military has killed fifty-two Gazans in the last twenty-four hours. This doesn't feel real. But it looks bloody real. As the ambulance speeds off, sirens screaming, the US State Department has 'encouraged' Israel to exercise caution to avoid loss of innocent life in Gaza.

I leave the Metro Supermarket with coffee, eggs, bread, cheese and longlife milk, walk to my apartment and start preparing for the *hafla*. By early evening, the bombing has intensified. The louder explosions make me flinch and I'm relieved when Shadi arrives with Saida. They have known each other for years. Shadi is wearing a blue paisley shirt and a determined grin. Saida is wearing a red *hijab*, a long-sleeved, red-and-white shirt, black trousers and heels; she looks extremely elegant and very tense. When I hug her, she feels rigid.

'*Habibti*, I cannot stay late tonight,' she says. 'My parents will worry too much because of the situation, especially my father.'

'I'm just so glad you've come,' I tell her. I know that she's here for my sake this evening; Saida doesn't go to mixed parties, never drinks alcohol and would no doubt rather be at home right now. Maybe having a *hafla* tonight was a really dumb idea. But it's too late to change my mind now.

I have also invited some work colleagues and *Ustaz* Mounir. Just as he promised, Mounir arrives early, before the dancing and drinking start. He doesn't stay long. After a quick cup of tea, he stands up to go. '*Yallah*, I am sorry, Louisa, but I have to be with my family. I am worried about them. I fear tonight is going to be very bad.' He offers me his hand. 'Come back to Gaza soon – we have more conversations to finish!' Mounir has never called me a friend, but I feel a great affection for him by now.

'Yes, *Ustaz* – we've lots more to argue about!' I say as he takes his leave. We look each other in the eyes and both smile at my parting shot.

Other guests start arriving. Niveen comes with the Smoothie, who greets me with a lingering kiss on the cheek. Muhammad the driver knocks on the door, then Mahmoud from Jabalya arrives with a couple of friends, and by this time Shadi has turned up the music because bombs are now exploding every few minutes. I start pouring drinks. Some of my friends don't drink alcohol, and those that do cannot often get their hands on it. I've long finished the booze I first brought with me, but have acquired a precious little stash from a few foreign friends and acquaintances who come in and out of Gaza for work. A few days ago one of them had a meeting with Tariq and dropped a bottle of vodka off with him. But now Tariq calls to say he can't make it tonight.

'*Habibti*, I'm so sorry, but you know I live next to Jabalya – and it's crazy here right now! There are all sorts of rockets going off and the Israelis are bombing us. No one is on the streets. I'm too frightened to leave the house.' As he speaks, I can hear explosions rocking down the line. 'When I told my mother about the party, she started screaming it was too dangerous to go outside,' he says, 'but I've got the vodka!'

I start laughing because I couldn't care less about the vodka right now.

'Stay at home. I don't want you getting killed on the way to my party!' I shout so he can really hear me. 'What would happen to the vodka then?'

Tariq jokes that even the belligerent local stray dogs have gone into hiding.

'I'll call you tomorrow and we will have coffee at the al-Deira Hotel,' he says. The tone of his voice has just changed; now he's using the same tone that Saida used on the phone the other night, the tone that deliberately masks fear and says this will all be over soon.

'OK.' I try to sound casual down the phone too. 'But take care – and drink the vodka!'

Half a dozen other friends call to say they won't be coming because of the bombing. But the majority do turn up, including some of my colleagues, one of whom arrives with a freshly home-baked apple cake that she thrusts into my hands. Within ten minutes she apologises, but says she has to go. There's a cab waiting outside and she needs to get back to her three young kids and see if they are managing to sleep though these blasts. Saida puts her arm on my shoulder.

'*Habibti*, I have to go too – my parents are very worried.'

She takes her coat and leaves with my colleague. I wave them goodbye and go back into my lounge, where a small crowd is dancing to raucous Arabic music. There are a few foreigners among them, including Dora, a middle-aged French woman with untidy hennaed red hair whom no one seems to know much about ... except that she has been roaming the streets of Gaza for some eight years, saying her book (which she carries round in a plastic bag) is almost, but never quite, finished.

'I really 'ate ze French,' Dora tells me, in her great smoke-crackled growl. "Iz my country, and still I really 'ate them. I love ze Gaza people.'

We smoke, drain the whisky and wine bottles, change the music, strut to the music. Tonight we're loud and defiant, full of passion and purpose and our joy reclaims the night. Niveen is holding court in the kitchen, pouring her great dirty laugh over several attentive men. Shadi is mincing on the dance floor. Mahmoud, who brought his beloved water-pipe with him, is smoking next to the balcony door. I feel a hand stroke my shoulder, then a body leans in close, lips brushing my neck.

'We should have a private *hafla* one night, *habibti*,' he croons. 'Just the two of us.'

'Let's see,' I murmur tipsily, as the Smoothie runs his fingers through my hair.

By three o'clock in the morning the bottles are dry, we're still a bit drunk, finally tired out, and the explosions have gone quiet. Everyone who left said what a great night it was for a *hafla*. A little later the Smoothie leaves too, home to his family. Just Niveen, Shadi and I remain.

Niveen is slumped in a chair, cigarette in one hand and a late-night cup of coffee in the other. She's staying with me tonight. Shadi, who is something of a chronic insomniac, stays for a final coffee and a cigarette too. As we linger in the smoky living room, a long, loud whistle screeches through the air. Niveen sits bolt upright. Shadi's face contorts and for the first time I see the stamp of fear in him.

'F-16 planes,' he says. 'I hope they are not going to use those on us again.'

Tom and Jerry

Before Operation Winter Heat, there was Operation Autumn Clouds: that was in November 2006 and also concentrated in northern Gaza, where the Israeli military killed fifty-three Gazans – including eighteen members of one extended family, the al-Athamnas – in less than a week. Five months earlier, in June 2006, Israel had launched Operation Summer Rains, a four-month military assault across Gaza, which Israeli spokesmen said was being carried out in order to stop rockets being fired into southern Israel and to secure the release of Gilad Shalit. Three hundred and ninety-four Gazans were killed by the Israeli military during the operation, and 1,000 more injured.

But these Israeli military operations have never stopped Gazan fighters launching rockets and mortars from open fields and waste-land towards Israeli cities in the southern Negev.

When Shadi has finally left and Niveen is tucked up in my guest room, I lie in my bed as F-16s stream overhead, that now-familiar knot in my guts clenched like a small fist. I am half-drunk, dreading the hours until dawn. Eventually I sleep.

The next morning, Niveen and I drink coffee, clear up the *hafla* debris and eat the remains of the apple cake for breakfast. The sky seems quiet.

'I don't want to go home yet,' she says, popping her daily blood pressure tablet out of its foil. '*Yallah*. Let's go and walk on the beach while it is still quiet.'

Just before we go, I call Tariq to see if he's OK.

'*Marhaba.*' His voice is sleepy down the phone.

'Are you all right after last night?'

'*Habibti*, we're all fine.' The bravado is back in his voice now. 'It was frightening for a while – but we have had much worse in Gaza! Listen, this is just Tom and Jerry compared to what they are *really* capable of!'

Outside the streets are very quiet and we suddenly remember it's Friday morning, when observant Muslims go to their local mosques to pray. After our night of revelry, everything outside looks very bright. Niveen and I take a slow stroll towards the beach. Hardly anybody is on the streets. When we clamber down from the road onto the sand, we both immediately pull off our shoes. The tide is out, the sand warm and dry. I have walked along this beach many times by now, savouring the salty fresh air and wide open space, because everywhere else inside Gaza always feels so crowded. This particular stretch of beach is the haunt of local men, wanderers and dreamers – and a few clusters of fishermen are usually nestled in the sand, mending their nets, singing softly as they work. We see them now and wave a greeting. They give brief nods in response and go on working. We walk, lulled into silence by the roll and sparkle of the waves, the sun on our faces. I can hear *zananas* circling above now, and what sounds like helicopters throbbing in the distance. But this is a tranquil space – a capsule separated from the fear and bloodshed just a couple of miles away.

Niveen walks on ahead of me, planting a trail of wet footprints at the water's edge. I've never seen another woman walking along the beach alone here. After a while she turns around, waves to me and shouts, '*Habibti* – I feel free!'

By now it is early afternoon; people will be coming home from the mosque, families will be starting to make lunch, married couples and rebels will be making love, children will be crying and playing, fighting and making friends. As these damned drones and helicopters infest the sky, life does go on.

A loud noise behind me. I flinch and reel round, more jittery than I realised. Four camels are swaying along the beach just behind me, each ridden by a man in shades with a black-and-white keffiyeh scarf wrapped round his head like a loose turban.[29] They look young and free, and incredibly sexy.

'Where are you from?' they want to know.

'Scotland,' I say. One nods, the others shrug their shoulders as the camels snort and threaten to spit.

'Why you came to Gaza?' the one who nodded asks me. 'It is dangerous here, you know. They are bombing up there' – he indicates northwards.

'But it's quiet here,' I say. 'Where have you come from?'

'From Rafah, in the south. We are riding towards Jabalya – there is nowhere else to go. We will go as far north as we can, and then we will ride back home. *Salam!*'

He raises a dark hand in salute, whips his beast into a comic, splayed-leg canter and races off up the beach, whooping as he races to catch up with his pals.

I wonder if I'm still drunk.

Twenty-four hours later, Operation Winter Heat is still ongoing, though the bombing is not so intense. I take a taxi to visit Saida. Muhammad the driver is sombre as we cross the city, which is sombre too. The shops have closed early again this evening.

'Those families in Izbat Abed Rabbo cannot escape,' he says as we turn into another unlit street. 'There is nowhere for them to go, they just have to sit and fucking wait for this bombing to finish.'

The district of al-Tuffah, where Saida lives, is near Jabalya and now we can hear the helicopters again. I clamber up the stairs of Saida's building and find her front door open. Her mother is sitting in the kitchen weeping. There's a power cut, but their battery-operated radio is on and a broadcast is crackling over the airwaves. Saida is sitting in the kitchen too, holding her mother's hand in the unsteady candlelight. I cannot understand much of what's being said on the radio, so Saida fills me in. Two local fighters have been injured in eastern Jabalya. The Israeli military are on the ground in the area, and the men have barricaded themselves into an empty house. They have phoned for an ambulance, but the ambulance cannot reach them because it's too dangerous right now. The two men are lying on the floor inside the barricaded house, both bleeding heavily. They have called this local radio station begging for help, because if no one reaches them soon they are both going to die.

I stand in the kitchen doorway listening to a voice rasping on the radio – I don't know if it is the voice of one of the dying fighters or the radio presenter. I feel like someone has just slapped me very hard across the face.

Saida's face crumples. She is a strong, proud woman, I've never seen her like this before, so young- and bewildered-looking. I stoop and take her hand. For a moment she clutches it, pressing my fingers into a tight bunch.

'Why do they want to kill us so much?' She shakes her head and bursts into tears.

'I don't know, *habibti*,' I say.

I don't know anything right now, except that the *hafla*, the jokes, the drinking, all of it was self-medication against the bloody reality that people are dying up the street.

༃

After four days and three nights, the Israelis pull out of eastern Jabalya. Their operation is over.

A few hours later, I am in the district of Izbat Abed Rabbo with a small team from the Centre. We've come to document what happened during the military operation and to interview eyewitnesses. I am standing with one of my colleagues, Samer, in a first-floor living room with bullet holes in the walls, a shattered cabinet of ornaments and a bloodstained carpet. The door to the children's bedroom, just off the living room, is open. Inside, the bedroom window is shattered and blood has congealed into a crust on top of one of the narrow single beds.

Abu Shebak, who lives directly beneath this first-floor apartment, is explaining what happened. Late on Saturday night he heard a burst of shooting, then screaming. He raced upstairs into this living room and found his young niece slumped dead on the floor. Her brother was lying close by, injured and bleeding, but still breathing. Abu Shebak called an ambulance, but as it sped the boy towards the local hospital, its sirens screaming, he died too. The children had been asleep in their bedroom. When gunshots shattered the window, they fled into the living room and were both hit by crossfire from Israeli and Hamas fighters.

Abu Shebak answers all our questions patiently and even offers us tea. But the living room is filling up with journalists and other human rights workers, all wanting their questions answered, and their pound of flesh as well.

Thanking the uncle, Samer and I tread back down the bloodstained stairs. The children's mother is next door, holding the traditional condolences, which can take place now that the Israelis have pulled out. Samer urges me to pay her my respects. I push the door open into a large room filled with women sitting on the floor. They propel me towards the children's mother. She is sitting on the floor too, her back against the wall. I squat down beside her.

'I am so sorry, so sorry,' I say to her in Arabic. I don't know what else to say to this thin-faced woman who is weeping violently, her shoulders shaking. She opens her mouth but no words come out. She tries once more, but the only sound is a gurgling sob. The woman sitting beside her puts a hand on my arm. 'She cannot speak,' she tells me. 'She just cannot.'

On every corner of Izbat Abed Rabbo is a condolence tent where the men are gathering to pay their respects to the families of the dead. So many Israeli tanks have driven through the main street, it looks as though it has been ploughed. Samer and I visit a dozen families and take testimonies about Israeli soldiers invading and smashing up their homes, tying them up, holding them and their children hostage without food or water, using their bedrooms for snipers' nests and ripping floors and beds apart for barricades. The unshaven men stare down at the torn floors, the women weep in humiliation. It doesn't look like Tom and Jerry to me.

In the late afternoon I follow Samer to one last house, where the front door has been torn from its hinges. His mobile rings and he pauses on the step outside. I step inside, to see if anyone is around. I call out and for a moment it seems there is no one and I am alone in this dark, cavernous hallway with debris scattered all around. But suddenly a group of a dozen women and girls appear. They make straight for me and demand to know if I speak Arabic.

'Er, yes,' I say.

They grasp my arms and march me along a dark passageway into a bare room with no windows. They shut the door, surround me, take my hands and begin to talk. Two or three of them wipe away salty tears, dirt streaking their faces as they gesture violently with wet fingers. Their voices are loud and shrill and I can catch only a little of what's being said because they are all speaking at the same time, demanding my attention. I am too drained to make much sense of it all, but realise this doesn't matter. They want to blurt out what has just happened to them and I simply need to listen. I do my best as we stand there pressed close together in this bare cell of a room until finally their anxious, quavering voices start to die down.

During Operation Winter Heat, the Israeli military killed 110 Gazans, almost half of them civilians, including 26 children. Gazan fighters launched some 200 rockets and mortars towards Israel during the operation. Some of them landed inside Israel, many fell to ground inside Gaza, and the fighters vowed to continue.

❧

The morning after our visit to Izbat Abed Rabbo, I am in a portacabin near the Gazan side of the Erez crossing, just beside the yellow barrier that marks the beginning of no-man's-land. I'm waiting for the go-ahead to cross no-man's-land and enter the main Erez crossing terminal building, where Israeli security admits people into Israel, or not.

A man called Hani has his work desk in the portacabin. Hani spends his day telephoning Israeli security operatives inside Erez, coordinating permission for individuals to proceed across no-man's-land, and still he manages to smile.

I have no idea how long it will take me to cross into Israel. Everything I'm carrying will be searched at Erez. The UN does not allow its female staff to walk through the crossing – they drive through in UN vehicles – as there has been a recent spate of incidents involving foreign women being subjected to 'humiliating strip searches' by the private Israeli security company working inside the crossing.

I have also heard about the room, deep inside Erez, with the grid floor where people are forced to stand, sometimes without their clothes, being interrogated by Israeli officials behind bullet-proof glass. I am not looking forward to this at all.

And I feel jittery too about facing the outside world, with its space and crowds and too many choices of where to go and what to do. Maybe I'm getting a bit institutionalised, like a prisoner gradually becoming fearful of being released from her jail.

Hani answers his phone again, speaks in fluent Hebrew for just a couple of minutes and gives me the thumbs up.

'You can go now,' he says, quite casually. I wonder if he ever gets to leave Gaza.

I stand up and reach for my suitcase and handbag.

'You coming back?' he asks.

I smile and nod. 'As soon as I can.'

'*Salam.*' He twinkles a smile back. 'Enjoy it out there.'

PART TWO

A Gazan rocket meets an Israeli rocket up in the sky.
'Where are you going?' asks the Gazan rocket.
'To Gaza, to kill terrorists!' says the Israeli rocket, 'where
are *you* going?'
'No idea,' says the Gazan rocket.

Gazan joke

the milking station

With one thing and another, it is almost six weeks later when I finally arrive back at the Erez crossing, armed with a new visa and a new Gaza entry permit. But the crossing is closed. When I get out of the taxi, I can hear explosions in the near distance, inside Gaza. While my Palestinian driver keeps the engine running, I speak to an Israeli officer inside a booth at the main Erez entry gate. She says there is shelling in Beit Hanoun – a town on the edge of northern Gaza – and she doesn't know whether the crossing will open today.

I hover outside the booth, considering my options. It's late morning, so I can wait here and hope the crossing will open some time today; or take the taxi back to Ramallah, stay another night with Saida's sister, Alla', and drive back here again early tomorrow morning. I decide to wait it out. I'm not alone; at least forty other people, Gazans and foreigners, are hanging around the crossing gate too. The Israeli plain clothes security operatives prowling just inside the main gate have tinted, wrap-around shades and their index fingers rest on the trigger of their M16s. When I tell my taxi driver I'm going to stay, he merely nods. Bags in tow, I take my place on the low wall just outside the main gate.

Waiting to enter a hermetically sealed strip of land that is being shelled is not a position I ever thought I'd find myself in. But I have switched on to auto-pilot, or maybe it's just denial. With nothing else to do, my mind drifts back to my six-week trip. I spent my first week outside Gaza snorkelling in the small Red

Sea resort of Dahab, as I had planned; but found the first couple of days bizarrely stressful. After constant power cuts inside Gaza, the light of Dahab dazzled me and sudden loud noises made me flinch. The Egyptian manager of my backpackers' hotel had tacked up a notice in the reception:

No Israelis, No Dogs

He told me it was a protest against Israel having just killed 100 people inside Gaza. I said it was pathetic. If he cared so damn much, why wasn't he protesting to demand that his government reopen its Gaza border? A few days later I got chatting to a middle-aged American 'living the desert dream' with her local Bedouin husband. She asked me where I lived. When I told her I was working in Palestine, she told me I was helping Palestinians because my heart was wide open – and by the way, did I know about a website exposing what those powerful Jews in America are really up to? I didn't know the website, and said I didn't want to know it, and she looked away. I never heard poison like that inside Gaza.

After Dahab, I went back to Scotland. I had been invited to give a reading in the far northern Orkney Isles, where, the day after the reading, I crouched amid rocks laced with lichen and watched blubbery seals snorting as they basked in radiant early morning sun. I filled my lungs with Atlantic Sea air, and at that moment Gaza felt like a dark tunnel that would just swallow me up whole. But as soon as I got news of my new entry permit, I flew from grey-skied London (which Gazans call *Balad al-Dabaab*, the City of Fog) to Tel Aviv, drove to Ramallah and spent a couple of nights with Saida's sister, Alla', and her family before heading back to the Strip.

'OK, now you have seen Gaza,' said Alla', 'you can see it is a hell.

Khalas! Stay here in Ramallah.'

But I missed the intensity of Gaza, I really did – and being away made me realise how much I wanted to go back. When I said this to Alla', she shrugged and bought presents for me to take to her family. But when my taxi to Gaza arrived at her place this morning, tears sprang from her eyes. She pressed her lips together and shook her head, as though trying to rid herself of her own thoughts, and kissed me hard.

'Kiss my family for me,' she said.

I flit between these occupied spaces of the West Bank and Gaza, visiting her family, but *they* never get to kiss each other.

The Palestinian driving me down to Gaza in his taxi asked me if we could give someone a lift to Gaza, a woman he knew whose son was in hospital in Israel. When we picked her up, she was a rake-thin, timid-looking lady who said barely a word for most of the journey. It was only during the last couple of miles to the Erez crossing, as we sped past emerald groves of orange trees lining both sides of the road, that she told me about her 19-year-old son, Muhammad. He had been shot by Hamas, she said, 'by mistake', during a row. After fifteen months in a Jerusalem hospital, Muhammad still couldn't walk, or use his right arm, because his brain was damaged. She had waited months for a permit from Israel to visit her son in the hospital and had no idea when she would see him again. She was going home to Beit Hanoun.

I told her that when we reached Erez, we would have to go through the crossing separately and she gave a passive nod. I felt rude saying it, but told myself I didn't know her or her son and didn't want to be refused entry into Gaza because I was in the company of someone the Israelis had their eye on. Gazing out of the car window afterwards, I thought to myself, 'Jesus, this place makes you paranoid.' When we got to the closed crossing, she took her bags, thanked me and walked away.

After an hour or so, the explosions go quiet. But the crossing remains closed. A few more people arrive and join our lethargic queue. I notice a young man carrying a backpack and clutching a book in one hand. He looks around, sees that I am alone too, walks over and asks me in stilted English if this is the way to Gaza.

'Yes it is,' I say, 'but do you have an entry permit?'

'Entry permit?' he repeats uncertainly. I glance at his book; it looks like a Japanese travel guide.

'Are you Japanese?'

'Yes.'

'Why do you want to go to Gaza?'

'I want to see the suffering of the Palestinian people.'

His reply is so straight-up, I am stumped for words. I point him towards the Israeli officer in the booth by the main gate and wish him luck.

Two hours later, maybe more, the Israelis finally start allowing us inside the Erez crossing main terminal building, in small batches of Gazans and foreigners. Once inside, we are still on the Israeli side of the crossing, waiting to be processed like suspect parcels. In order to cross over to Gaza, we each have to go through Israeli passport control. This can take anything between ten minutes and five hours, depending on lots of factors, including whether the shelling resumes and how long the Israelis feel like keeping us waiting. One of the passport control officers is sitting in her bulletproof booth now, just a few metres in front of my nailed-down plastic chair, filing her nails, clearly in no rush at all.

'Erez' means cedar tree in Hebrew, an Israeli symbol of nobility. These days, the crossing looks like something out of a James Bond film. But when first rigged up, in the aftermath of the 1956 Suez/ Sinai war – Israel's first brief military occupation of Gaza – it was a simple wooden checkpoint.[30] In 1967 Israel re-invaded Gaza and the Egyptian Sinai peninsula; during the early days of this second Israeli occupation, Gazans continued to work as labourers in Israel and Israeli soldiers didn't even bother checking the few Palestinian cars going back and forth across Erez. The right-wing Israeli Likud Party's Zionist mantra – that all Palestine was part of Eretz Israel ('Greater Israel') – was one of the main reasons that Erez was dismantled in the early 1970s. And with the checkpoint gone, Palestinians moved around their own country more freely than they had done since 1948.

But after the infamous 'Bus 300' hijacking in April 1984, the Erez crossing was re-erected and reinforced.[31] On some days, the queue of Gazan labourers at the crossing stretched for up to 2 miles in either direction. On the Gazan side, Palestinians were corralled into metal walkways like cattle and they cursed the fortified crossing as *al-mahlab*, 'the milking station'. Israel handed over the administration of Gaza to the new Palestinian National Authority (PA) in 1994 – but kept control of Erez (plus Gaza's airspace, land borders and territorial waters) and built the 37-mile barrier that encircles northern and eastern Gaza, severing it from the outside world.[32]

I perch on a moulded plastic chair, trying to read my novel. But it's hard to concentrate when I know that every flicker of my eyelids is being recorded. Most of the other foreigners waiting to be processed are medical aid workers. I know this because they are wearing

sleeveless vests branded with the names of their organisations. As I
look around this vast fortified chamber a couple of people catch my
eye, and we smile, but without moving from our seats, like pieces of
chess waiting to be played. The woman who drove down here with
me hasn't appeared inside the terminal. Maybe she got stopped at
the first gate. Or turned back. Or maybe she is being interrogated.
I hope she makes it home today.

Eventually, just when I really need the toilet, one of the
foreign aid workers gets called into a passport booth. Most of us
immediately stand too, scooping our bags and suitcases together,
wired and nervous in case we are next. My name is called by the
woman who has long finished filing her nails. I step up to her booth,
slide my passport and documents under the glass towards her.
The knot in my guts is taut because I'm nervous and intimidated,
and I resent her for this. She asks a few questions about why I'm
going to Gaza. I go into role play, giving very little information,
feigning polite boredom while maintaining direct eye contact. She
stares me down, turns to the computer screen in front of her, eyes
flickering right to left until she finishes scanning. With a slight
nod, she stamps my passport and slides it back.

'Thank you,' I say, picking up my bags and walking out of the
booth. Foreigners' luggage is rarely searched en route into Gaza –
just on the way back into Israel.

In front of me, on the far wall, is a signpost:

→ **Gaza**

I follow the sign into a long windowless corridor, suddenly amused
by the clinking of glass inside my suitcase. Come to think of it, I
could do with a swig right now.

In front of me now is a high metal gate. As I approach, it opens with a loud click. I step through. Ahead is a solid wall. I approach it slowly too and whoever is watching me presses a switch or a computer key. A section of the wall glides upwards, like the door to a secret passage. And there is Gaza. I step through the open section of wall and it glides back down, sealing me inside.

Now I am on a wooden walkway, with lines of razor wire on either side. The walkway leads to the tunnel that spits pedestrians out into no-man's-land, the final stage of walking into Gaza. Gazan porters work on this Palestinian side of the Erez crossing, ferrying people's luggage back and forth across no-man's-land; I can see one of them hurrying towards me now, from the other end of the wooden walkway, eager to carry my bags for a fee. But I stand still, distracted. Staring out at the fields just beyond the razor wire, where, no more than a few hundred metres from the perimeter of Erez, there is a small row of white cottages. I remember them from the first time I crossed Erez. Then, as now, I wonder who the hell lives there and why, because that's a crazy place to stay, so close to the Israeli border. Maybe I can get someone to come and visit them with me and meet whoever is living there, right on the front line.

why no one visits the Swailams

At work, I spend a lot of my time editing documents and reports
that the Centre publishes in both Arabic and English. But I get out
of the office as much as I can. Recently I suggested we could interview ordinary people across Gaza about their experiences of living
under siege and publish the interviews on the Centre's website.

These narratives have proved to be popular, so I have been
encouraged to continue writing them. When I get back to work,
I speak to my immediate boss, Hamid, and suggest I could go and
interview whoever lives in the row of white cottages next to Erez.
Hamid sits back in his chair, thinks about it for a moment and then
agrees. He tells me a family called the Swailams have been living in
those white cottages for generations (in Gaza people can usually
be identified by area, as extended families tend to live within sight
of each other, often in the same building). The Swailams used to
farm citrus, especially oranges. But Hamid isn't sure how they are
surviving now.

He suggests I take another colleague, Majd, with me to act
as interpreter. I'm happy to do so: Majd is broad-chested, has a
booming voice and speaks English better than I do. We get on very
well. This morning we take a taxi and drive north. We stop briefly
in the grimy town of Beit Hanoun to pick up a local contact, a
community worker called Samir who knows all the farmers in
this corner of Gaza. Samir is young, but has the silver-streaked
hair of an older man and a searing gaze. When we meet him, he

is polite, but brief, saying little except to direct the driver out of Beit Hanoun, then onto a rutted dirt track amid the fields. A little while later the driver pulls over to the side of the track. He says he will wait for us here. We are 400 or 500 metres south of the white cottages, which look as if they are about the same distance from the razor-wire Erez perimeter.

Majd, Samir and I clamber out of the taxi and start walking towards the cottages. There doesn't seem to be anyone around, just what looks like a big dog on a chain. It's late morning, the sun is shining and the warm air is spring fresh. But Majd isn't happy at all.

'Why', he hisses towards my left ear, 'do we have to walk? Why can't the driver just wait for us outside the white houses? I have a wife and four children you know, and this ... situation is making me absolutely nervous.'

Majd is not from northern Gaza. He lives in the city of Khan Younis, down in the southern Strip, and doesn't know this area. Samir scowls at Majd – who doesn't notice – and strides ahead. As we approach, the dog stands and yanks its chain with a sullen growl. Still no one is around – and if we can see that Israeli watchtower, there is no doubt they can see us too. A few other farmhouses are dotted around this area, but the Swailams' cottages are closest to the buffer zone – the 300-metre military zone that extends along the entire northern and eastern perimeter of Gaza, bordering Israel. The Israeli military patrol the zone day and night and fire warning shots if anyone approaches: anyone reckless or desperate enough to attempt crossing the zone into Israel will be shot dead.[33]

I felt almost fine a minute ago, but now Majd is making me nervous. We are almost at the row of white cottages, close enough to see the large allotment at the front, facing east, where bright flowers are growing between rows of well-tended vegetables. A few hens are scratching in the dust. It looks for all the world like a traditional smallholding, the kind of place where men and boys have calloused hands and filthy nails, and women and girls bake steaming fresh bread. As long, that is, as you blot out the watchtowers built into the wall ahead and the white sphere suspended above the wall, like a tethered moon, and which I now know is listening to Gaza.

We haven't seen anyone yet. But hang on – a heavy-set man has just emerged from a doorway and is pounding towards Samir with strong strides. He must be one of the Swailams. Then half a dozen kids appear from nowhere, just as the dog starts barking enthusiastically. Samir and the heavy-set man reach each other and embrace as other men, and women, stream out of doorways to see who has just arrived.

Majd looks at this small crowd, and I hear him exhaling.

'Louisa, don't worry, you are safe with me. Everything is hunky-dory now.'

As we all start shaking hands, my anxiety evaporates like clouds in a hot sky. Three or four generations of the Swailam family are here, from chubby toddlers to elders with stooped shoulders and faces like old maps. The man who first strode towards us introduces himself as Jamal Swailam. He is large, handsome and wide-shouldered, with a silver moustache that would make a walrus proud. He beckons us to follow him into the last cottage in the row of four, nearest to Erez.

Samir, Majd and I enter a big kitchen. Jamal offers us white plastic chairs, warped slightly out of shape by previous occupants. There is very little other furniture. Despite the sunlight outside, the kitchen feels cold and slightly damp. Jamal and Samir sit to-gether, heads bent towards each other, talking between themselves.

I shuffle in my chair, trying to get comfortable. Majd nudges me. 'Look at these walls.'

The kitchen walls are bare and white, the upper sections spattered with bullet holes and embedded with shrapnel. The corner of one wall looks as though it has been torn or blasted away.

'This kitchen does not get used much,' says Majd.

There are no signs of cooking, dirty dishes, cups or even food. I nod, taking in the nakedness of a house that no one actually seems to live in.

Two boys sidle into the kitchen, one balancing a tray of small cups. The older lad scrapes a chair across the floor and sits next to Jamal, the younger passes round the coffee cups.

'This is my big son, Imad.' Jamal pats the narrow shoulders of the teenager beside him. Samir sits back in his chair, his conversation over. I lean slightly forward.

'How long have you lived here?' I ask.

'I was born in this house nearly fifty years ago,' says Jamal. 'I have always lived here, my father too. This is his land. He's resting now, but you can meet him when he wakes up.'

'Are you farmers?'

Jamal flashes an amused smile.

'Of course we are farmers! We used to have groves of orange and lemon and grapefruit trees – guava too – because our land here is very rich. This area all used to be orchards; our district of Beit Hanoun was the garden of Gaza.'

This is not just the view of 'Hanounis' (Gazans' nickname for those from Beit Hanoun). I have heard other people, including my teacher, *Ustaz* Mounir, reminisce about the exquisite orange orchards that used to flourish all across northern Gaza.

The tenth-century Iraqi historian, al-Mas'udi, known across the

Middle East as 'the Herodotus of the Arabs', described orange trees arriving in the Arab world from India around AD 912. The trees, he said, were first planted in Oman, but quickly spread across Syria to Palestine and its neighbour, Egypt. Oranges were yet another strand of the burgeoning medieval spice trade. Oranges exported to Palestine were traded in Gaza, and trees were planted en masse in Beit Hanoun because it is blessed with the highest rainfall in Gaza and with rich, dark, moist soil. Trees planted by Hanouni farmers flourished and blossomed into vast perfumed orange orchards. Even now, twelve hundred years after these small fruit first appeared in Palestinian *souqs*, the intensely sweet oranges of northern Gaza remain the most sought-after.

'We used to have so many trees on our land ...' Imad interjects, then falls silent as his father continues speaking.

'We farmed citrus fruits for many years,' says Jamal. 'But when the second intifada started, the Israelis came and bulldozed our trees. We replanted all of them. When they bulldozed the trees again, we replanted them again, all of them. The Israelis damage and destroy, and we rebuild – this is our life. But the fourth time they bulldozed our trees, we did not have the energy or the heart to begin again. Some of the trees we lost were fifty years old. We still farm 17 dunams, but now we only grow vegetables.'[34]

'Do the Israelis still come here?'

He tells me the Israeli military enter the area in tanks and jeeps. Sometimes they just come up to the Swailams' houses or around their land, sometimes they go on to Beit Hanoun. But they always pass by these white cottages. Jamal says they shoot indiscriminately, so his whole extended family – forty adults and children share this row of cottages – have to stay inside whenever they see the military coming. There have been times they have all had to stay inside for more than two days, to try to be safe. Two years ago, his farmer neighbour was shot and killed by Israeli soldiers. He shakes his big head.

In the past, the Israeli military have instructed Gazan farmers living in the northern and eastern border areas not to plant crops that grow taller than knee height. The Israelis claim that they uproot trees and crops planted close by borders and buffer zones in order to protect Israeli 'national security'.

All along the eastern border areas are fallow fields and empty homesteads, abandoned by Gazan farmers who are frightened to work their own land for fear of being shot by Israeli snipers. The villages close to this eastern front look half-empty and feel haunted. The silence is skin-prickling.

The few farmers who are as tenacious as the Swailams have vowed to stay put. They now harvest a mere fraction of what they could grow if they were safe to work their own fields. But Israeli bulldozers roll into eastern Gaza almost every day, levelling land, crops, sometimes entire farms. Since September 2000, the equivalent of 15 square miles – more than 10 per cent of the entire Strip – has been bulldozed.

This wanton destruction is one of the reasons that the bulk of fresh produce in local *souqs* like al-Zawiya does not actually come from the fields of Gaza. Israel turns hefty profits dumping thousands of tons of its own agricultural leftovers into the Strip every year, while denying local Gazan farmers access to markets outside the Strip. Gaza is stuffed to the gunwales with Israeli goods. It is, quite literally, a captive market.

Young Imad interrupts the conversation again. 'We do not ever go outside after five o'clock,' he says. He has a tight, furrowed brow and deep-set eyes the colour of coal. 'Our life is fear and tension.'

He looks at me. 'And it is lonely here. No one ever visits, people are too frightened.' He radiates an intensity that is unnerving in such a young face.

'How far is Erez?' I ask Imad.

'Four hundred metres from our door,' he replies.

Jamal shrugs shoulders as broad as his son's are narrow.

'This house and our land is all my family know. We are not leaving.'

He eases himself out of the tight-fitting plastic chair.

'Come. I want you to see something.'

Jamal moves towards a flight of stairs I haven't noticed until just now and starts to climb them, his plastic sandals smacking the bare concrete. We follow him upstairs, along a narrow landing to a room at the top of the cottage. He pushes open a door – and the stench almost knocks me sideways. Inside is a floor-to-ceiling cage, where at least a dozen green-and-yellow budgerigars perch, fluttering narrow mottled wings. They look clean and bright-eyed ... and they stink to high heaven. Majd backs away, hands clamped over his nose and mouth like he has just seen something dead. Jamal opens the cage and puts both hands inside, his fingers outstretched. Two of the birds hop aboard his thick dry fingers, their tiny heads bobbing.

Jamal looks at me. I'm holding my breath. He's smiling serenely.

'They help me feel peace,' he murmurs.

A memory slips through my mind: of strolling through a refugee camp over in the Palestinian West Bank a few months ago. Seeing small cages of birds being hung from balcony railings and store-front awnings by men who looked like Glasgow pimps, but who handled them with the greatest delicacy. As the fresh air ruffled their feathers, those caged birds sang. But these tiny creatures have nothing to say.

Jamal places the budgerigars back in their cage. We peer inside the other upstairs rooms, and each is utterly bare, except for curtains flapping across the part-open windows. In one room I move towards the window to look outside. But Samir blocks my way with his arm.

'Keep back from the window!' he snaps at me. 'They might shoot you.'

Samir radiates intensity too, like a man hunted, or haunted. I step back and he drops his arm.

'We don't sleep up here,' says Jamal. 'Downstairs or next door is safer.'

The last bedroom looks directly towards one of the Erez watchtowers, so we don't linger. Instead Jamal takes us to meet his father.

Abu Jamal is sitting on a rough-hewn chair inside what looks like a garden shed on its last legs, tucked in between two of the white cottages. The shed door is open, ribbons of sunlight streaming inside. When he grasps my hand in greeting, his feels like an old claw. His voice is thick, his tongue coated white. His small eyes are milky too, dimming inside cataracts. Abu Jamal is almost 100 years old.

'When I was young, this was all trees – just big orchards of fruit,' he says, opening wide his stiff arms, as though embracing the land around him.

When Abu Jamal was a young man, back in the early 1940s, neither the state of Israel nor the Erez crossing existed. This area was part of southern Palestine, with its small, traditional farming communities. The village of Dimra, a settlement of some 500 or 600 people who farmed citrus fruit and cereals, lay a kilometre or so north of these cottages. Dimra had a small village school, and no doubt a small mosque too. But in October 1948 the villagers fled.

Either they panicked for their lives as Israeli troops advanced south – or else they were forced from their homes by an armed Zionist militia, possibly the Givati Brigade.[35] Or both. Whoever invaded the village in 1948 destroyed it.

A year later, an Israeli kibbutz, also called Erez, was established on part of the ruins of Dimra. The Erez kibbutzniks still harvest, and sell, their own oranges and other citrus fruit. The Swailams and their handful of scattered farming neighbours who lived beyond the boundary of Dimra escaped the 1948 onslaught and survived with their homes and land more or less intact. When the Erez checkpoint was first erected in 1956, their homes were just inside the boundary of Gaza, where Abu Jamal has been living for almost a century.

Majd and I leave Abu Jamal warming himself in a small pool of sunlight, like a stiff old cat, and go to admire the allotment out at the front, which is flourishing with peppers, aubergines, beans, tomatoes, potatoes and clusters of small red chillies. At the end of the allotment, a fence has been cobbled together from old bedsprings and scraps of metal.

Majd shakes his head. 'That is the Swailam demarcation line,' he says. 'The Israelis have watchtowers and *zananas*, and these people have the remains of an old bed no one can sleep on any longer!'

We exchange a wry smile. These white cottages feel like an island stranded in a dry, hostile sea. Local fighters launch their missiles towards southern Israel from this area – though not from right here, because we are in full view of the military watchtowers, where patient Israeli snipers wait. This is why no one visits the Swailams, or any of the few other farming families who refuse to budge.

No one yet knows whether the recent tantalising rumours of a Hamas *tahdiya*, or 'period of calm', with Israel will soon bear its own fruit.

Catherine and the Tulip

Saida and I are at the al-Deira Hotel, on the café terrace overlooking the sea, eating warm grilled meat sandwiches and drinking melon juice.

'I missed you, *habibti*, while you were outside,' she says.

'I missed you too,' I smile. 'Did you get my emails or my texts? I never heard back from you.'

She doesn't reply. I look at her across the table, a half-eaten sandwich in my hand.

'What is it?' I say, because there's something wrong. Saida has lost weight and looks slightly braced, like she is holding something in.

'I did get your messages, but ...' She wipes her long fingers with her napkin and lays the napkin on the table. '*Habibti*, it's easier for me not to reply when you are away. Because I am still here. I work and see my family and – what else is there, here? Being in touch with you outside just reminds me how I am stuck here in Gaza.'

She holds my gaze and I hold hers.

'I understand.' I put my tepid sandwich back on the plate. 'You don't need me going on about my foreign travels ...'

'No – listen to me!' She interrupts. 'When you are back here it's fine, because you are with us in Gaza again. And now I want to hear everything.' She extends her hand towards me, inviting me to speak. 'You understand what I am saying?' she adds.

'Yes. I'll tell you my news – but first, tell me yours.' Now I extend my hand towards her.

Saida rolls her eyes.

'Nothing new – I work long hours because I can forget about the situation when working, and in the office we are always busy. But we have no generator at work, and often no electricity during the day. When I get home we have no electricity either! So I go home and rest, and then I get up and do my work in the evening when we have electricity at my home. This is Gaza. Sometimes I see my friends, but not very much because I don't have many friends here ...'

This is why I love Saida. She's completely straight with me about her situation, neither playing it up nor down. She gets on with her life, making the best of what she has here, accepting the choices she has made. She treats me like a sister – still protective, sometimes stern. I, in turn, fret that Gaza is eating away at her. Things have not been any easier here since I got back. The power cuts continue ad nauseam, and despite the talk of a Hamas/Israeli ceasefire being negotiated, Israel is now ramping up the fuel cuts too; maybe to put pressure on Hamas to accept the ceasefire. Fuel stations are closing across the Strip because the pumps are dry. Only a fraction of public transport is working, hospitals are taking ambulances off the roads, and taxis have almost doubled their prices to cover costs. The fuel coming through the tunnels from Egypt is expensive, filthy stuff that clogs up engines, so drivers have resorted to converting their cars to domestic oil (the stuff they use to fire kitchen ovens), cooking oil, even bottles of (potentially lethal) domestic gas. The city streets reek of stinking, uncollected garbage and oily fumes. To quote the Israeli prime minister, Ehud Olmert, 'The residents of Gaza can walk and have no fuel for their cars because they have a murderous terrorist regime.' It is a strange and sad privilege, seeing a people being collectively bullied because they live in a land they cannot leave.

Saida and I finish our lunch, order coffees and I tell her about my trip away. She asks about my family, and an hour later we're still at our table. When she asks what I am doing after work tomorrow, I give a brief shrug and realise that, while I've been here, I have picked up this gesture of not knowing. These days I do the Gaza shrug.

'You want to come to my aerobics class?' Saida asks.

'Ha ha! No way!'

I went to Gazan-style aerobics with Saida once and still cringe at the memory. The instructor was a female gladiator. Ten minutes into her class, I was whimpering, as she lambasted me: 'Louisa! One two three four! *Yallah*! One two three four!'

I shudder and reach for my cigarettes.

Saida rolls her eyes again, but now she's smiling.

'OK, *kaslana* (you lazy thing)! You can sit and talk to Catherine. I will do aerobics and then we can see if the sauna is working.'

We shake on it and arrange to meet at the Tulip Beauty Salon tomorrow after work.

The Tulip is situated on the second floor of a tower block, just a couple of minutes walk from my place. When I arrive, slightly late, Catherine is at the reception desk. She looks me up, then down.

'You fat bitch!' she says, grinning at me.

'Nice to see you too, Catherine.'

'You haven't been around for weeks – where did you go?'

'I was visiting Scotland.'

'You must have stuffed your face the whole time!' she chortles.

'Your double chin's doing very well these days!' I shoot back.

She's something of a Gaza legend, Catherine – a pale-skinned, dark-haired English rose from the Lake District, her Cumbrian accent still strong after twenty-four years in Gaza. She speaks rapid-fire Arabic and has a mouth like a sewer, but she's really a big softie. While Saida works out in aerobics, she and I sit behind reception, drinking tea with milk and chomping on biscuits.

Catherine and her husband Muhammad met in Israel in 1980. She was on holiday with a pal and he was working in a hotel, back in the days when hundreds of thousands of Gazans worked in Israel. They got married the same year and moved to London. But her husband – she calls him Mo – couldn't settle in London, and a few years later they decided to make their home in Gaza. Catherine often reminisces about their decision to do so.

'It was 1985 and we were back here in Gaza again, on holiday. We were sitting at a restaurant on the beach, having a nice fish dinner. Mo asked if I thought I could actually live here. There was a beautiful sunset in front of us and I remember thinking – why not?' She drains her cup. 'This place, even now, it's got *something*. Mind you – I've been slappin' myself ever since!'

I dunk a biscuit in my tea and chuckle. I've heard this story before, but I still like it.

As we sit and chat, a stream of local women flow through the reception. Catherine and Mo opened the Tulip in 1999; it has a gym, hairdressers and a beauty salon. But the *pièce de résistance* has to be the ever-popular 'breast vibrator'. Apparently it does wonders for droopy boobs.

At least half the Tulip staff are foreigners – Russian and East European women who met their husbands when they (the men) were studying at Russian and East European universities. There are several thousand long-term foreign residents living inside Gaza, most of them women married to Gazans. I get my hair cut by a lithe Russian blonde called Vera, who hails from a city called Kalashnikovo and is a dab hand with short hair. Vera has been in Gaza for six years now; she lives with her husband and children in the sprawling Beach Camp (another of the refugee camps), which begins practically next door to the al-Deira Hotel, but is a different world altogether. Once they marry and settle here, foreign spouses are obliged to apply for Palestinian ID cards and, as far as the Israeli authorities are concerned, they effectively become Gazans. The subsequent travel restrictions make it difficult for them to leave Gaza but, ironically, often even harder to return. Catherine hasn't left Gaza for five years now and Mo has not set foot outside the Strip for almost a decade. He cannot secure a permit from the Israelis and she won't go without him.

Catherine asks about my holiday. I tell her the news from the world outside, then ask what she's been up to these last six weeks. She gives me the Gaza shrug.

'You know what? While you were away, I don't think I even left the building ... you've seen our flat upstairs, on the thirteenth floor. It's quiet, and we've got a nice view of the sea. I know it sounds a bit sad, but I don't go outside for weeks at a time. I haven't even been to the beach since about 1996.'

I stare at her and shake my head. 'You know what, you need to get out more!'

Catherine tilts her head back and chortles. 'C'mon, Lou – where is there to go?'

※

Catherine lives within a fragment of an already restricted space, a bit like confining yourself to one wing of an open prison. Most of the Gazans I know get out more than she does, but many people seem to have interior maps that restrict their lives even within the claustrophobic confines of the Strip. When I asked one of my friends recently if she liked the city of Rafah, in southern Gaza, she said, 'I have never been there. I am from al-Rimal, where you live. The rest of Gaza is a dump.' She had never been to the camps or swum in the sea. She wasn't interested.

There *are* people who criss-cross the Strip, like my colleague Shadi. But the majority seem to stay within their neighbourhoods because of ties to families, or clans – and because there is nowhere new to go. As part of his work, Shadi monitors the traffic going in and out of Gaza, human and otherwise. He estimates that 2 per cent of Gazans are permitted to travel outside the Strip on any kind of regular basis. Tens of thousands of Gazan teenagers and those in their twenties, even their thirties, have never seen a day outside this Strip. Many pace or rage in silence, like caged animals; the pressure builds and explodes, at home or out on the streets. Men beat their wives, their children and each other (one afternoon I saw a man on the street pull off his heeled boot and use it to batter a young girl about the head and when I screamed at him to stop he screamed back at me, 'She's *my* daughter!'). Others take to alcohol – some brew their own hooch here – or drugs, like hash, or Tramadol, self-medicate themselves into lethargy, and start to slowly rot.

Meanwhile, as we wait to hear news about the *tahdiya* between Hamas and Israel, civilians, young and old, are being summoned to Hamas police stations as their political connections and allegiances are probed by this increasingly paranoid regime. I can see, and feel, the direct repercussions on the streets, where people are slightly more guarded about what they say and more nervous about hosting mixed parties with dancing and alcohol. These changes are subtle, like a fluctuation of one or two degrees in the air temperature, but isn't that always how it starts? My local friends tell me that more moderate members of Hamas are struggling to keep the movement's political militants at bay because the regime is isolated, and no match for Israel's military might, and because they cannot do anything about lifting the siege. So instead, Hamas is beefing up its local military presence. Military training camps have opened up and down the Strip – including one on a piece of wasteland opposite the bottom of my street, next to Gaza's Al-Azhar University where lines of masked men practise target shooting every afternoon, within range of thousands of coming-and-going students. With these added internal pressures, there is even less space for ordinary Gazans to breathe. Sometimes when I step outside my door, I can feel the tensions crackling round these streets.

I tell Catherine that, while back in the UK, I had a telephone conversation with the BBC journalist Alan Johnston, Hamas's former hostage. We didn't talk for long. But what stuck with me afterwards was his comment about how remarkable it is that Gaza still actually manages to function as a society, given the almost-unbelievable pressures on ordinary people. And this is from a man who spent his last four months here imprisoned in a basement.

rocket talk

Abdul never left Gaza either. He lived in Beit Hanoun, on the ragged northern edge of the town, in an apartment in a grimy tenement building where his mother keeps the heavy curtains closed. Thanks to its proximity to Erez – and Israel – Beit Hanoun is one of the most battered places in Gaza, a dreary town that no one else wants to visit.

Abdul attended the Beit Hanoun Agricultural Secondary School, just down the road from his home. After school he sometimes used to hang out and play football in the school yard, like most 13-year-old boys do. On 21 August 2007 Abdul and two of his friends, Fadi and Ahmad, were in the yard after school. They kicked the ball around for a while, then scampered over the low fence dividing the yard from a scrubby field with a small copse of buckled trees at the back. Abdul was small for his age, and wiry, good at climbing trees. At 5.45 PM that afternoon, while the three boys were climbing round the twisted branches and trunks, an Israeli officer pressed a button that launched a surface-to-surface missile at them.

Abdul's mother, Sabah, is draped in black when we meet at her home. She sits beside a lamp which casts her half in shadow, half in light.

'He was a good boy,' she says of her dead son, but her thread of a voice is so fine I have to lean forward to catch her words. A photograph of Abdul hangs on the wall above her, framed in gold, next to an identical framed photograph of his elder brother, who was killed by the Israeli military the previous year in circumstances I know nothing about.

Sabah sees me squinting up at the two framed photographs in the half-light and bows her head. She didn't witness either of her sons' deaths, but has the bearing of a woman emptied by grief. Abdul was dismembered by the Israeli missile and died in the field among the trees. Fadi died as he reached the local hospital. The third boy, Ahmad, was injured by shrapnel, but lived. The Centre where I work gathers data on everyone killed in Palestine by Israeli or Palestinian forces and I am helping to collate information on children who have been killed by the Israelis inside Gaza over the last twelve months.[36]

I am in Sabah's home with Samir, the local community worker with the searing gaze and silver-streaked hair who recently took me to meet the Swailams. When we have finished drinking the coffee served to us by Sabah's young daughter, Samir says he will show me the spot where Abdul was killed. As we rise to our feet, Sabah extends her hands towards me and for a moment she and I stand in silence together, our fingers clasped. I thank her for her time, tell her I am very sorry about both her sons and we say goodbye.

I follow Samir out of the tenement and down the dirty street. We walk side by side. Samir looks straight ahead, silent. A donkey cart trundles towards us. The beasts' hooves are overgrown as calluses and the man riding the cart has a barrel of a belly. As they rattle past, he gives the donkey a surly whack with a hefty stick. But apart from them, the street is quiet; the local children are at school. I am not used to this near-silence inside Gaza; it makes me jittery.

At the end of the dirty street, I follow Samir through a gap in a crumbling stone wall, into a scrubby field with a handful of trees at the back. We walk towards the trees. As we approach, I see that a few of them are budding small white blossoms. The long, oblong building of the Beit Hanoun Agricultural Secondary School is to our left, just over a low fence. Samir stops and squats down beside a scoop in the ground at the edge of the trees, where the impact of the Israeli missile still marks the spot like a shallow grave. I squat down beside him, trying to make sense of what happened. Families from around Beit Hanoun have told me, and my colleagues, that they believe their children are targeted by the Israeli military to pressurise them into confronting the fighters launching rockets towards Israel.

'Why do you think the Israelis killed the boys?' I ask Samir.

'Come.'

He stands up and walks away from the trees towards a ragged path that slices through the field to the school. I follow just behind him. When he stops, I look round but see nothing until Samir points out a rusty contraption lying on the ground among the grass and weeds near the side of the path. Neither big nor small, it looks like a stepladder with just one large rung in the middle. I squat down to touch it but Samir puts his arm out, blocking me, just like he did inside the Swailams' house.

'Don't touch it,' he says. 'It is a rocket launcher.'

I whip my hand back to my side.

'The fighters were firing rockets next to the school?'

'It is an old rocket launcher, it is not being used any more. But the two boys who died were playing very close to it when they were hit.'

'How do you know?'

'I was here just after the attack, I filmed everything. I have the video if you want to see it.'

'OK.'

When we stand up, I search Samir's face for a reaction and he stares back at me with an expression I cannot read. Though my throat is dry, I light up a cigarette and realise that my hands are trembling.

※

My Gazan friends do not shy away from rocket talk. We have had many evenings in the al-Deira Hotel discussing the pros and cons of Gazan militants firing rockets at Israel. The al-Deira is a haven where we don't see Hamas operatives – not in uniform anyway – and people seem to talk quite freely here.

I'm quite black and white about the rockets: I think they are provocative and do nothing but give Gaza a bad – or worse – name. And Gazan civilians, especially those in the flashpoint border areas, pay a horrific price for what local militants do. At the beginning of February this year, a teacher at another Beit Hanoun school was killed while walking across his crowded school yard to begin morning classes. The Israeli military had spied Gazan fighters nearby; they launched a missile, missed the fighters and blew the teacher to pieces in front of his students.[37] But in spite of such horrific cases, my local friends – including those whose families live in and around the border areas – are more ambivalent about the rockets. They stress that it is a myth the Israelis merely 'respond' to Gazan rocket fire. The Israeli military fire missiles, and bombs, into Gaza at will, claiming this is in defence of their 'national security' as though this is a one-sided privilege.

'The rockets are a message to Israel that they can't just stamp over us,' argues one of my friends. 'It is ugly, but it's resistance. We have this *tahdiya* now because Israel has been forced to negotiate with Hamas – because Hamas resists the Israeli occupation.'

The *tahdiya* has just been confirmed: it will begin at dawn on 19 June. But no one inside Gaza is holding their breath. They have, literally, been here before.

'My family lives in Shaja'iya, right up by the border,' another friend tells me. 'I've seen fighters by the local school yard: they use it for cover. I have to tell you, I really have mixed feelings about it. I wish they didn't use the schools, but people here don't confront them because without the rockets Israel will just do what it wants with us. The rockets are a warning to Israel that we will not lie down.'

'And the children who get killed ...?'

'Louisa,' she says, 'do you really believe that if Gazan fighters stop firing rockets, then so will Israel?'

❦

Just a day or two before the *tahdiya* is scheduled to begin, Samir walks into my office at the Centre.

'*Marhaba*. I have the video for you.' He brandishes a USB stick.

'*Marhaba*, Samir. Would you like a coffee?'

He shakes his grey head, says he doesn't have time to drink coffee. I take the USB stick from him and upload the video onto my computer. Samir scribbles something on a scrap of paper lying on my desk.

'The film is very short,' he says. 'This is my number. Call me if you want to visit Beit Hanoun again; I know everyone there.' With a brief nod, he walks out again.

I press Play, sit back in my chair and reach for my cigarettes. The film opens with a grainy shot of the ground. The cameraman, Samir, is running; I can hear him panting as the camera jerks up and down. Then I see people running in and out of that scrubby field in Beit Hanoun, screaming at each other. An ambulance screeches as a man sprints towards the camera, a dark bundle in his arms, howling at people to get out of his way. Just behind him is another man, his eyes wild with terror, and in his arms this second man is brandishing a leg – a child's leg that has been torn from the child's body. As he runs, the man raises the leg up until he is holding it against his chest. Now that he's almost level with the camera, I see the terror speared inside his eyes, and then I know that he is the father of one of the boys whose body has just been ripped apart because never before have I seen such wild animal terror in anybody's eyes. The camera speeds over the road, though a gap in the wall, and races across the scrubby field, zigzagging towards the buckle trees at the back, zooming between yellow earth and blue sky. And when it comes to a stop, the body of Abdul lies crumpled in the scoop in the ground, his belly imploded, like a small dead bird.

shortly before six in the morning

I wake just as darkness is retreating and dawn begins to finger the long lace folds of my bedroom curtains. Nestled warm and soft in my bed, I know that, whatever time it is, I don't have to get up for a while yet, can just lie here drifting in my sea of sleep. The neighbourhood is quiet; even the belligerent cockerel down the street is still dreaming. I roll over, grunt, then remember – the *tahdiya* begins at six this morning.

Tahdiya means 'period of calm'. There have been many *tahdiyas* in Gaza – like punctuation marks between the storms of wars and occupations that have battered this land over the centuries. When Julius Caesar's carousing and hard-bitten military general, Mark Antony, married Cleopatra, the vengeful, venal queen of the Egyptian Ptolemies, circa 37 BC, he bequeathed her a whole swathe of land including Gaza as a wedding gift, and from her bloodstained hands the territory of Gaza was swiftly passed on to that insatiable brute, Emperor Herod. The English historian Gerald Butt describes the Roman Empire's greatest triumph as 'the bringing of peace, helping to create a second great Hellenistic age in which men could travel from one end of the Mediterranean to the other without hindrance.'[38] But over in Judea, the Romans were culling the Jerusalem Jews. In the year AD 135, soldiers of Emperor Hadrian butchered half a million Jews during the Bar Kochba

142

revolt, leaving the pitiful survivors to starve or to rot slowly from their putrefying wounds. Hadrian – whose wall once marked the limit of Roman Britain – renamed the entire territory of Judea as 'Palaestina', after the Jews' ancient enemy, the Philistines. Jews were transported down to Gaza to be sold in the busy slave markets for handsome profits.

In Gaza the Roman era was a boon, a golden time when the city and its surrounds flourished alongside its burgeoning land and sea trades. At the end of the fourth century, Palestine became part of the Eastern Roman Empire – Byzantium – and the Eastern Orthodox Christians swept into Gaza. Two hundred years later, while the Prophet Muhammad was receiving revelations from God, the Persians swept through Palestine and briefly invaded Gaza. As Zoroastrians – worshippers of the creator, Ahura Mazda – the Persians despised the Christians. They ravaged Gaza's churches before they, in turn, were cast out by the Roman emperor, Heraclius, who briefly returned Palestine to Byzantine rule.

And so Gaza was tossed from one empire to the next, like a small gold coin, as invasions, occupations, *tahdiyas*, power struggles and the inevitable eruption of some new bloodthirsty empire followed on from each other, like concentric circles of history.

When I reach for my little clock on the bedside table, it says 5.50 AM. The *tahdiya* starts in ten minutes. Will it last? Right now I don't care, I just want to go back to sleep. As I put the alarm clock back on the bedside table, I hear a deep, now familiar, boom strike the earth. Then another and another – until all I can hear is the pounding of bombs. The Israelis must be striking northern Gaza. I wonder if the Gazans are at it as well.[39] Now the bombing is louder and more furious – waves of strikes. I think of farmers like the Swailams, and families in Beit Hanoun, and the knot in my guts contracts, the pinch making me wince. I can't sleep through this bloody racket, so I just turn over and lie on my back, thinking not of England, just this mirthless drama playing out around me. Sometimes Gaza feels like a theatre where all of us – Israelis, Palestinians, expat journalists and human rights workers – have our ascribed roles in an unending script that the rest of the world is bored of watching.

When the bombing stops, I check my alarm clock again: 6.00 AM exactly. But I might as well get up and have a coffee now.

PART THREE

There's a small secret. If you know it, then it is possible to carry on. In order to live in Gaza, you must create your own secret world [...] which contains you and those like you; those who carry small dreams

Soumaya Susi, Gaza poet

pleasure at the weekend

That first morning of the *tahdiya,* I arrive at the Centre early for work. I don't know what to expect, but there are press releases and reports for me to edit, and correspondence to write, and somehow things feel almost the same as the day before. But of course they are not the same; if anything, my colleagues are a little subdued this morning; as though everyone is waiting to see whether this *tahdiya* is real or just imagined. But it holds all day. That night, the skies are clear and the dawn is quiet.

As the first few days of the *tahdiya* pass – and hold – Israel allows fuel to trickle back into Gaza, a surge of cars return to the roads and the greasy reek of engine-choked cooking oil begins to lift. On the streets the atmosphere shifts a shade, into a tenuous fragile calm. Both sides are holding their fire.

When the weekend comes, for once I have nothing planned; as though the *tahdiya* has given me the luxury of idleness. I wake early as usual, pad into the kitchen in my bare feet to make coffee, drink the first cup out on my shaded balcony and take the second back to bed. Here I read and daydream until sated with rest, then rouse myself with a tepid, salty shower, enjoying the slow beat of having nothing to do. I don't actually spend a lot of time in my apartment these days. For breakfast I have pomegranates, which are now in season – great thick-skinned fruits the size of boxers' fists. I slit them open, scooping the juicy ruby seeds out with my fingers into a bowl, and devour them with Israeli yoghurt and spoonfuls of local Gazan honey. My spacious apartment is silent, the surrounding streets ripple with low noises. I wonder how long this peace will last and what real difference it will actually make to life inside these stagnant walls.

I'm writing my journal when Saida calls.

'*Habibti, ta'lli* – come to our house for lunch this afternoon.'

'OK, *habibti, shukran.*'

I often have lunch with Saida and her family at weekends. We eat mid-afternoon, round the kitchen table, feasting on a steaming mound of *mahshi* (aubergines stuffed with rice, meat and vegetables), one of Hind's favourite dishes. When I mention the *tahdiya*, Hind says *Inshallah* (God willing), it will last, but only God knows.

Saida says, 'We will see, *habibti*, this is Gaza,' and she stands to clear away our plates. Her gesture tells me this *tahdiya* means almost nothing, yet.

Afterwards, the five of us – Hind, Saida, Maha, their brother Muhammad and I – watch Arabic music videos in the bedroom that Saida and Maha share. When Hind goes to pray, Maha stands up too, yawning that she's bored of watching TV. Shooing Muhammad out into the hall, she starts to dance from one side of the bedroom to the other. I have never seen her dance before. She's loose-limbed as a cat, lithe, confident and graceful.

'Come on – dance with me!' she demands, extending her arms towards Saida and me.

By now I know some Arabic dance moves, but when I attempt to join in, Maha just rolls her eyes. 'No – not like that!' She is a teenager, after all. As she gives me an impromptu dance lesson, Saida watches, her quiet smile growing, until the music lifts her from the cushions too and the three of us shimmy across the room together, as Maha sings aloud to the music. I've danced at a lot of mixed parties in Gaza, and quite a few weddings where men and women dance separately – but this is something different. Spontaneity is rare here, where people spend their lives glancing back over their shoulders.

Saida is laughing, her hair loose round her shoulders. For once she looks carefree. Despite her close-knit family, she has often told me that she pines for her friends back in Ramallah, and for her sister Alla'. She finds Gaza lonely.

'I don't have many friends here now, *habibti*, apart from you,' she has said more than once. 'I have been away too long, I don't fit in now.'

Usually she holds herself in check and just carries on: stoic, respectful, dedicated to her work, her prayers and her family – but not very joyful. I've never seen her as carefree as she is right now, arms and fingers outstretched, her whole face smiling, lost in the music.

Maha ties a scarf round her hips, then mine. As she tries to teach me 'the shiver', a shimmering vibration of the hips, Saida cracks up laughing. By now the three of us are raucous and aroused. Suddenly a loud rap at the door, then a fierce push, and Hind stands in the door frame, scowling like an enraged queen.

'*Khalas*! (Enough!)' She berates us for making such a racket, especially on a Friday when people should be praying. As a new song kicks in, we three stand still, scolded into silence. But suddenly Maha and Saida get the giggles and they catch their mother's eye. Hind gives a loud, head-tilting tut, but a smile is breaking across her angry mouth. She glances back over her shoulder and as though having reassured herself no one else is around – for her husband is still at the mosque – she steps lightly over the threshold into the bedroom, clicking the door shut behind her. With a mischievous smile I have not seen before, Hind slowly kicks off one slipper then the other, moves into the centre of the room, spreads her big arms wide open and begins to sway her hips.

We dance ourselves tired, and laugh ourselves hoarse, and I end up staying the night, sleeping in Maha's bed while she curls up on a mattress on the floor. In the morning, after splashing our faces with cold water, we breakfast and drink slow cups of thick coffee. Then Saida and her mother fix their *hijabs* and get ready to visit Hind's elderly mother and father who live nearby. They ask me along, but I decline the invite and come back to my apartment instead, to potter round and maybe go for a walk later. My quiet apartment looks, and feels, like home by now. I've tacked postcards and pictures on the walls and even bought some plants to brighten up the balcony. But instead of pottering at leisure, I wander from room to room, picking things up and putting them down again, unsettled by the pleasure of dancing and maybe the *tahdiya* too. I want more pleasure today.

I have just finished watering the wilting balcony plants when my *jawaal* rings. It's Wafa'. She is one of Saida's friends, a TV journalist with taut, catlike features and a faint twang in her voice from her years as a student in the US. We've met before, together with Saida. I don't know her very well, but I like her sly wit. Wafa' says she's at home too, bored to death. She wants to go out somewhere this afternoon. Am I free?

'Sure!' I say. I suggest the al-Deira café. Wafa' groans. She was there just yesterday. Can't we think of anywhere else to hang out? We chat for a while, trying to decide how to amuse ourselves. At times like this I realise how small our world inside Gaza is, and how limited our options within it. We can walk – but where to?

The beach will be crowded, and the sun blazing hot. If we want to swim, we have to do so fully clothed. There's a public swimming pool, up near Jabalya camp, but it's full of gawping *shabab* – Wafa' would never go there. Back in the better old days, there actually used to be three cinemas in the city – one even had a bar – but that was almost two decades ago; and after the first intifada they never reopened. Concerts and theatre performances are popular, but rare; and I have often been warned about the gropers lurking in the small, tree-filled city park. For us women, even the cafés are restricted – most of the traditional coffee shops in the old quarter of the city are men-only.

But suddenly I have an idea: 'I know – let's go to the lingerie market at Souq al-Bastat.'

A slight pause on the other end of the line. Then Wafa' says, 'OK – why not?'

I heard about Souq al-Bastat a while ago, but none of my local women friends have actually been there. Neither have I, or Wafa'. I tell her I'll pick her up in half an hour.

I call Lebanon Taxis, and soon a cab arrives. It's not Muhammad the driver, but an older, grey-haired man called Harb. His name means 'War' but he drives through the streets as though meditating. We collect Wafa' outside her home and head towards the *souq*.

Souq al-Bastat lies just down the road from the al-Zawiya vegetable market, in the old quarter of the city. It's a long covered market with a series of narrow side passages lined with clothes stalls that you have to push past in order to enter the main body of the *souq*, where I've been told the lingerie section is located. The sun-drenched streets around the *souq* are crowded. Saturday is the busiest shopping day of the week.

Harb brakes to a gentle stop beside one of the side entrances to Souq al-Bastat.

'What are you shopping for?' he asks, with an innocent raise of his grey brows.

Wafa' and I glance at each other and start to giggle.

'Oh, we're just looking around,' I say, feeling suddenly young and a bit naughty.

'Ah, enjoy your afternoon,' he blesses us with his quiet smile.

Wafa' and I push past stalls of black robes and embroidered *jilbabs*. Waves of women are surging in both directions, and our bodies rub as we squeeze past each other. Suddenly we are surrounded by bright lights and the passage ends, emptying us into aisles of brimming stalls. We're in the heart of the *souq* – and as we look around we see that every stall is decked out in lingerie. It is the most decadent sight I've seen in Gaza. I turn to face Wafa', my mouth wide open. She gives a small shudder of anticipated pleasure.

'*Habibti* – let's shop!'

In a slow, happy trance, we wander from one stall to the next, determined not to miss anything. Wafa' links her arm through mine, seeming just as thrilled to be here – surrounded by these glorious, flimsy fripperies – as I am. We stop to gaze at an entire section of stalls devoted to belly-dancing outfits: ornate sequinned bras with matching hip-hugging skirts, each fringed with layers of jangling silver coins. There are belly-dancing dresses too, with plunging sequinned necklines and thigh-high splits. This would impress Saida, Maha and Hind next time we decide to dance!

I hold one or two of the outfits against me, Wafa' laughs her approval and the stallholder – an elderly Bedouin resting on embroidered cushions among her wares – tells me how beautiful I look ... and that she will give me a very good price. But for now we're just browsing, and thanking her we move on. The next temptation is the fur-lined negligees in transparent pink, orange and baby blue ... spread next to stashes of low-cut, silky nightgowns, gossamer black-lace bodices embroidered with red ribbons, and seamed black fishnet stockings with red suspender belts to match. There are sheer camisoles too, and piles of transparent panties with sequins spelling out LOVE ME just above strategically placed holes, sparkling thongs of every shade, ruffled French knickers, balcony bras and lacy boleros, dressing gowns that cling to curves, and bolts of sheer, shining fabrics for women to make their own creations.

I'm starting to feel a bit drunk. Wafa' and I are exclaiming and laughing as we rummage and browse, though I see her glance over her shoulder a few times, making sure we are not attracting too much attention. But the whole shebang is rowdy with shoppers and traders, and young boys with smooth brown faces who flit past with bunches of fresh mint and sage to sell, the fresh earthy fragrance wafting in their wake. I catch the eyes of other browsing women and we exchange easy smiles because we're all sharing the same playful joke.

Many of these purveyors of lingerie are *munaqabas*, and those not fully veiled are clad in black from head to toe. We are on the edge of Shaja'iya, the 'mixed quarter' that used to lie just outside the ancient city walls, a district where Christians, Muslims and Jews historically lived side by side. These days Shaja'iya is one of the most conservative districts of Gaza City, yet the atmosphere here is nothing but jovial. The stallholders encourage us to pick up fabrics and run them through our fingers, though sometimes there is very little fabric to feel at all.

I have money to spend, and want a stash of Gazan lingerie. But many of the items I pick up are definitely too petite for me.

'Do you have anything, er, bigger?' I ask one of the traders, holding up a black lace bodice with crimson roses spread over the décolleté.

'No, I am sorry. That is the only size I have,' is his solemn reply.

He is a bearded older gentleman wearing a traditional white lace *taqiyah* cap. The stallholders are almost all men. Many have beards and are wearing flowing robes to show they are pious; some are scarred with the revered *zebiba* prayer callus on their foreheads, from years of devout, five-times-a-day prostrations. Yet these middle-aged fathers and grandfathers seem perfectly at ease flogging sexy lingerie in downtown Gaza City. The only female traders I can see are a handful of older women – like the lady selling the belly-dancing outfits – who all look like Bedouin.

'Why are so many men working here?' I ask Wafa'.

'It's considered shameful, y'know, for young women to work in a place like this,' she says. 'Like it's shameful for unmarried women to come here. I can come with you because you're a foreigner – but not with another unmarried woman or alone. No way! That's why I've never been here before.'

This treasure house of lingerie is not a Gaza secret; but it's discreet, tucked away inside a *souq* in the old quarter, where women can shop for pleasure and indulge their senses; especially *munaqabas*, or veiled women, whose husbands will be the only other witnesses of whatever they select. I'm as fascinated and repelled as most Westerners by the *niqab* and the accompanying black robes that swallow the woman wearing them. I have met proud *munaqabas* who told me how they love their veil, the respect and anonymity that it gives them, and how they would never go outside without covering their face. For them the veil is freedom. Others have told me that the veil protects their skin from the sun and the winter cold, so they look younger. My unveiled friends say *munaqabas* have many different motives, including being pious, being seen as pious, being forced to wear the veil by pious male relatives, indulging in anonymous love affairs – or slipping away unnoticed after pickpocketing or pilfering from market stalls, their veil cloaking their crimes.

Munaqabas or not, Muslim brides-to-be choose lingerie for their wedding trousseaux in *souqs* like this all across the Middle East. Under Islamic law, if a husband cannot satisfy his wife sexually – or vice versa – it is considered legitimate grounds for divorce. And, like people everywhere else in the world, Gazans who are not married to each other, straight and gay, find places to meet, dream and make love. Empty apartments on the edge of the city are lent out to friends for afternoons or evenings of pleasure, and I too have found a lover here.

Wafa' and I agree that the lingerie here in Souq al-Bastat looks better than it actually feels. The fabrics are not sensual and silky to touch, but synthetic and scratchy. Like most of the clothes in the street stores, they are mass-produced in Egypt, Turkey or China and enter Gaza via the tunnels down at Rafah. I wonder whether the smugglers realise, or care, that some of the sacks they are hauling through the tunnels contain black lace bodices and crotchless panties.

I pick out several outfits and, with Wafa''s approval, purchase three sheer negligees with matching thongs, several bras, and a shimmering camisole embroidered with fake pearls. But Wafa' does not buy anything.

'If I did get something, where would I keep it, *habibti*?' she says with the Gaza shrug. 'I sure can't take it home with me.'

Wafa' is in her mid-twenties, she studied journalism at university in the States and since returning home to Gaza a year ago, has been working freelance and looking for a permanent job in international media. Like most young unmarried women, she lives with her parents. Hers is a religious family, and she too prays with diligence, studies the Qur'an and dresses with utter modesty, her *hijab* always covering her hair, throat and neck. She never stays out late in the evening. We once had a long, intense discussion about the rise of female Qur'anic scholars and why she passionately believes Islam needs its own Reformation.

When we are finally ready to leave the *souq*, Wafa' turns to me.

'How about going to Café Mazaj for a while? I can smoke in there.'

She raises one immaculately plucked eyebrow in question (it's another local gesture I'm practising because I think it looks really cool). Wafa' never smokes at home, but always keeps a stash of cigarettes in her red patent-leather handbag – and wouldn't be seen dead without her carefully applied make-up. She is a *muhajaba* with attitude.

Café Mazaj is in al-Rimal district, where I live, and is close to Wafa''s home too. The café looks out over central Umar al-Mukhtar Street, has comfy beige chairs and framed soft-focus photographs of coffee beans and frothy cappuccinos. Wafa' chooses a table where she can sit with her back to the rest of the café and enjoy a furtive fag with her caramel latte. Though Islam does not prohibit smoking, respectable and, especially, religious women are expected not to indulge.

'Women here live in fear of our reputations being spoilt,' she says. 'It's – you know – the mixture of religion and culture that makes people here so conservative ... and our isolation.'

While we wait for our coffees, she tells me about her time away, studying in the US.

'I really partied in the States,' she says, glancing round again. 'I did everything I wanted to; I even took my *hijab* off. I could be someone else while I was out there.'

'But doesn't that make it really hard to be back here now?'

'Sometimes. But this is my home. My family is religious and traditional, so I just have to learn to manage my life here as a Gazan. It's OK because I know it's not for ever, just maybe for the next few years; then I will make another plan and move on.'

'I know,' I say. Because I'm sure that she will.

'Y'know, I like hanging out with you, *habibti*, because you live in the moment.'

She says this with a small sigh as smoke curls from between her painted lips.

'What else is there here, apart from the moment?' I reply without even thinking.

We look each other in the eyes. And both shrug.

As Wafa' sips her latte, I look around the busy café and muse on the fact that it wouldn't be out of place in central London. When I shift my gaze down onto the busy street just below us, two horse-drawn carriages, one with flashing fairy lights draped across the carriage hood, are parked at the opposite side of the street, waiting for passengers. I smile down at them. Gaza is filled with such surprises.

The waiter comes over with our lattes and glasses of water. He is a small man called Ali, with a big, beaming smile. When he is gone, I look around again, unwrap a new pack of cigarettes and pass one over to Wafa'.

'It's OK, *habibti*,' I say. 'No one is watching.'

# of all the ports ...

As the *tahdiya* continues, the initial uneasy calm morphs into a sense of stasis. Israel allows more goods to enter Gaza (no mineral water though, even at this humid height of summer). But the volume of people crossing through Erez has barely increased. The Rafah crossing to Egypt is apparently 'open' for three days a week, but few people actually manage to leave Gaza; the Egyptians manning the crossing have a reputation for demanding bribes and taking their instructions from Israel.

I've lost count of how many Gazans have told me that all they want in this world is two weeks outside the Strip; then they can cope with another stretch inside this interminable siege. Their dreams of having their own sovereign state have faded, just as Gaza has faded from the news. During one of our lessons, *Ustaz* Mounir tells me he is totally fed up and is against the *tahdiya*.

'At least we used to resist the Israeli occupation!' he says with angry passion. 'But now what do we have? Nothing. Nothing has changed, life in Gaza has just stopped.'

And much of the time that is exactly how it feels.

Bar the resident aid workers, and the occasional visiting journalist, there are not many foreigners around either. But now there are rumours circling about a flotilla of international activists who are apparently about to brave the Mediterranean and sail from Cyprus

to Gaza – just like the ancient Philistines – in order to break the
siege.

On my way home from work one afternoon, I stop to buy fruit.
The weather is hot and so humid that dust and salt stick to my wet
skin. While I'm in the store my *jawaal* rings. As I struggle to locate
it inside my handbag, the bulging bag splits and the fruits tumble
out around my feet.

'Where are you?' Shadi hollers down the phone, as pomegranates, bananas and mangoes hit the floor and roll around me. 'Did
you come to the port?'

'What's going on?'

I can hardly catch a word he is saying; it sounds as though he's
in the middle of a riot.

'Quick – come to the port! The Free Gaza boats have arrived!'

I scoop the loose fruits up from the floor, tell Muhammad the grocer
I'll be back later and hurry for the port, which is just five minutes
away, down a sloping street. Crowds are surging towards the narrow
port gates as cheers rise up the street. It's a thirty-two-hour sail from
Cyprus to Gaza. The boats that have just reached the port are the
first international vessels to dock here in more than forty years.

I reach the port and start wading through the crowd towards
the waterfront. People beam at me, grasping my right hand as I
push past. '*Ahlan wa sahlan fi Gaza!*' Welcome to Gaza!, they call,
as others applaud – and *shabab* elbow their pals and point me out.
They must think I'm just off the boat. An elderly, wrinkled man
blocks my way. '*Mabrouk*! Congratulations! All Gaza welcomes
you! How long will you stay here with us?'

His family turn towards me with such eager faces, I'm tempted
to pretend to be with the siege-breakers; but I play it straight and
confess I have actually been living in Gaza for nine months.

'I'm sorry, I don't even know who the people on the boats are,' I
tell the elderly man. 'I just came down to welcome them, like you.'

'Oh.' His loose face droops, his family turn away. He stands
aside to let me pass.

I press on towards the waterfront. Pushing and shoving to
the front of the crowd, I snatch a glimpse of two white vessels
crowded with passengers and draped in international flags, just as
a contingent of Hamas police start to bear down on us with batons
and rifles. Their faces clenched, the police swing the batons, cock
their rifles and bay at the crowd to back off. One of them eyeballs
me and sneers.

The crowd parts like the Red Sea, the foreign passengers
disembark from the vessels and begin to walk between us, towards
a waiting line of empty minibuses. The foreigners are draped in
Palestinian flags, and grinning like people in love. We cheer and pat
their shoulders as they give the Victory salute. The exchange of sheer
mass joy suddenly makes me want to cry. There is so little collective
joy here. I try to count how many foreigners there are and lose track.
But one or two of them stand out: an old gentleman with thick white
hair and the raw complexion of a sailor; a serene young woman with a
pale face; and a swarthy young man with a strut of a walk, and a pipe
sticking out of the corner of his mouth. He's Italian, no doubt about
it. His name – though I don't know it yet – is Vittorio Arrigoni. The
foreigners clamber into the minibuses, pressing their faces against
the windows and chanting, 'Palestine will be free from the river to
the sea – Long Live Palestine!' The air is electric.

I wade back out of the port to call Shadi, and meet up with
him at the al-Deira Hotel, just up the street from the port. He is
ecstatic.

'Six thousand, six hundred and sixty-six welcomes to the Free
Gaza movement!'[40]

The foreigners – it turns out there are forty-six of them in total – all arrive at the al-Deira later, to stay at the hotel. And from that moment onwards, Shadi can be found among them: networking, fixing, advising, introducing them to local community activists they want to meet, almost desperate to immerse himself with them. Shadi struggles more than most Gazans I know with being locked inside the Strip. He is defiantly, manically cheerful; but occasionally forgets to apply his public smile and then I see a different, and quite broken, thin grey face of a man. He has not been outside the Strip for two years now, which isn't very long by Gazan standards. But sometimes I fear Shadi's imprisonment will extinguish the light still guttering inside him.

A week or so later, one of the Free Gaza activists, an American called Debby, asks if I want to join them on a Day of Solidarity, accompanying local Gaza City fishermen out to sea.

Fish is a traditional Gazan staple – grilled or barbecued, spicy and fresh. In 1993, as part of the Oslo Accords, the Palestinian Authority and Israel agreed that Gaza fishermen could cast their nets 20 nautical miles (37.04 kilometres) out to sea.[41] But the Israeli navy have imposed increasing restrictions on the fishermen, claiming they are a security threat and that some are involved in illegal smuggling, including arms. The fishermen say they just want to work, but are now restricted to 6 nautical miles. Israeli naval officers, they say, still shoot at them inside this limit, deliberately damaging their vessels and forcing them back towards the shore. The shallow coastal waters have been totally overfished, supplies have dwindled and prices have shot up. These days fish is a luxury item.

Debby tells me the fishermen hope that, if foreigners accompany them out at sea, their vessels are less likely to be attacked. I have wanted to go fishing for months, but never quite had the nerve to ask a local crew to take me with them, especially as women are traditionally banned from boats as they are thought to bring bad luck. When I tell my colleagues that I'm going fishing, one of the lawyers takes me aside.

'You are fucking crazy,' he says. 'You have no idea how dangerous it is out there; the Israelis will just shoot you.'

❧

I meet the activists at the port at dawn. The early sunlight is soft, and the air damp and salt-tinged. The port is already bustling, fishermen giving their nets a final once-over and loading gear onto their boats. I spot Debby standing by the boats. She waves me over.

'Hey! We're just sorting out who's going out on which boat – you wanna come in a boat with me?'

Debby has the short grey hair and round, wire-rimmed spectacles of an archetypal middle-aged activist. She sailed here with her twin sister, Dorothy. They are not quite identical, but both look slightly undernourished and nervy, like a pair of ageing sparrows. Debby leads me to one of the larger boats in the port, we hop aboard and one of the men on deck downs his tools and comes over. Though young, in his early thirties at most, his shoulders are stooped, giving him a slightly cowed expression, and his dry face has deep frown lines gouged between dark brows. His name is Suboh and he is the captain of the boat. He welcomes us aboard and we meet his crew: four men, and one young boy with a tangle of hair the colour of carrots. They make room for us to sit out on deck as we wait to cast off with the other fishing boats going on this collective voyage. Sunlight spangles the calm sea.

The activists' audacity in sailing to Gaza seems to have bolstered me too. This morning I feel stronger, braver. I'm not frightened of setting off to sea at all, just excited about the adventure.

'Isn't it beautiful, this morning?' I say to Debby, who is busy writing in a notepad.

'It's a good morning for a solidarity action,' she replies, head bent over her notes.

Our boat shudders and starts chugging towards the harbour gateway to the sea. We are in a fleet of about a dozen boats, two activists on board each boat. We wave to each other, cheering in the sunshine. Within minutes Gaza begins to recede into a low skyline of crooked white buildings and palm trees lining the seafront. Along the road that stretches along the entire length of Gaza's coast, pale nets are staked out like windbreaks, to snare the small sea birds that are a local summer delicacy.

We sail south-west. Two hours later my *jawaal* beeps with a text: 'Welcome to Egypt.' We are not in Egyptian territorial waters, but outside the Gaza telephone network range. Captain Suboh calls over from the wheel, saying we are now almost 6 nautical miles out to sea.

'We cannot go out any further,' he says, though we've already dropped anchor once, but caught little. The fishing fleet has dispersed into clusters of three or four vessels that move together, but with plenty of space in between for the nets. The fishermen use two-way radios to communicate with each other, and can also change frequency, to listen in on the Israeli navy – and to make contact with them as well. The other fishing boats in our cluster are slightly further out than us, right at 6 miles. But one rebel Gazan vessel has just struck out beyond the limit, towards the richer, deeper fishing waters, to harvest shoals of fresh sardines.

'*Yehud.*' One of our crew gestures ahead. *Yehud* are Jews. An Israeli gunboat is speeding towards the rebel fishing vessel. We can hear the Israeli tannoy blasting orders at the vessel to turn back. Debby and I stand side by side. As the Israeli gunboat circles the Gazan vessel, Suboh hands me a pair of binoculars. I focus on the scene ahead and take a sharp breath as the Israeli navy begin to water-cannon the fishing vessel. I can see the arc of water pounding into it. I pass the binoculars to Debby.

'Oh my God,' she says, 'they are violating human rights.'

'They use dirty water to hit us,' says one of our crewmen. 'It ruins the fish. Until you have seen it for yourself, you cannot believe the situation we are facing.'

He sits down heavily and lights a cigarette. His name is Abu Mahmoud; he's been a fisherman for more than twenty years. His skin is wind-scoured, his eyes are the colour of the sea.

The two-way radio crackles and we hear the captain of the boat that is being water-cannoned shouting that he's going to retreat before his vessel capsizes. Then another voice takes over the radio, roaring at the Israelis in thick-accented English to stop abusing the fishermen and stop breaking international humanitarian law.

'That's Vittorio,' says Debby.

'The Italian who arrived with you?'

'You've met him?'

'Briefly. Is he staying in Gaza for a while?'

'We all are,' she says. 'How can we leave now, after what we've seen?'

I watch her as she sits down and writes more notes. She's earnest all right, and it's easy to mock the activists' pious, ideological altruism – but I have seen delegation after official delegation of the Great-and-the-Good traipse through the doors of the Centre while nothing has changed for ordinary Gazans. This lot at least walk the line.

'Suboh,' I call over to our captain, 'how often do the Israelis attack the fishing boats?'

'Every day,' he says. He's at the wheel, chain-smoking, his face warped with anxiety.

He looks towards the Gazan fishing vessel now in retreat.

'My family has always fished,' he calls back to me. 'This boat belongs to my father, but now he is too old to work, so he gave it to me. What else can I do? I have three small boys and there are no other jobs for men like us.'

He says he is out at sea almost every day, and many nights. He has to support his family, maintain his boat and pay his crew.

The crew have dropped anchor again. But the second haul is also disappointing. Suboh rubs his hands over his face, closes his eyes and shakes his head. He tells his crew that we will stay within the 6-mile limit, but change direction. We are going to sail north, towards Israel.

We leave the other vessels behind and sail north alone. The atmosphere on board is sombre. We need to catch fish. But the crew are pessimistic.

'They will come for us today,' says another of the crew, with a grim laugh. This is Imad, who is 23 and saving all his money to get married. 'I'm giving up on fishing,' he says, 'it is too difficult and dangerous now. I want to leave Gaza, reach Dubai and find work over there.'

The carrot-haired young cabin boy – the men nickname him Gingee – is Suboh's 12-year-old nephew. Gingee wants to carry on fishing.

'School's boring,' he says with a freckled grin. He is easily the most relaxed of all of us on board.

When Suboh slows down the boat, we are more than a mile from the border with Israel, and the crew say we are still 6 miles out at sea. They begin preparing to lower the nets.

Debby and I are at opposite ends of the boat, on lookout. Debby calls out, 'Israelis,' and we see a streamlined grey gunboat speeding towards us.

Suboh hands me the two-way radio.

'Speak to them,' he says. 'Tell them you are a foreigner and we are within the limit.'

As he tunes me to the Israeli frequency, his face looks as though he's in physical pain. My throat is dry. I have no idea what to say. I cough, and force myself to speak into the radio.

'Hello ... this is, er, we're two foreigners on board this, er, fishing boat and ... look, can you just stop pursuing us? We are within Gazan territorial waters ... You have no legal right to harass or attack us ...' I think of Vittorio roaring at the Israelis and raise my voice: 'These men just want to fish. *Leave us alone! Please!*'

The only response is the stutter of the frequency.

Suboh tells Debby to stand at the stern, and me to stand at the bow. He wants us both on deck, in full view of the Israeli navy.

'They have to see you,' he says, 'then maybe they will not attack us.'

Without a word, Debby walks to the stern and stands out on deck.

I hesitate, because now I'm really scared.

'*Please,*' he says to me, gesturing towards the deck. 'They have to see you.'

I stand out on the bare deck, blinking and biting my lip as the Israeli gunboat cuts through the sea. It is so fast, for a moment it looks like it might plough straight through our vessel. But instead, it begins to circle us at high speed, creating a violent wake that pitches our boat almost ninety degrees either side. I grasp at the narrow railing on the side of the deck, terrified of being flung overboard and drowning. I feel sick. The gunboat continues circling, like a predator closing in on its prey, as we are knocked one way, then the other, by the wake; then it retreats a little, positioning itself close enough for me to see the figures on board quite clearly. One of them turns a heavy piece of equipment and aims it directly at our vessel. It is not water that flies towards us, but bullets, which crack right over my head. I duck and leap towards the small cabin where Suboh is standing at the wheel.

'Please stay out there!' he shouts at me. 'They need to see you are not afraid!'

'I *am* afraid!' I scream.

Suboh looks me straight in the eye, the way a good friend or a lover does, and suddenly I see who he really is: he is a man trying to make a living to provide for his family. A man who chain-smokes because he's violently bullied almost every day of his life. A young man whose shoulders are stooped from stress, whose face is warped with anxiety, and who still somehow finds the guts to sail 6 miles out to sea, knowing exactly what he and his crew will face. His boat is scarred with bullet holes. He has nowhere else to go.

I step back onto the deck, stand tall and stare down the Israeli navy. They can see I am a foreigner. No Gazan woman would be out on a fishing vessel. They will not want to shoot me or Debby.

'Come on, Louisa,' I say to myself, 'let's have a bit of class here. Six nautical miles out to sea and being shot at – at least it's not another day at the office!'

My heart is hammering with such violence, it feels as though it could burst out of my heaving chest. But I am not moving from here. I stare over at the Israeli gunboat, where the machine gun is still trained on us. One of their officers on board has binoculars glued to his eyes, and I've no doubt they are so powerful, he can see my lingerie. I'm so exposed right now, it is almost comic. Almost. So I do the only thing that I can think of doing right now. I raise my right hand in a slow arc and wave to the Israeli navy.

❧

We retreat from the Israeli gunboat. Once we are at a safer distance, a good way back from the 6-mile limit, the crew lay the nets once more, and this time they yield: 240 kilograms of fish – a decent catch. Our captain smiles, and we all exhale and relax. We sail back towards Gaza port for a hour. Then Suboh kills the engine and Abu Mahmoud and Gingee cook lunch as we drift in the Mediterranean. When the food is ready, we sit out on deck together and share a big pot of fish simmered with rice – simple fishermen's fare, plain, fresh and delicious. We are all starving. The sea is shining. These men have just fought for their lunch.

When the food is done, most of the crew sit back and smoke. Debby makes more notes, then begins an impromptu Arabic lesson with Imad. I sit beside Suboh and we smoke and talk about fish. He tells me it is the sardine season now, and after that they will be fishing for crabs.

'Come to my home and we will prepare fresh crab for you,' he says. I've never lived in a place where people invite you to dinner so much.

He lives in Beach Camp, just down the street from the al-Deira Hotel, where most of the Gaza City fishing families live. These days, Beach Camp is a sprawling concrete jungle. Suboh, his wife and their three sons share two rooms between them. His neighbours include the Gazan prime minister, Ismael Haniyeh, who still lives in his family home in Beach Camp, though Haniyeh's place is cordoned off to casual visitors these days. Suboh tells me about the ugly tensions between Hamas and Fatah supporters, how neighbours refuse to speak to each other because of political allegiances that are now splitting the close-knit camp into factions.

As the sun begins its slow, molten descent towards the sea, the crew kick back. Suboh and I fall silent too. We sit back and watch the light shift; the Mediterranean is calm, infused with streaks of silver, then burnished pink, orange and gold. The sky is ablaze, the soft air almost cool by now. It has been a long, stressful day and we still have a couple of hours' sailing back to Gaza port. But the men have made their money and they'll be back out at sea tomorrow at dawn.

I offer Suboh a cigarette. He accepts it with a small nod of thanks.

'You know, this is the first time I have ever been fishing,' I say.

He makes a small noise from the back of his throat; it sounds like a dry chuckle.

'This is my life,' he says, watching the waves.

sea creatures

While the fishermen fight their corner out at sea, Gazans on dry land have invaded the beaches. On these long midsummer evenings, the only breeze to be found is a ruffle of warm air down at the seashore. Makeshift cafés have sprung up along the main stretch of Gaza City beach, serving coffees and fresh juices from early afternoon until late at night. Every table is busy with families. Many other families just bring their own chairs which they set down at the lapping sea edge, to watch their children swim, and catch the lights winking from Gazan fishing vessels in the late evenings, like stars suspended just above the waves. There are camel and donkey rides for hire, and at one end of the beach two ancient carousels creak as men spin them slowly round by hand and the small children sitting in the carved wooden seats squeal and shriek with high-pitched joy. Half a dozen makeshift lifeguard towers with look-out balconies are stationed along the beach too, where young men pose in the afternoons and play cards and smoke all night.

Other men have set up stalls selling fresh corn-on-the-cob – boiled or grilled – and hot wedges of fluffy sweet potato they bake in small portable tin stoves, then wrap in twists of paper, selling each wedge for a shekel. But the most delightful sights of all are the donkey carts that trundle along the sand, laden with buckets, spades and such an abundance of brightly coloured balloons that the whole spectacle looks as though it might just rise into the warm air thermals, donkey and all, and drift away across the shining sea.

I spend many evenings down on the beach with my friends and their families, though Saida's family tend to stay at home even on these long, sticky evenings. But one evening she calls to invite me to a beach picnic at the weekend.

'*Habibti*, you remember Mata'm Haifa (Haifa Restaurant) – outside the city? We are going there for our picnic. It is more quiet than the city beach. *Ummi* (my mother) and Maha are coming too, and some friends. We will have fun, maybe even swim.'

Mata'm Haifa is perched above the sea, two or three miles outside Gaza City, on the southern coastal road. At Saturday lunchtime, a posse of twenty-five of us descend on the clear stretch of beach below the restaurant. I know many, but not all the women, who have brought their children with them, but not their husbands.

The women quickly shed their *jilbabs*, but leave the rest of their clothes, including *hijabs*, in place. After a splendid picnic, we lie around smoking narghile under palm-leaf umbrellas until the sun begins to cool a little. Then, in the late afternoon, most of us run into the sea fully clothed, and as we hit the waves it feels like a vast, warm bath. Saida holds my hand at first, frowning and nervous. Like most Gazan women, she cannot swim. But her sister Maha just flings herself backwards into the water, shrieking with delight. I take a swim, then float on my back for a while as the tide washes me gently back and forth. We spend hours playing in the sea with the kids, splashing and laughing. Even Hind takes a paddle.

Afterwards, most of us loll around in the still-warm shallows, weary, salty and happy. I lounge between Saida and Hind. Saida scoops up handfuls of wet sand and gazes out to sea. She's wearing soaked cut-off jeans and a baseball cap instead of her *hijab*. I watch her, wondering where she is right now. She catches my eye and smiles.

'How is your friend?' She says it in English, so that her mother won't understand.

I smile back. 'He's fine.'

'What about his wife?' She holds my gaze.

'He says the marriage is over, his wife lives in the States now ...'

'You believe him?'

'I think so.'

She nods, then touches the inside of my arm.

'Be careful, *habibti*.'

I nod back, still smiling. He is a foreigner I met a couple of months ago, an older man with a silver-washed mane of thick hair. I call him Sakhar, after the grizzled male lion in the bare-boned Gaza zoo.

Hind nudges me, wanting to be included in our conversation. She pats her big belly. 'Leeza, I am fat,' she says.

There's no denying she is a big lady. I give a sympathetic nod and Hind pats my belly.

'You were quite fat when you first came here, Leeza,' she says cheerfully. 'You look much better now. What exercise have you been doing?'

She looks so innocent, I am suddenly convinced that she has understood everything we've just said. Saida begins to giggle. I start laughing, then Hind, and the three of us lie back in the shallows until we're all gasping for breath. I love them both so much.

As the sun begins to set, Hind leaves us to prepare herself for the Maghrib prayers, which are recited between sunset and dusk. In just a couple of weeks it will be September, and Ramadan will begin.

'*Habibti*, you remember last time you and I came here together?' says Saida.

'Those sonic booms?' I nod.

She nods too, then shakes her head.

Saida and I came to Mata'm Haifa for lunch a couple of months ago, just before the *tahdiya*. But we had to eat our meal in a rush and leave because the Israelis started detonating sonic booms that threatened to blow out the restaurant windows.[42]

I don't know what to say because I don't want to spoil our wonderful day. We sit in silence, watching the sea, drinking in its rippling vastness. I know why people loiter on the beaches in Gaza – it is because this is the only view without some kind of barrier, the only wide open space to be savoured, the only tangible sense of freedom that there is here.

Behind us, the other women are making mint tea and I can smell apple-flavoured smoke from the shisha pipes.

I hear Saida sigh, a gentle sound of evening contentment.

'You know today is special, *habibti*,' she says. 'Because today I love Gaza.'

❧

The manager of Mata'm Haifa is a grizzled fella with a face full of moles. Known for his rancorous moods. However, he is also a talented chef, especially when it comes to home-made pizza. Which makes his restaurant very popular.

A week before Ramadan, I'm back at Mata'm Haifa, this time with Niveen and the Smoothie. The restaurant is busy, but the beach below is deserted, and we ask the manager if we can have a table right down on the sand. It would be such a treat to sit there and watch the sunset while we eat. He seems to be in a good mood this evening and says that's no problem at all. A waiter lays a table for us, takes our order and leaves us on the tranquil beach. As we sit, the Smoothie winks at me and I wink straight back at him. We are both in a good mood too.

Niveen is smiling, but she's jittery this evening, lighting one cigarette after another. I haven't seen her for quite a few weeks. She says she has a lot on her mind.

'My daughter, Sarah – you know she's studying in Cairo; but now she has applied to do her Masters in Canada,' she says, 'and if she goes there, then I will not see her for a very long time. And my son, he needs to see his sister.'

In the next week or so, Niveen has a telephone interview with a British educational trust that may agree to fund her to resume the PhD she had to abandon when her husband died five years ago. If they do, she will try to leave Gaza and take her children with her to the UK.

'Imagine – I could be in London next year, finishing my PhD!' she says, her voice quite breathless. 'If my son and daughter could be there with me, I would be the luckiest mother in the world ...'

'How will you get out?' I ask.

'I have some professional contacts; I will try to leave by Erez. If not, *habibti*, then it will be the tunnels for me!'

The three of us chortle.

The Smoothie also intends to leave Gaza. He is being harassed by Hamas, who have summoned him to his local police station for regular interrogations about his work, his political views and who he mixes with. He is a youth worker, says he has nothing to hide and is contemptuous of their attempts to bully him.

'I'm going back to Sweden,' he says, 'not staying here and putting up with this shit.'

The Smoothie used to live in Sweden. After his Swedish wife was killed in a car crash, he says he went half-mad and had to return home to Gaza for a while, to heal himself. But now he wants to go back to Sweden. Gaza is no place for a free-thinking poet like him, he says. He has several children here in Gaza now. But I've no doubt he *will* make it out and take his kids with him. Some people always manage their situations and the Smoothie has the sheer chutzpah to carry it off. It's going to be much harder for Niveen, I think. She is independent and free-thinking too, but also really fearful of whatever lies ahead. She's torn between loving Gaza and being quite desperate to escape the claustrophobic confines of her life here.

Both of their situations depend a lot on whether this *tahdiya* lasts, and cracks are already appearing in the calm. Fighters have launched a few rockets and mortars towards Israel – rumours are circulating that businessmen who own tunnels down in Rafah are paying them to do so because they don't want the border crossings opening and spoiling their monopoly on business. Hamas is arresting fighters from various militant groups, including the Fatah-aligned Al-Aqsa Martyrs Brigade, which Hamas claims is violating the *tahdiya* in order to undermine its rule. It is an ugly scene: Gaza under Israeli siege, and now turning in on itself, politically self-destructing from pressures inside and out. No wonder so many people are talking of escape.

A few days ago, a foreign radio journalist called me. 'I will see you in Gaza soon,' he said, 'when the *tahdiya* breaks down and things go back to normal down there.'

Our pizzas arrive, along with bowls of fresh Greek salad. The food is tasty, especially out here on the warm beach with its winsome evening breeze. We eat slowly, then linger for a long time afterwards, smoking as we watch the slow setting of the sun. Eventually, stiff from sitting so long, we decide to take a stroll across the beach, groaning as we get up because we're all stuffed full of good pizza.

I go barefoot, trailing just behind Niveen and the Smoothie. I have spent a lot of time on the beach over the summer. The sea flows through so much of life here, freeing but also imprisoning Gaza, almost like another wall. Imagine, I think to myself, if this sea was open for fishermen and sailors, if there was political reconciliation and if the crossing down at Rafah was *really* open as an international border. Imagine what Gaza could be ...

I press my feet into the still-warm sand. Suddenly the entire beach appears to be quivering as though it has just come alive. Niveen, the Smoothie and I all stop at the same moment, then crouch in the dusk, gazing at a carpet of tiny white crabs making their slow sideways dance towards the retreating waves.

Ramadan for Christians

The Islamic calendar is lunar, so every month begins in sequence with the new moon, and each Ramadan starts about eleven days earlier than the previous year.

On the first night of September, a silver sliver of new moon is cradled in the sky above Gaza. I go to sleep early and am startled awake by what sounds like a drum being beaten. I totter onto my bedroom balcony, which looks out over the street, to see who the culprits are. Two men are pushing a bicycle down the street, a large drum resting on the saddle, shouting and bashing the drum. Their job is to wake people in time for *Suhoor*, the meal just before dawn, when fasting begins.

Last year I spent Ramadan over in the West Bank. In Ramallah, restaurants heaved every evening with people breaking their fast; the city centre streets bulged with temporary street markets; even some of the bars were open at night, and serving beer. But in Gaza, Ramadan looks and feels like a threadbare affair. During the day, the streets are nearly deserted – the weather is still very hot and humid. People do come out at night, but the crowds seem subdued in the under-lit streets. The exception is the lamp-lit al-Deira Hotel, which at night sparkles like a jewel in the dust, as the waiters preside over the lavish daily *Iftar* evening break-fast buffet. But the vast majority of Gazans cannot afford to sample its decadent fare. Most break their fast at their own kitchen table.

At the beginning of Ramadan in Gaza, I briefly wonder whether to try fasting, just to join in with my colleagues. I ask *Ustaz* Mounir what he thinks. We're still having our twice-weekly lessons, still fiercely debating but still listening to each other.

'It would be interesting for you to try fasting,' he says. 'But you know, Louisa, many people in Gaza are fasting for the wrong reason – just so they can tell everyone they are fasting like good Muslims. *Khalas*! The question we have to ask each other is not whether we are fasting during Ramadan – but what will we do *after* Ramadan?'

And that puts me straight. Nobody at work expects me to fast anyway – just to be discreet and to keep my office door closed if I eat or drink anything during the day.

In Gaza almost everyone conforms to the thirty-day Ramadan fast ... bar a handful of rebels. And the local Christians, of course.

I'm curious about the Christian community here in Gaza and how they are faring under Hamas. In September 2007, a few months before I first arrived here, a young Gazan Christian was abducted by unknown assailants and murdered. He was the owner of Gaza's only Christian bookshop, and his death – his punctured corpse was dumped in a back street in the old quarter – ignited Christian fears that Hamas extremists were targeting their local community. The killer or killers were never found, but the murder seems to have been a horrific one-off.

The first Christian I met in Gaza was our receptionist at the Centre, Rawiya, a placid woman with a long uncovered mane of thick hair and deep-set brown eyes. We greeted each other every morning, sometimes chatted, and one morning she asked me if I was Christian. I gave her the simple answer – that I was brought up as a Christian – and we had a brief chat about the local Orthodox church of St Porphyry, which she sometimes attends.

One afternoon during the first week of Ramadan, Rawiya comes into my office and shuts the door behind her.

'We are celebrating a Christian engagement tomorrow night, at one of the hotels,' she says. 'Do you want to come and join us?'

'Yes I do!'

'Welcome – it will be a good party,' she says, with a wink.

Rawiya, her husband, Adil, and their two daughters pick me up at my place at seven in the evening. The engagement party is being held at the Commodore Hotel, on the same seafront street as the al-Deira. I know everyone will be all dolled up – Palestinian engagements and weddings are usually big, showy affairs – so I wear my smartest outfit and my only pair of decent shoes. Rawiya looks elegant in a sparkling dress and her husband has donned a sharp suit. Adil has a neat brown moustache and a merry glint in his eyes. He asks if I have brought anything to drink. When I tell him I have a bottle of red wine in my handbag, he rubs his hands with glee.

The Commodore is busy. We join the throng clambering up the wide, carpeted stairs, past windows of delicately stained glass, from better days when tourists, including Israelis, stayed in these hotels. Tonight's party is being held in the upstairs function hall. Muslim engagement parties are traditionally celebrated by women and men separately, with just the groom attending the women's party. But as we enter the function hall, I'm confronted by the sight of at least 300 women and men sitting at long tables side by side, and not a *hijab* in sight. I cannot quite believe I'm still in Gaza.

I turn to Rawiya: 'Wow! – This really is something else!'

'Welcome to our world, *habibti*,' she says.

There is also a dance floor, and a stage at the front, where two empty white thrones await the lucky couple.

We sit down, Rawiya on my right side. On my left is a middle-aged man I've never met before. His name is Adham and he's also amused at my amazement. I ask him what things are like for local Christians now, and he gives me the Gaza shrug.

'Do we look scared?' he twinkles.

'No, you don't, to be honest. Not at all.'

'We have parties like this all year,' he says. 'Our community is very strong, we enjoy celebrating together. But you know, I only go to church for weddings, feasts and deaths!'

'What are things like between your church and the local mosque?'

He chuckles and takes a sip of what looks like wine from his glass.

'Our church, the Greek Orthodox Church, is the most conservative in the Middle East, you know, and we Gazans are the most conservative Christians in Palestine. We reflect our society, just like the local Muslims. I would say my views are pretty close to theirs.'

On the table in front of us, small plates of hummus and other dips are congealing in the heat beside baskets of bread. Adil, sitting across the table from me, quietly takes a bottle of whisky from inside his jacket and unscrews the cap. I pass him my bottle of wine. He pours three drinks, then tucks the bottles under his chair.

'Usually we have the bottles on the table,' says Rawiya quietly, 'but we will keep them under the table this evening because it's Ramadan and the waiters are Muslims.'

The hovering young waiters look bored, and oblivious, as we raise our glasses to toast the party. Our bottles, and a few others, are passed around, glasses are filled, other toasts raised. I offer Adham a top-up of wine.

'I thought you would never ask!' he chuckles again.

We clink glasses and drink to the engaged couple, who have yet to make an appearance.

When the bride- and groom-to-be finally make their entrance, the young woman – trussed into the traditional meringue of a dress and caked in white make-up – stares straight ahead, swallowing hard. Her fiancé is beaming like he cannot believe his luck. Schmaltzy romantic music fills the room as they move towards the dance floor for the obligatory slow twirl in front of hundreds of pairs of prying eyes. The bride-to-be looks mortified.

When the couple retreat to their white thrones on the stage, the guests take to the dance floor. At first the dancing is stilted, but as more people join in, the crowd starts to warm up. Rawiya wants to dance too. As she and I squeeze our way towards the floor, two older, immaculate women look me up, then down, curling their shiny lips as they sneer.

Ustaz Mounir, and other friends from outside the city centre, often complain to me about the snobs in al-Rimal looking down on everyone else in Gaza, especially people from the camps, their sense of self-importance inflated by their sense of being from a better class. I follow Rawiya onto the dance floor, feeling a bit mocked and self-conscious.

As we dance, people smile and my confidence returns. Adil joins us, taking our hands in turn and spinning us around. The floor fills up with small, excited children, teenage girls in beaded, strapless ballgowns and portly older men whose faces become flushed and damp as the music gets louder and bolder. Rawiya and I dance for most of the evening, pausing only to drink water and a little more wine. A posse of long-limbed *shabab*, their eyes bright with testosterone, come over and I share a slow dance with one of them later; he is a tall teenage lad who holds me at arm's length, giggling nervously, his breath smelling of coffee, cigarettes and cardamom. Women and men mingle, the atmosphere is relaxed and easy, and I do spy one or two *muhajabas* in the flowing crowd.

'Come. I want you to meet someone special.' Rawiya takes my hand and escorts me to the table nearest the stage, where she introduces me to a man with a full dark beard and dressed in flowing black robes who is sitting back watching the dancing. Father Artemius is the resident Greek Orthodox priest. The Christians call him *Abunah,* Our Father. I've seen him before, at the al-Deira Hotel, smoking shisha in the café.

'Come, visit the church any time you like. You are most welcome,' he says, shaking my hand. His feels soft and fleshy, and his smile is warm. I thank him and say that I will.

❧

By the end of the fourth century AD, thanks to Greek Bishop Porphyry and his messianic disciples, the majority of Gazans were at least token Christians. A hundred and fifty years later Islam erupted from the Arabian peninsula, following the death of the Prophet Muhammad. Armies of Muslim Arabs marched along the ancient caravan route from Mecca to Damascus and swiftly captured Syria from Emperor Heraclius's ailing Byzantine Empire. The Arabs then stormed south towards Gaza and Egypt, seizing Gaza City with little apparent resistance from local inhabitants. Due to its long history of trading, many Arabs were already living in Gaza. The Prophet's great-grandfather, Hashim Ibn 'Abid Manaf was buried there. The new Islamic rulers permitted Gazan Christians and Jews to practise their own religions, so long as they paid the requisite taxes. But just as the Christians had laid waste to Gaza's pagan temples at the first opportunity, so the Muslims tore down Gaza's remaining churches, creating mosques over the ruins and sparing only the Orthodox St Porphyry, one of the oldest churches on earth. There are around 3,500 Christians left in Gaza. The majority are Greek Orthodox, plus a few hundred Catholics with their own (fairly modern) church and a mere handful of Baptists.

❦

Eventually the party winds up. We crowd downstairs and into the hotel car park, where people linger, talking, laughing and smoking.

'Did you like the party?' Rawiya asks me.

'I loved it!'

'Tonight was like we were not in Gaza at all, but in another place,' her husband says, unlocking the car.

I know exactly what he means; but the fact that we *are* in Gaza is what made it so special.

I ask for the following Sunday morning off work, to attend a service at the Orthodox church. The service starts at eight in the morning, and when I arrive the church is already almost full. It lies slightly below ground level, like a sunken bath; the interior is inlaid with gold, the vaulted ceiling is heavily frescoed, the walls lined with paintings of solemn saints. Towards the front of the church a majestic chandelier, apparently donated by Empress Catherine the Great, is suspended like an oracle.

I sit in a pew amid older women, some wearing lace veils over their hair as they chant prayers in Arabic and Greek. Father Artemius is absent and the service is taken by a younger priest draped in the same loose black robes. After the mass, as the congregation slowly file outside, this young priest stands at the church entrance, greeting people as they leave. He singles me out as a newcomer and offers me his hand. His name is Alexius; he says he has only been in Gaza a few months.

'You know, this building was a pagan temple until Bishop Porphyry built this church in its place,' he speaks, with a slight nasal squeak, and pats the outside church wall to make his point.

'How many churches were there before the Muslims arrived?' I ask him.

'At the beginning of the fifth century, we had about 400 churches,' he says, his eyes smiling at the thought. 'But then the Persians came and destroyed them.'

'Ah,' I say, thinking they really are all as bad as each other.

Gaza stabilised under Muslim occupation until the arrival of the Seljuqs – medieval Turkic nomads from southern Central Asia. The Seljuqs' feudalism stagnated regional trade, and the restrictions on pilgrims visiting the Holy Land sites outraged the Christian world. Pope Urban mobilised a massive force of Crusaders, who eventually reached Jerusalem in mid-summer 1099, intent on the violent salvation of this most Holy City. The Crusaders smashed their way through the city walls and massacred some 10,000 people, without sparing Arab Christians. The lands of the Eastern Mediterranean were then divided into four Latin kingdoms and a Crusader named Baldwin was crowned King of Jerusalem, including Gaza. Resistance to the Crusaders gathered momentum in the mid-twelfth century, led by a sadistic Seljuq with a penchant for torture, Imad al-Din Zengi, who united the Muslims against the infidels whom they regarded as nothing but barbaric and bovine.

In the year 1170 one of Zengi's dynasty, the Kurdish warrior and father of seventeen sons, Salah al-Din Yusuf ibn Ayyub (also known as Salah al-Din or Saladin) gathered an Egyptian army to attack the Christians. But it was seventeen years before Gaza finally surrendered to Salah al-Din's fighters, in the autumn of 1187. A month later, Salah al-Din seized Jerusalem too. There were three bloody Crusades in all. After the third, the Mongol hordes also swept briefly through Palestine, reaching the gates of Gaza before they too were routed by the next wave of invaders, led by a ferocious, flame-haired pagan slave.

There is a tantalising footnote to the Muslim invasions of Gaza: local Muslims used to whisper of a ghost, a monk who haunted the old quarter of Gaza City, casting incense as he drifted through the dank streets where the Orthodox church still stands. Was this, perhaps, the ghost of Bishop Porphyry, or Mark the Deacon, or another lost soul? Whoever he was, this restless spirit has not been seen for a very long time now.

Despite the rigours of fasting from sunrise to sunset every day for a month, many Gazan Muslims tell me they welcome Ramadan.

'I love this time', says Saida, 'because it brings me closer to my God.'

I share many break-fasts with Saida and her family, and they are not fasting merely in order to conform or to appear pious. For them, Ramadan is something sacred.

Just before the end of September, at the tail end of Ramadan, I get an unexpected phone call from Samir, the community worker up in Beit Hanoun. We exchange greetings, then Samir asks what I am doing for Eid, the four-day festival that immediately follows Ramadan, when Muslims traditionally give each other presents, buy outfits of new clothes, visit relatives and eat a lot.

I tell him I haven't made any plans yet, wondering what he has in mind.

'I want you to come to Beit Hanoun,' he says. 'We are planning an operation.'

Operation Smile and Hope

On the last morning of Ramadan, a dozen of us meet at the community centre in Beit Hanoun, where Samir works, to carry out the operation. There is a minibus waiting for us outside the centre, with the engine running. We are going to visit farming families living along the northern Gaza border, to distribute traditional Eid presents and, in Samir's words, 'remind these families they have not been forgotten'. Samir calls this Operation Smile and Hope. Before we leave, each of us is given a sleeveless vest with the community centre logo branded on the back, so we will look more like aid workers and hopefully will not be shot at by Israeli snipers. Apart from me, Samir and the minibus driver, the rest of our contingent are all local teenagers.

Samir looks different this morning; his face seems softer and his mood lighter, as though some weight has been lifted from his narrow shoulders. He catches my gaze, giving me a brief warm smile I haven't seen before, which crinkles the skin around his fierce eyes.

'Welcome, Louisa. Welcome to our resistance!' He almost sings the words.

I clamber into the minibus beside him, happy to see this chink in his shell. The minibus has 'Operation Smile and Hope' hand-painted on both sides.

We drive north from Beit Hanoun, towards the border with Israel. The driver stops at the Hamas checkpoint stationed close to the

Palestinian side of no-man's-land. Samir asks me to go with him, to speak to the officers at the checkpoint and explain what we are doing today, so hopefully they won't hinder us. The bearded Hamas officers look blank, then baffled, when we tell them we have come to distribute presents to local farming families; especially as we now have an entourage of local media following us in several cars. There hasn't been much news in Gaza recently, so these journalists are keen to film us. To my surprise, the Hamas officers just wave us on our way. We park the minibus beyond the checkpoint and start walking along a dirt track to visit our first family. We are in open fields, about a kilometre from the Israeli border. The Gazan paparazzi trail behind us, TV cameras at the ready.

Before we reach the first house, the entire family comes outside to see what on earth is happening. They don't get many visitors around here. Samir steps forward.

'Eid *Mubarak*! (Happy Eid!) – may every Eid be happy for you and your family,' he greets them as they gawp at us all, looking as baffled as the Hamas officers back at the checkpoint. For a moment no one moves. Then the Beit Hanoun *shabab* begin distributing presents – toy cars for the boys, sparkly hair clips for the girls and small boxes of toiletries for their parents. The children begin to gurgle with pleasure and skip around and the parents and grandparents break into smiles as the journalists zoom in for close-ups of this fleeting joy. But we have a dozen more families to visit today, and cannot tarry. So after brief handshakes with the adults, we start walking back towards the minibus as they wave and call their thanks.

This operation is quite mad, I think: but it's also quite beautiful because it is so innocent and at the same moment so utterly real. Samir steps up beside me.

'Now we are going to see the Swailams,' he says.

The driver parks the minibus much closer to the Swailams' house than I expected. As we walk towards the row of white cottages, the *shabab* are boisterous and laughing, like this is just a good day out. I fall into step with one of the older ones, Khalil, who is carrying a box of presents. Khalil works with Samir, and like the rest of this friendly, rowdy crowd, he lives in Beit Hanoun.

'You know, when I was little, this place was paradise,' he says. 'It was just one big garden of trees ...'

As Khalil reminisces about scampering round the orchards of Beit Hanoun, I recall Niveen telling me about her time in the West Bank, where she was studying at Beir Zeit University in the 1980s. Whenever she used to return to visit Gaza in winter, Niveen told me she could always smell the Beit Hanoun orange blossom before she even caught sight of the trees; it was, she said, the most exquisite welcome home possible. Palestinians' connection to their land is as visceral as blood and bone.

The Swailams come out of their cottages, curious to see these unexpected visitors. I shake hands with Jamal. He acknowledges me with a nod and a faint smile. I ask him how the situation is now, three months into the *tahdiya*.

'Not so bad,' he says, as though measuring out his words. Then he shrugs and I read this as resignation to the continuing pressure of not knowing if and when things will get better or worse. It must be like holding your breath for three months. One of the Swailam women, Sayra, tells me things *are* easier. They can go out into their fields around their home every day now. But the young children are still frightened and nervous.

'My little one will not leave my side at all,' she says, as her young daughter pushes up against her legs, eyeing me jealously. While we are speaking, Sayra is also baking flatbread in a *taboun*, or traditional clay oven, for tomorrow's Eid feast. I admire her willpower, baking fresh bread while still fasting.

I ask her where Abu Jamal is and she directs me to a narrow arch tucked between two of the white cottages. I slip through it and find myself in a small courtyard. Abu Jamal is fast asleep on a narrow cot beneath a lone olive tree. His ancient face is tranquil, his chest rising and falling with a quiet rattle, as though he and this tree belong to each other. Leaving him undisturbed, I go back to the others and find the Swailam children gleeful with their small presents too. As we take our leave, Sayra presses a plastic bag into my hands. It is filled with flatbreads, hot from her stove.

'Eid *Mubarak, habibti*,' she says with a smile.

For the next few hours, we move from one family to the next, carrying out our operation. The families – all of them farmers – say their land is not being invaded by the Israeli military, or by Gazan fighters, and they feel safer now. A few have even started planting spindly orange and lemon seedlings.

'Our old trees were all destroyed,' one farmer tells me. 'God willing, this peace will last long enough for these new trees to give us fruit.'

By early afternoon, we are all beginning to flag. Everyone in our group is fasting, except me, and I can't bring myself to drink from my bottle of tepid water in front of a dozen thirsty activists. The Gaza paparazzi have long gone. But Samir insists we have one last round of visits to do, along a strip of the north-eastern border known as Siafa, where local Bedouin live. Siafa is usually inaccessible because it lies so far inside the buffer zone. But the *tahdiya* has given us a rare opportunity to visit this remote, cut-off corner. As we drive towards the eastern border, the only vehicle we see is a donkey cart driven by a hunched woman with a face like a windfall apple. As she trundles past, she waves, and the *shabab* stick their heads out of the windows and cheer.

'You people are crazy!' shouts the driver. 'I am from Beit Hanoun and I've never come this close to the border in my whole life!'

When he parks the minibus at the end of a faint track, I see a white house a little way ahead, perched alone on the crest of a shallow hill.

'Now we'll visit my Bedouin friends,' says Samir, with another rare smile. He really does remind me of *Ustaz* Mounir.

We stroll up to the white house. Samir leads us through a narrow gate into a courtyard, where two women and a man are sitting on plastic chairs beneath a canopy of dry palm leaves. The older of the two women sees us first and rises to her feet. She's wearing a long yellow robe embroidered with small white flowers, a scarf tucked loosely around her head and draped over one broad shoulder. She has a gap between her teeth and shining, sun-darkened skin.

'*Marhaba*, Samir!' she cries. 'Eid *Mubarak*!'

Samir introduces us to Manah al-Tarabin.

The other woman and man in the courtyard are Manah's daughter and son – Sharifa and Sa'ed – both of them shy compared to their exuberant mother. Sharifa giggles and blushes, looking overwhelmed by this boisterous invasion. Sa'ed shakes hands but says nothing, his face closed and sullen. He smiles only for Samir. We present our small gifts and Manah insists on gifting us back; clasping a dagger, she hacks great clusters of ripe red dates from a tall palm tree in one corner of the courtyard, around which an outside staircase appears to be wrapped.

I cannot take my eyes off her. She beckons me up the stairs, onto an empty roof terrace, and we stand there together, looking out eastwards. Maybe 100 metres ahead of us is the Israeli border fence, and immediately behind the fence, a road, presumably for Israeli military patrol vehicles. After visiting the Swailams, I didn't believe anyone *could* live any closer to the border. I am trying to take it all in, but Samir is already calling for me. I know I have to come here again.

'Can I visit you another time?' I ask Manah.

'Whenever you like, *habibti*!'

We go downstairs. The *shabab* are waiting. When I kiss Manah goodbye, her cheeks smell of sunshine and earth.

Our final visit of the day is to some neighbouring Bedouin, who live in a camp on the other side of this shallow hill, a mere 50 metres from the border. As Samir leads us towards the camp, even the *shabab* are unsettled.

'This is *too* fucking close,' Khalil hisses to me.

But like obedient children we traipse after Samir across this open, exposed land, even when he circles around a blackened Qassam rocket lying spent on the ground like a firework. At the other side of the hill, we squeeze through a gap in a fence of wild prickly pear bush, one at a time, recoiling as vicious-sounding dogs begin to howl. Inside, we find a makeshift camp of tents, wooded outhouses, scratching hens and the skin-and-bone dogs yanking at their chains. Samir calls out. There is no answer.

Most of us stand together, feeling uneasy and watched, though we don't know who is watching us. After a tense couple of minutes, four men appear from one of the outhouses at the same moment, their unsmiling eyes fixed on us. One aims a kick at the nearest dog, which dodges the blow by sinking towards the dust, tail curled under its backside.

When Samir steps forward with our Eid greeting, the men stare him down. A stream of thin small children run from one of the tents, then stop dead, and they stare too.

We are not visitors, but trespassers, and right now it feels like this could all go very wrong.

Khalil clears his throat, opens up one of the boxes and begins to hand out presents to the children, who push and shove each other forward. The first gift goes into the cupped palms of a girl who could be anywhere between 6 and 12 years of age. Skinny and stunted-looking, she clutches the earrings without even looking at them, as though they will be snatched straight back off her. Backing into her own space, she holds them up to the light and begins to jump up and down, screaming, 'I have a present – I have a present!'

Her joy ruptures the tension. Women begin to emerge from another tent. We all begin to smile. But the children's delight is tempered by their parents, who accept their gifts with reticence. Few words are exchanged between us and the Bedouin's faces never lose their wariness. I cannot begin to imagine their lives, at this jagged edge of Gaza. I ask one of the women where the border with Israel is, and she walks a few of us to the other side of the camp. We stand on a small sandy tussock and witness for ourselves the breath-catching closeness of the Israeli fence. We can actually see the rooftops of an Israeli town just across the border.

'*Yehud*,' the woman points at the red-and-white roofs, meaning the Jews are over there.

'It is Sderot City,' says Samir.[43]

As we walk back into the camp, he says to me, 'Everyone's life here in Gaza is hard. But these people: no one understands what they go through, no one visits them. They are forgotten.'

I think he is referring to all the families that we've seen today, but especially these Bedouin, who inhabit a small, separate, isolated world. I don't know anything about the Gaza Bedouin and have never heard other Gazans talk about them.

'Can we come back after Eid and see your friend Manah?' I ask him. Samir nods. 'She has already told me she wants you to visit.'

bedouin

Over the next few weeks, Samir and I go back to Siafa several times to see Manah and her family. Manah has a lightness, a joyousness about her that is infectious. We laugh a lot together. She has a second daughter, called Abir, the kind of young woman that my mother would call 'strapping', who is often out tending to the family's small herd of sheep. Manah has lived on this piece of land for thirty-five years now; yet these sheep seem to be the family's only source of income, apart from a grove of lemon and olive trees. I never figure out how they actually make enough money to survive. I do, though, quickly learn that they have no electricity in their home, or running water. Manah never mentions a husband, and I never ask, sensing that whoever he is, or was, he has long gone. Once a week she hitches her donkey to a cart and trundles off to the Beit Hanoun market, but she and her daughters spend most of their lives in and around the small world of their hilltop home. Only her son, Sa'ed, comes and goes, sullen and nearly silent whenever I see him, seeking only the company of Samir.

After seven months in Gaza, this is the quietest place I have visited. No cars, rowdy neighbours or people in the streets. No planes or helicopters. Noise is such an essence of Gaza life, it is the texture of calm that I crave these days, and here the silence feels like a quiet tide.

'What was it like here before the *tahdiya*?' I ask Manah one afternoon as we sit drinking very sweet mint tea.

She smiles, flashing her crooked white teeth.

'It is better here now.'

'And before?'

'Before the *tahdiya*? *Aayy*!' She gives a loud howl that makes me flinch, holding her hands in front of her and shaking them as though she has just burnt her fingers; another local gesture of fear.

'They [the Israeli military] used to fire rockets and bombs from planes and helicopters – and the *zananas* – terrible! We would run from the fields.'

She mimes covering her head with her arms, like the brace position you adopt as a plane hurtles towards the earth.

Sometimes, when Manah and her daughters are talking, they use words I don't understand, words that don't sound at all Arabic to me.

'What language are you speaking?' I ask her another afternoon, as we sit in her sunny tranquil courtyard.

'Our Bedouin language, *habibti*,' Manah winks.

Bedouin, 'those who inhabit the desert', are an ancient tribal culture of Arab nomads and camel breeders who traditionally lived in camps of extended families, called *ashiras*, presided over by a local sheikh. Some Bedouin women used to ink their faces with distinct blue tattoos, but these can only be seen on very elderly female faces now. A minority of Bedouin cling to their traditional semi-nomadism, but the vast majority have been pushed into squalid settlements in Palestine and Israel, and left to quietly rot. In pre-1948 Palestine, some 90,000 Bedouin were scattered across the southern Naqab desert (also known by its Hebrew name, the Negev) in eight tribes. Manah and her family are from the al-Tarabin tribe.

Not all Bedouin are black like Manah and her family, and communities of black non-Bedouin still live across Palestine. Some trace their roots to neighbouring north-east Africa, especially Sudan;

others to a tribe of black Muslim Arabs, the al-Salamat, who settled in the Hijaz region of western Arabia bordering the Red Sea. As trade and migration flowed through the Mediterranean, and along the ancient Way of the Sea through Gaza, so North African traders, Muslim pilgrims and members of the al-Salamat tribe journeyed back and forth through Palestine, and some inevitably stayed on.

Rheumy-eyed old Palestinian Bedouin also tell stories – passed down through generations of tribes – of young African children being kidnapped, or purchased in markets, and brought to Gaza to live with Bedouin as their young slaves. Only prominent Bedouin families, so the story goes, owned and traded the *abid*, or slaves, and by the same accounts remnants of slave labour lingered until the late 1950s in a smattering of remote Bedouin *ashiras*.[44]

Manah welcomes me fiercely into her small, isolated world – but she has no time for her Bedouin neighbours down the hill.

'Those ignorant people! Been at that camp thirty years and will only mix with their own kind, no one else,' she says, dismissing them with a flick of her hefty hand.

There are thousands of Bedouin living across Gaza; some are in the cities, many on the outskirts, and there are several established Bedouin villages. Poor Bedouin families, though, are mostly confined to squatter camps, and treated by many Gazans, especially liberal city-dwellers, as social outcasts, and backward petty criminals who'll do anything for cash. I have often seen Bedouin families riding their rickety donkey carts down Salah al-Din Street selling scraps of firewood, scavenging bits of scrap metal, or herding their goats in the shallow sandy hillsides surrounding Khan Younis. The only people in Gaza, it seems, who have fewer visitors than the Swailams are these Bedouin.

bell jar

I have my small secret world inside Gaza too, these days. I am still having a fling with Sakhar, the silver-maned lion I met at a UN party a few months back. His tenth-floor apartment is just a few minutes' walk from where I live and we always meet at his place, discreetly. Our affair is no one else's business. We enjoy cold beer in his lounge, with its sea view, and go to bed early, or lie in his big jacuzzi-style bathtub with its endless hot water.

'You UN guys are spoilt!' I tease him, and he laughs and flicks soapy bubbles at me.

Many of the expat UN staff stationed in Gaza have done other 'hardship postings' in places like Darfur, and say they cannot believe the seafront, air-conditioned luxury of their Gaza accommodation. They don't get out much though; despite the *tahdiya*, they still have to travel round in armoured vehicles and can visit only a handful of local hotels that have been vetted, like the al-Deira. They are not allowed to visit any private homes either, which is why Sakhar never stays at my place.

'Why do we get on so well, you and I?' he murmurs into my ear late one night.

'Because you're an oddball and I'm a misfit,' I reply, and we lie back on the pillows and laugh out loud, because we both know there is truth in it.

In the mornings, we always leave his building separately. I

ignore the looks from the armed Gazans half-heartedly patrolling the front door of his building. I don't want to care what they think. I'm happy.

But then Sakhar goes on leave. He is gone longer than I expect and when he does return, a few weeks later, he is still charming and affectionate, but a little distant, and he stays later at his office in the evenings so I don't see him quite so much. Something has changed. I don't ask what happened while he was away because I'm not sure that I want to know.

One morning at the beginning of November, the Centre director calls me into his office and tells me that he is sending me to a conference in Brussels. The flight is tonight. So I need to go home early, pack and make sure that I reach Erez before the crossing closes this afternoon. The director was meant to be going to the conference himself, but cannot secure a permit to leave Gaza. I, on the other hand, only need to telephone the Palestinian District Coordination Office (DCO) and inform them that I'm leaving Gaza today. Ironically, getting out of Gaza is much easier for me than getting back in.

I don't want to go to Brussels tonight.

'What's the matter?' he asks me. 'Do you have other plans for this evening?'

I do have other plans for this evening: Sakhar has assured me that he is free tonight. But I give the director a wide smile and tell him I'd be delighted to go.

Sakhar is not the only reason I am so reluctant to go to Brussels tonight. I don't want to leave Gaza because it involves crossing Erez, and I can already feel the knot in my guts pinching at the thought of the X-ray machine, the cameras, the security checks and questions, and the nagging anxiety that on my return I will not be allowed back inside the Strip. But no one else from the Centre can attend this conference; I'm the only one who *can* leave for Tel Aviv airport this afternoon.

When I leave the director's office, Shadi is standing outside in the corridor.

'Six thousand, six hundred and sixty-six *mabrouk*!' he cries out. 'You are so lucky!'

He gives me a hug and I wish with all my heart that it was him going to Brussels tonight. Shadi is still spending much of his time helping the Free Gaza crew, some of whom have decided to stay here for quite a while. Being a human rights activist is not only Shadi's job, it dominates most of his life. I promise to bring him back a bottle of decent whisky and a box of his beloved red Gauloises.

As I finish off bits and pieces, so that I can leave early, Joumana and a dozen other colleagues all pop into my office to tell me how lucky I am and how pleased they are for me.

'Put me in your luggage, *habibti*!' says one of the Centre fieldworkers, a young woman with a radiant, smiling face and a neat three-month pregnancy bump.

By the time I leave the Centre, I am clasping a long list of duty-free perfumes, cigarettes and drinks to bring back from the world my colleagues cannot reach.

I walk home and start packing. I am nervous and smoke while I'm packing. I've already tried to ring Sakhar but his work number is engaged. I call Saida to tell her I will be away for the next week or so.

'*Mabrouk, habibti*!' she says, like everyone else. She asks if I can visit her sister, Alla', in the West Bank while I'm outside. I am their go-between, bringing gifts, hugs and kisses from one arm of the family to the other. But I have to tell Saida that I don't think I can visit Alla' this time; I will be coming straight back to Gaza from Brussels. Even speaking these words aloud sounds strange now. I ask Saida if she wants anything from outside.

'Just come back soon, *habibti*, and come back happy. We need you to be happy for us,' she says, in that calm, restrained voice that I know so well.

I call Sakhar's mobile. But that number is busy too. He calls me when I'm in the taxi en route to the Erez crossing. It's mid-afternoon, a good hour before the crossing closes, but Erez is never predictable.

'You're leaving me!' He croons down the phone and even though I know something has changed between us, I feel myself flush. I can't say much because I am sitting next to Harb, the taxi driver. I tell Sakhar I will call him from the airport.

Harb and I have to stop at the Hamas checkpoint close to the Palestinian side of no-man's-land. A bearded Hamas officer (most of them have beards) writes my name down with great care and asks politely whether I am coming back to Gaza. I tell him I expect to return in about a week – and we are done.

When we reach the edge of no-man's-land, I ask Harb if he would like something from outside. Muhammad the driver has a new job with an international organisation, so I take a lot of taxis with Harb these days and have become very fond of him. Harb shakes his grey head and tells me that he doesn't need anything.

'Belgium,' he says slowly, rolling the word around his mouth. 'I cannot imagine Belgium.'

He turns his taxi round, to drive back into Gaza. I wave, then walk over to the portacabin, to hand in my passport and wait for coordination to cross no-man's-land. It is strange and unnerving how relatively easy it is for me to leave Gaza. And this afternoon I don't even have to wait very long to cross. After just twenty minutes or so, I am told that I can proceed.

When I step out of the portacabin, I see Debby and a few of the other Free Gaza crew sitting on a bench. They must have just arrived while I was in the portacabin.

'Where are you going?' they want to know.

'To Brussels.'

'Wow!' they chorus.

'When are *you* leaving Gaza?' I ask Debby.

'We can't leave. We can't get permits to cross Erez; and we tried to get out at Rafah, but the Egyptians turned us back,' she says. 'We are Palestinians now.'

'No you're not!' I snap at her. 'Someone will get you out – you'll be able to leave Gaza soon. Because you're *not* Palestinians.'

Apart from the Free Gaza posse on the bench, the crossing is very quiet today. The only other people around are a few taxi drivers waiting for arrivals, and the local porters who ferry people's luggage to the gates of the Israeli side of the crossing. The porters are all Hanounis; they earn tips for carrying luggage and bicker bitterly among themselves about whose turn it is to take my suitcase this afternoon.

A skinny man with a small head wins the job, hoicks my case onto his narrow shoulders and we set off across no-man's-land, towards the mouth of the tunnel that leads into the main Erez crossing terminal. Though it is mid-November, the sun still feels like it's roasting the earth. I have the strangest feeling about this trip; in fact, I have an almost violent urge to turn round and run straight back into Gaza. I don't know what's up with me today;

maybe I am just nervy about the bloody crossing. I walk on beside the porter. There is no path for me and him to follow; we weave our way around rocks and rubble. To my right, I can see the Swailams' row of white cottages and a thick splash of green where their vegetables are ripening. To my left, the shattered remains of some other buildings, reduced to tottering wooden frames and piles of stone. Just a few hours from now, I will be in another universe; sitting at a hotel bar drinking cold beer from a frosted glass shaped like a vase. I'm aware that I have barely said a word to the porter. I have nothing to say to anyone right now. As we approach the tunnel, I'm just possessed by the thought that everyone has heard of Gaza and most people will never see inside this Strip for themselves.

We reach the tunnel. Inside, the air is cooler. The roof, high as a cathedral, is covered with a ripped red tarp that flaps like a bird's torn wing. The uneven floor is made of stone. I'm thirsty. At the end of the tunnel is a gate of metal bars that opens onto the walkway leading into the main building. When the porter pulls the gate, it swings open with a whine like human nails scraping a board.

This porter can go no further. I thank and tip him, and with a brief nod he is gone. As I step onto the walkway, a second porter appears like a magician's assistant. They each have their pitches. Taking my bags, he escorts me along the walkway to a series of metal doors embedded in a wall. He presses a buzzer. One of the doors clicks open. We step into a wide passage, where two tables lie side by side, in front of another barred gate. The porter lifts my bag onto one of the tables, opens it and waves towards a camera tilted towards us. I wonder how he does this every day, ferrying travellers' bags almost to the border, then going back for the next job lot, without any hope of crossing himself. But this is no place for small talk. A light above the gate flicks green. I offer the porter a tip. He looks aghast. I think it's generous and refuse to give him any more. I step through the gate; he retreats back inside the Gaza wall.

I'm inside the main terminal building. The walls are straight and hard-edged. I enter the security area, where my bags are lifted onto an airport-style conveyor belt and opened. I lay the contents of my handbag out on a tray like a meal. The security guard and I acknowledge each other briefly.

My luggage moves away. I step through a glass door, then another, and enter a transparent tube, where I place my feet over the footprints painted on the floor and raise my arms. The doors shut and rotate with a swoosh as I am X-rayed. When the door opens in front of me, I step forward. A disembodied voice says in English, 'No. Go back inside, please.'

I reverse back inside and am X-rayed again and again. After the third X-ray I know something is up. The voice instructs me to go through the door on my right and wait. Fuck, fuck, fuck! This is the door that Gazans and foreigners crack morbid jokes about – the door that leads to the interrogation rooms. As I open it, I remember the reports from earlier this year of women being subjected to humiliating strip searches by the private security firm inside Erez. I feel as disembodied as the voice giving me instructions. I step into a narrow corridor, with a door at either end.

'Walk to the door straight ahead of you, open the door and go inside,' says the voice. I do so and the door clicks shut behind me. Now I am standing on a grid floor, and between the bars I can see the ground, maybe 10 metres below me. I feel wobbly, brace myself. Because I know this room.

In August 2008 a prominent NGO (Physicians for Human Rights) – Israel published an exposé of Gazan patients being subject to extortion by the Israeli security services at the Erez crossing.[45] During the first half of this year, 35 per cent of Gaza patients who required treatment outside the Strip were refused exit permits by the Israeli authorities. Some of the 100 patients interviewed for this report, who included individuals with terminal diagnoses, said that they had been interrogated in underground rooms, or rooms with a grid floor, by Israeli officers who spoke to them from behind bulletproof glass. While undergoing interrogation, patients were asked to become informants for the Israeli security services in return for being allowed to proceed across Erez and receive their medical treatment in Israel, the West Bank or a third country. According to patients' testimonies, if their responses did not satisfy the Israeli General Security Services (GSS) interrogators, they were sent back to Gaza. One Gazan patient was told by an Israeli security officer: 'If you want to go to the hospital, take my private cellphone number, talk to me and give me information about people.' Patients who were refused permission to cross into Israel after such interrogation included a man diagnosed with cancer of the lymph glands and a man with a degenerative eye disease who was going blind. These patients' testimonies were gathered by the Centre where I work, and I have read them, including the testimony of a Gazan patient who was brought into a room with a grid 'iron floor' where he could see the ground several metres below.

An Israeli officer is standing in front of me, behind what looks like bulletproof glass. She speaks into a microphone.

'Take your clothes off,' she says.

To my own surprise, I stand tall and stare straight at her.

'Why?' I ask.

She repeats the instruction.

'Why?' I say again, louder.

I am thinking of the patients who have been brought into this room, stood on this grid floor and refused to collaborate. I am thinking of the men and women who haunt our Centre, month after month, desperate for permits to cross into Israel or the West Bank for treatment for themselves or their children. One man I know from his frequent visits to our Centre has had throat cancer for six years and cannot receive the treatment he needs inside Gaza. Another man is trying to secure a permit to visit a Jerusalem hospital to visit his baby son, whom he has never seen and whose little twin brother has already died. I am thinking of the deliberate cruelties of this military occupation and of the cold decisions made here inside Erez about who will be allowed to cross, and who will be pushed back into Gaza as punishment for refusing to betray themselves.

Until this very moment I have been really frightened of Erez, and of the Israelis working here, because of the absolute power they wield over everyone who crosses. But though the knot in my guts is taut as wire, I am calm. I have nothing that the Israeli security services want. They cannot harm me. Right now, standing on this drop-away iron floor inside one of the most fortified borders in the world, the resident fear inside me has just cracked.

When the Israeli woman repeats her instruction for the third time, I pull my blouse over my head and stand before her, legs splayed, in my bra and jeans. She points to an X-ray machine on my right and tells me to place my blouse inside it, which I do. The machine clunks and my blouse is X-rayed.

When she says, 'That's fine. You can put your clothes on now and proceed back to the passport control,' I do not look at her.

I collect my suitcase, which is meticulously searched in front of me by an Israeli officer, and proceed to passport control. Three other people, Gazans, are waiting to go through into Israel, but the passport control booths are empty. I know we will be kept waiting for a long while; this too is part of the procedure.

I need the toilet, but there is no toilet on this Palestinian side of passport control.

Above the chairs where we are sitting is a long glass corridor, where Israelis walk the length of the crossing and watch us from above, like scientists observing lab rats. Erez, I think to myself, is not a milking station; it is a bell jar.

I will make the plane to Brussels tonight, but I won't be coming back here for a while. I can already feel it in my guts.

※

Israel sealed the Gaza borders in mid-November 2008. Its military forces launched Operation Cast Lead on 27 December 2008, the biggest Israeli assault on Gaza for four decades. It lasted until 18 January 2009. I was unable to return to Gaza until the Israelis had withdrawn, when internationals were permitted to re-enter the Strip and Gazans who had been outside when the assault was launched were allowed to begin returning home.

PART FOUR

All the invaders who set up camp in the city or on its
borders left their mark, before moving on. But what the
invaders left in the psyche of the people of Gaza was a
hatred of occupation [...] and the spirit of resistance [...]
From Gaza, too, sprang hope and the rivers of dreams.
And Gaza has remained, as it is today, a city on the sea,
dreaming of the sea.

Ibrahim Darwish[46]

the fridge

January 2009

The row of white cottages where the Swailams lived has been reduced to rubble, the land around it laid waste. No-man's-land has expanded across this whole stretch of northern Gaza. There is nobody living here now.

As I walk through the Erez crossing into Gaza, I have violently conflicting emotions. I have been obsessed with returning to Gaza, but now part of me wonders what the hell I'm doing back here. And I never heard another word from Sakhar.

It is the last week of January. The Israeli military pulled out of Gaza just a few days ago and the aid workers and journalists swept in. So much has already been written about this assault, Israel's most devastating offensive inside Gaza since it occupied the Strip in 1967. Gazans refer to it as *al-harb* (the war). The Israeli military killed 1,414 Gazans; the vast majority were civilians, including more than 300 children and 9 local paramedics. Up to 5,000 Gazans were also maimed and injured. The Israelis damaged or destroyed more than 14,000 homes and 219 factories across the Strip, mainly in northern Gaza and Gaza City itself. Thirteen Israelis were killed, including 10 soldiers and 3 civilians – though 4 of them died from 'friendly fire'. Twenty-eight Israeli families had their homes destroyed by Gazan rocket attacks, and across southern Israel students were only allowed into schools with fortified classrooms and bomb shelters. Gazans sheltering inside UN schools were bombed with rockets containing white phosphorous, which burns through human tissue until it is deprived of oxygen. But these statistics say very little about what actually happened inside Gaza. The facts do not speak for themselves.[47]

A few days after arriving back in Gaza, I enter a shabby apartment building in Shaja'iya, in eastern Gaza City, with one of my colleagues from the Centre, a woman called Noor. We have come here to speak to surviving members of the 'Olaiwa family. We are gathering testimonies from families whose children were killed during this war. The fieldworker who brought us here this morning has a thin face framed with long, dark hair and burning eyes; he looks like Jesus. He introduces us to a woman called Fadwa 'Olaiwa and then leaves. He has a lot of work to get on with.

Fadwa is slender and middle-aged. She takes us upstairs to the fifth floor, where her brother, Hayder, has his apartment, two floors above hers. She has a key to his front door. As the lock releases, I hear her draw breath. The layout of the apartment is simple. It has a long living room with a kitchen and two bedrooms off to one side. I can see through the kitchen doorway to the balcony, which has a black wrought-iron railing. Sunlight is streaming into the kitchen, striking the back wall streaked with dust and congealed blood, and highlighting the dirty white kitchen cupboards, their doors hanging off. A stack of plates and bowls are still mouldering in the sink. On the other side of the kitchen, a square of the linoleum is faded, where the fridge used to stand before it was dragged away. In front of the faded square is a hole in the wall big enough for me to climb through.

On 5 January 2009, Hayder 'Olaiwa, his wife Amal and their

eight children were having a barbecue in this kitchen, with the door to the balcony open because Hayder was grilling meat. Families have barbecues during wars. They have to eat. And no doubt they were all hungry because it was four o'clock in the afternoon. As Amal stood next to the fridge, making salads to accompany the meat, a 122-millimetre Israeli tank shell burst through the window of the bedroom next door, where their daughters slept. The shell slammed into the wall between the bedroom and the kitchen, decapitating Amal and killing three of her sons and one daughter. Amal's headless body was pinned beneath the fridge.

Fadwa was at home when the tank shell struck the apartment upstairs.

'When I heard the explosion, I ran upstairs,' she says, her voice quiet and flat. 'After just a few seconds I came to this apartment and there was smoke everywhere. When I pushed the door, I saw Hayder: his face was black, with blood pouring down it, and he could not speak. He just raised his finger to the sky. Then I heard Ghadir [one of the 'Olaiwa daughters] shouting, 'Help me!' I ran to her room and she was underneath her dressing table. It had fallen on top of her when the missile had passed right through her room into the kitchen. As I was helping Ghadir, I was calling for Amal because I couldn't see her. Then I went back into the kitchen and I saw Amal underneath the fridge without her head. The four children were dead too. And Muntassir was there in the doorway, alive.'

Sixteen-year-old Muntassir, Amal and Hayder's eldest son, saw it all.

Fadwa falls silent. The three of us stand in the ruins of the flat. I have written down everything she has said, but cannot take it in. Noor and I ask if we can look around and Fadwa nods, but does not move from the spot. Noor and I cross to the bedroom where

the shell first entered the apartment. The dressing table is still over-
turned, the contents spilt across the room. I push my head through
the gaping hole in the wall and wonder whether the blood at the
back of the kitchen belongs to Hayder or Amal. But it doesn't matter any more. Noor shakes her head and wipes her eyes. We enter
the kitchen and stand in the middle without touching anything.
The balcony door creaks.

When we walk back into the living room, Fadwa has not moved.
Her small shoes are coated in a fine layer of dirty white dust, her
face ashen with grief. She looks at us.

'I cannot find any more words to describe what has happened
to my family,' she says.

But it is Noor who begins to cry quietly, and Fadwa who steps
forward to comfort her. The three of us stand close together in this
devastated dusty home. Then, behind us, set against the back wall
of the living room, I notice a bookcase, crammed not with books
but with shoes, each pair slightly warped into the shape of its owner.
I step over for a closer look. A small child's tattered sandals rest on
top of a large pair of men's shoes. There are grimy pumps and boots
of all sizes, a single red high heel and a scuffed pair of women's lace-
ups that must have belonged to Amal, the dead mother. If she were
alive, we would be exactly the same age. I stare at these shoes until
Noor clears her throat, making me jump.

'Muntassir is waiting for us downstairs in my apartment,' says
Fadwa.

We had also asked to speak to Hayder. But his jaw and face were
so badly injured in the attack, he has trouble speaking to anyone now.

Muntassir is waiting for us in his aunt's living room. He is a
sallow-skinned boy hunched in an armchair that looks way too
big for his slender limbs. He was injured in the attack too, and
after two operations at Gaza's al-Shifa Hospital, still has shrapnel

embedded in his right leg. We sit down facing him and he stares at us with eyes so startled, yet blank, they are frightening. Noor speaks to him in her soft voice, explaining who we are and what information we need.

'I was in the kitchen doorway,' he says. And stares straight ahead without another word.

From that doorway, he saw half his family slaughtered in front of him. Now Muntassir sits in the armchair, staring, drowning, already oblivious that we are even here.[48]

Noor and I spend weeks travelling up and down the Strip by taxi, interviewing bereaved families, asking detailed questions and making precise notes. We need this information, and the parents answer all our questions. Some weep while telling us about their kids; others just stare blankly at the walls, speaking in dull monologues as if they are trapped inside fog. The men are uncharacteristically silent, often letting their women speak while they sit cross-legged and stare at a small space just outside themselves. I deliberately switch my emotions off while taking these testimonies. But Noor, who has just lived through this war with her husband and their three small children, often weeps during the interviews. And there are days when I cry in the taxi afterwards, on our way back to the Centre. Noor and I even laugh about how we take it in turns to weep, one of us always dry-eyed, propping up the other.

'You know why I cry so much?' she says to me one afternoon. 'I cry because every time I look at those parents, I think that really could have been me.'

While I was stuck outside Gaza, I rang Saida repeatedly, frantic with worry when Israel launched its assault. Now that I'm here, Saida says little about it but she looks thin, tired and pinched. Her family hid beneath the stairs of their building for two days and nights, then fled to stay with friends as their area was being heavily bombarded. But their immediate relatives who lived in the apartment just below them in the same building stayed. On 7 January Saida's young cousin, Muhammad, was walking in the street just outside his home when he was hit by exploding shrapnel that sliced off both his legs.

My friend Wafa' and her family had to evacuate their first-floor apartment when the UN told them the area was going to be bombed.

'I woke up in the morning and my family was frantically packing,' she tells me. 'We literally had minutes to get out of the house. I took nothing. My cousin is a journalist – he put us in his armoured car to drive us to my relatives, and as he raced down the road we could see the bombs exploding behind us.'

Up in Siafa, Manah and her family spent the war inside their remote hillside cottage. On the night of 17 January, they were ordered out of their home by the Israeli military, who used a loudspeaker to tell them: 'You have fifteen minutes to leave your house. This house is going to be destroyed. No houses are allowed in this area.'

Manah, her daughters and son fled outside, then stood and watched as Israeli tanks rolled in and over their home and crushed it into the ground. Eight hours later, the Israeli military withdrew from the Strip.

When I walk the streets, many people still look dazed, their eyes dull and exhausted, like they have just emerged from a train crash.

As I settle back into my apartment and my work, I *am* glad that

I returned. I'm proud of the work the Centre is doing, meticulously documenting how Israel has pounded Gaza. (One of my colleagues spent every day of the war at the door of the morgue at al-Shifa Hospital, writing down the name of each corpse that arrived.) But sometimes in the evenings, I slump on the couch in my living room, trying to slow my spinning mind. I didn't call Sakhar when I first came back; I was too proud. When I bumped into him at a dinner party at Catherine's a week or so later, the atmosphere between us was glacial. I tried to speak to him alone, but he skilfully avoided me. Now I feel scalded and angry, hackled with hurt and spite.

Late one windswept night, unable to sleep, I sit out on my living-room balcony, swaddled in blankets. I watch the near-full moon for a long time, as clouds storm across the scowling sky. The biting winter sea air clears my mind. I smoke, swig neat vodka, cry furious tears and fling Sakhar into the tempest, knowing I just have to let go: he will never tell me what happened. And then I brood over the awful inevitability of this war, the governments of Gaza and Israel locked in their terrible, fearful embrace. The wind begins to howl then scream around me, as angry clouds swell. I can almost hear the Mediterranean waves rising and hissing. This elemental violence heralds the end of this particular chapter of war in Gaza. But I can't stop myself thinking that very soon, this too will be history.

Bruno does tension zones

The Israeli military may have withdrawn from Gaza, but now we are facing another invasion: the hacks have stormed into town. Their HQ is the al-Deira Hotel, which is doing a roaring trade, packed to the rafters with journalists and film crews. By day they stalk the Strip, and when dusk falls they surge into the al-Deira café, hollering into mobile phones, striding around at full speed as though they're fully charged, greeting each other bloody loudly. Through the collective roar I can hear snatches of conversation: 'Hey, Charlie! Haven't seen you since Kurdistan!' and 'Serina – It's been a while! Debbie says Hi. Y'know she's embedded back in Eye-raq.' They really do speak to each other like this.

Shadi, my friend and colleague from the Centre, spends most afternoons and evenings in the al-Deira café too, doing round after round of interviews with radio and print journalists from Europe, Scandinavia and the US. The second that an interview is finished, the journalists start typing their notes, mobile jammed between ear and shoulder. Shadi and his family spent most of the war sheltering in the basement of his brother's house. Now he sits back, another interview done, lights up a cigarette and catches my eye. He is endlessly patient and gracious, and thinks that some of these journalists are very good. But there's an air of them consuming details as fast as possible because they won't be staying very long. This week, and maybe next, Gaza is on the front page. But we all know it won't last. Very soon they will all be moving on to the next breaking story.

But while they *are* here, certain places in Gaza – most of them sites where numerous members of the same family have been killed together – have become press stomping grounds. It's strange – all these journalists are competing to scoop news stories from the aftermath of what Al Jazeera calls the Israeli 'war on Gaza', yet they have a curious herd instinct. Most seem to visit the same places and interview, photograph and film the same survivors, one after another. For example, they head off to Zeitoun, on the south-eastern edge of Gaza City, to interview survivors of the al-Samouni family.

On Sunday, 4 January 2009, the Israeli military corralled up to 100 members of the extended al-Samouni family into one building within their large family compound. The following morning, the Israelis shelled that building, burying many of the al-Samounis alive. Those who could ran for their lives. The Israeli military refused to allow ambulances into the compound for the next seventy-two hours. Upon entry, medical personnel found twenty-seven corpses, including eleven children. Scrawled on the walls of Helmi al-Samouni's house, which Israeli soldiers had used as a temporary base and a toilet during their assault on the compound, were the words, '*Arabs need 2 die.*'[49] Having survived hell, the al-Samounis are now besieged by journalists all wanting their piece of the action. Others, like the Abdul-Dayem, al-Dayah and Shurrab families, also face this worst kind of fleeting fame of being international war victims.[50]

Bruno has no doubt already 'done' the al-Samouni story too. And from the way he's crowing right now, it's clear he has just emerged from another press stomping ground – the tunnels down at Rafah.

'Right down the shaft!' he exclaims. 'I tell you – I got some great photos ... really shot the atmosphere.' As hacks raise their hands in greeting and call out his name, Bruno can hardly contain his glee, strutting cock-like across the sunny al-Deira terrace, where Shadi and I are having a late lunch with a few friends. I cannot take my eyes off this man called Bruno. Even when I realise that I'm sitting bolt upright with my mouth open and a glass of fresh orange juice poised half-way to my lips, I keep staring until he stops right in front of me.

'What is it?' His voice is not aggressive, but punchy and clipped. He looks and sounds northern European.

'Where are you from?' I ask him.

'I am Bruno and I come from Belgium. You?'

'I'm, er, Louisa. From Scotland.'

'Oh.'

'Who do you work for, Bruno?'

'A few different agencies ... I go wherever the contracts are.'

'And you've just been to Rafah – to the tunnels?'

'Yeah!' And for a few seconds his pale, sun-blushed face lights up. 'I dropped 25 metres right to the bottom and crawled along there with one of those local boys. Got some mean shots ...'

Bruno, I should add, is smothered in cameras. They are draped around his neck, his torso and his back; he has one strapped either side of him, like gun holsters, and another resting on top of his money belt, resembling a slightly out-of-place codpiece. They are all black.

I am staring at him because I'm trying to count them, but when I get to fourteen I start feeling crossed-eyed. Damn it – I wish I had my little pocket camera with me. I would love to take his photograph. I don't know why I am so fascinated by Bruno. He's pale, thick-skinned and middle-aged. I don't fancy him – but I have never seen or heard anyone like this before.

'You're a war photographer?' I say. It is not so much a question as a witness statement.

Bruno is already gazing over my shoulder, but now gives me a look that says: 'Oh, for fuck's sake, what does *she* want?'

'I am a well-known professional photographer. But, my dear! – my work is not restricted to war zones.' His voice curdles with each word. 'It is more complicated than that, you see. I go wherever the tension is. I do tension zones.'

☙

Not all the foreign press are assholes like Bruno. Some are very competent and there are a few excellent investigative journalists, like Amira Hass. The only Israeli journalist to have lived in Gaza, she moved here in 1993 and stayed for more than three years. In November 2008 she returned here, on another vessel chartered by the Free Gaza movement, but just a few weeks later she was ordered out of Gaza by Hamas. Incandescent at being locked out during the war, Amira crossed back into Gaza via the Egyptian border within days of the Israeli military pulling out.

When I first meet Amira at the Centre, she looks exactly the way I expected her to: a bespectacled academic dressed in baggy clothes, with a stern gaze. She tells me she will be staying here for several months and we exchange numbers. For weeks afterwards I catch fleeting glimpses of her as she strides through the Centre on her way to various meetings. But then one evening she calls out of the blue, and invites me to dinner. We meet at the Palmyra Restaurant, named after the birthplace of the legendary Syrian Queen Zenobia, lover of philosophy and poetry, who briefly ruled Gaza in the third century AD.

As we chomp our way through plates of kofta and salads in the busy restaurant, we talk. Actually I do most of the talking. Amira is an exceptionally good listener – which probably explains why she is such a formidable journalist – and I find myself offloading at length. I tell her about the bullying immigration police officer who held me at the Erez crossing as I was on my way back inside.

'This is the last time you are going to Gaza,' he warned me. 'I am giving you one more month [inside Gaza] – but you need to be back here before the end of that month. It will be better for you.'

I have already been back inside Gaza more than a month, and intend to stay until my visa runs out in eight weeks. But I know that the day I leave, he will be waiting for me at Erez. Amira jokes that we could leave Gaza on the same day and get arrested at the crossing together.

'My family came from Bosnia,' she tells me a little later. We are still at the restaurant, lingering over dessert, and she has finally dropped her guard and opened up a little. 'When people ask me why I chose to live in Gaza, I tell them it's because here I found my own shtetl,' she adds, and we both smile.

Amira calls herself 'a Gaza addict' and says the only people she is frightened of here are Hamas. 'But it is my job to stay here for the next few months to document the scale of what my country is doing to the people here.'

'You are the bottom line,' I say.

She doesn't reply but concentrates on finishing her slice of cake, her face closed. She is one of the very few Israeli dissidents who have defiantly made their home in the Palestinian West Bank, a small community who dedicate their lives to unravelling Israeli government myths about Palestine and Palestinians. She's not sentimental about Gaza, though, and deplores the internal violence and the die-hard patriarchal attitudes. But she wants Israeli society to confront its military occupation of Palestine, and she is their witness.

While we are talking, her mobile phone rings: it is her lawyer calling from Israel and she apologises because she needs to take this call. Sitting across the table from an Israeli journalist speaking Hebrew in a crowded Gaza restaurant, I feel my spine tense. But when I look around, nobody is taking any notice at all. Hundreds of thousands of Gazans have worked in Israeli restaurants, factories and workshops over the years and I'm sure that many would go there to work, even now, given the opportunity. Many Gazans speak fluent Hebrew and Amira's presence does not cause a whiff of fear or anger. When we finally go to pay our bill, Amira and the Palmyra Restaurant owner greet each other in Arabic, then Hebrew, exchanging news as the tables fill up around us.

How-How

A couple of weeks after the spectacle of Bruno strutting across the terrace of the al-Deira Hotel, Shadi and I are on our way to Rafah. We have come to visit one of his friends, who lives near the tunnels where Bruno took his mean shots.

'You know the Israelis have not stopped bombing the tunnels of Rafah,' he says, as we drive south down the coast. His 'best-in-the-West' rust bucket is somehow still roadworthy. 'My friend Farrah and her family are still evacuated every week. They're facing six thousand, six hundred and sixty-six dangers every single day.'

'You really do have your ear to the ground,' I say.

'I told you, *habibti*, if they whisper in Rafah, then I hear it up in Beit Hanoun,' he grins, steering the best-in-the-West with one hand, a half-smoked cigarette in the other.

We drive through the tattered centre of Rafah City, then head west, towards Salah al-Din Gate, where the Rafah International Crossing lies. Taking a smaller road that curves towards the Egyptian border, we enter the district of al-Salam, which lies adjacent to the network of smugglers' tunnels snaking between the Egyptian and Gazan sides of Rafah. Now we are beyond the boundary of Rafah City itself, in an area of sandy streets and ragged buildings, where children play against a backdrop of broken walls smothered in graffiti. It looks like the worst parts of Beit Hanoun, another lonely edge of Gaza. Except that now we are at the eastern tip of the Sinai desert.

Shadi parks beside the last house standing at the end of a track. When I climb out of the car, I can see tarp-covered entrances to the tunnels just metres away. Gazans started building tunnels at least twenty years ago, back in the mid-1980s, maybe just to bypass Israeli and Egyptian customs. Since the Israeli blockade tightened in June 2006, the tunnels have burgeoned into Gaza's most lucrative domestic industry. There are hundreds of them now, and more are still being built. The market in Rafah is the best-stocked *souq* in the whole Strip.

I've visited the tunnels before, and watched the men being lowered 20 metres below the earth by electric winches. The tunnellers I met were from all over the Strip, young men proud of the money they were earning for their families (I once hailed a cab in the centre of Rafah and the teenage driver asked with a cheeky wink whether I would like to see his tunnel). Hamas have cashed in on the trade, taxing the owners of the tunnels, who still stand to make fortunes smuggling goods, including car parts and livestock, into Gaza. This is why some of the tunnel owners apparently paid renegade fighters to fire rockets towards southern Israel during the *tahdiya*. They did not want to lose their cash cow.

A woman is walking from her gate towards us. Her loosely tied silver *hijab* sparkles as it catches the light.

'*Ahlan wa sahlan*,' she calls. 'Welcome to my home.'

'This is my friend, Farrah,' says Shadi.

Farrah laughs out loud as she greets Shadi with affection, though they do not touch each other. He has already told me they are old school friends. She has deep-set green eyes, almond-shaped and fringed with thick lashes, and a voice that rings with confidence. We follow her through a low gate. Her home is a long, low building with a flat roof, flanked by a wide yard. In one corner, a few hens are scratching inside a wire coop. In another is a shaded sitting area of mattresses, embroidered cushions and wall hangings, with a tarpaulin roof. But suddenly I realise that we are surrounded by cats, prowling and watching us, slit-eyed, from the roof.

'Cats,' I say, dismayed. I hate cats. They make me itchy and asthmatic.

'Ah, we have too many cats,' says Farrah breezily.

'How many?' I ask, suspiciously.

'Twenty-five, I think, maybe more – it is too hard to tell now!' Tinkling with laughter, she goes off to brew coffee.

'I trained as a teacher,' Farrah tells me a little while later, as we slump against the cushions, slurping our coffee. 'Then I worked as a private tutor for a few years, with local kids who are struggling at school. But there is no work around here now. Many people have left and my neighbours have no money to pay a tutor. It is a shame; many of the kids are still struggling at school. And after this war they are very nervous.'

Israel launched its assault on a Saturday morning, just as thousands of children were entering and leaving their schools. As the bombs began to explode, Shadi dived in and evacuated classrooms of screaming children from the school near his home.

I lean back against the cushions, still keeping an eye out for the damned cats.

'How is the situation for you now?' I ask Farrah.

'Difficult,' she replies, with classic Gazan understatement.

'This is the hardest place to live in Gaza,' states Shadi, stubbing his cigarette out in a tin ashtray.

Farrah nods. 'We have to leave our house maybe three times in a week. We are just 500 metres from the border with Egypt, and the men in the tunnels, they dig all day and night – except for Fridays of course! Sometimes we cannot sleep because of the noise. If we hear the *zananas* or the Israeli planes coming, we know they are going to bomb the tunnels, so we have to run.'

'Where do you go?'

'To our neighbours who live a few streets back. It is a bit safer there. Or to my sister's house – she lives in the next district.'

'How long have the Israelis been bombing the tunnels?'

'For years.'

'How long have you lived here?'

'All my life.'

'Do you ever feel safe?'

This time she shakes her head. One of the skinny kittens is sitting in her lap, rheumy-eyed and purring. She strokes it. 'Who feels safe here in Gaza? I want to move away from this area, it is too dangerous. But my father is old and stubborn; this is his land and he refuses to leave.' Farrah's father also has his own corner of the yard, a tatty mattress beside a small fire of smoking twigs. He looks as though he has camped here since the day he was born.

Farrah's mother strides across the yard with a dish of almonds. She greets Shadi enthusiastically and berates him for not having visited for too long. Then she returns to the kitchen to prepare lunch. It's a makeshift kitchen that has been built onto the side of the house, with a roof of corrugated iron stapled over the top.

'We used to have a kitchen inside,' says Farrah, following my eyes. 'But a few years ago our house was damaged by a bomb and the kitchen was ruined. So now we cook out here.'

She insists we stay for lunch and Shadi and I gladly accept. It's a Saturday and we are in no rush. This is a welcome break from the constant demands of work. Shadi stretches, then flops down

among the cushions, and for once makes no effort to check his
jawaal.

'If you like, we can stay here all afternoon,' he says, clearly relishing this time out.

Our lunch is a mound of rice and vegetables and fresh,
homemade bread. Afterwards, Farrah and her mother pray
while Shadi and I smoke. Then she offers to show me around the
neighbourhood. Shadi opts for a snooze in the shade of the shelter
as Farrah and I set off together.

I follow Farrah through a gap in the fence to the garden next door.
Right where her neighbours' house should stand is a crater half-
filled with rubble where the building has collapsed in on itself.

'Where are your neighbours?' I ask, hoping they're not dead.

'They are OK, they left before the house was destroyed last year.
Now they live there.' She points to a domed tent in the garden,
set in a small grove of olive and orange trees. As we're talking, a
woman steps out of the tent door. She is small, elderly and her face
is inked with faded blue tattoos. Like Farrah her *hijab* hangs loose
over her hair; her name is J'meeah.

'*Marhaba* – You are the foreign lady who has come to visit?'

Word gets around here fast. J'meeah begins to ask me questions,
but I am gazing at her inked face. Only elderly Bedouin women
still bear these distinct tattoos.

'Are you Bedouin?' I ask, slightly hesitant.

'We are both Bedouin,' cries Farrah, slapping my shoulder to
make her point. 'So many of the people round here are Bedouin.'

This makes sense: the Gaza Bedouin mainly seem to live in
isolated enclaves on the Strip, like here and in Siafa, and in the
unvisited Bedouin camps.

J'meeah invites us in for tea, but Farrah says we are going for

a stroll and we'll see her later. As we take our leave, J'meeah says
something to Farrah, making a sound like a growl or a bark. Farrah
nods, and takes my arm.

'What did she say?' I ask as we cross the garden to the lane outside.

'*How-How* are outside, so we have to be careful,' she answers,
jerking her chin towards the road ahead, and guiding me towards
a gap in the fence.

'*How-How?*'

Her green eyes flash. 'The Hamas police.'

After this war, many Gazans have hardened against Hamas.
Where were the fighters, people ask, when Israeli ground forces
invaded the Strip? Many people mock them as cowards who hid in
the other network of subterranean tunnels, up in northern Gaza.[51]
As they lose popularity, the Hamas leaders become more militant,
and the rank and file more heavy-handed and paranoid, especially
with dissidents and outsiders, and the Bedouin are both.

Farrah and I cross into the small lane. It is lined on both sides with
bombed-out and shelled houses. An occasional single wall has
been left standing, or half a room. The scale of destruction is like
the worst bombed-out sites in the north of Gaza. I know some of
these houses were bombed back in 2005, when Israel carried out
large-scale house demolitions across the district of Rafah. But here
on the front line, it seems they have never stopped.

We walk for maybe an hour, through rubble-strewn streets.
Farrah tells me the men in her neighbourhood spend much of their
lives repairing their homes, which are badly damaged by Israeli
bombs that penetrate deep into the tunnels, burying alive anyone
who is inside. Meanwhile the smugglers accuse the Egyptian
authorities of sealing tunnels with cement, and even pumping gas

inside, to scare them off. It's a dangerous, dirty business; dozens of Gazans have been buried alive in these tunnels. But even so, the money is a magnet that attracts new hopefuls from all across the Strip every day.

I ask Farrah what she thinks of the tunnels.

'I don't like them – I worry they will dig right under our house!' she says. 'But the siege means we cannot get aid or goods into Gaza. Israel controls it all. So they have to dig tunnels or we will have nothing.'

Personally, I think this is a bit of an exaggeration; but I get her point. Israel controls and monitors everything that enters the Strip, ensuring there is enough for life to be tolerable, but never releasing its list of what can enter the Strip, and when. Yet unpredictability ensures that people can never plan ahead. Israel dumps its surpluses here, banning all exports from Gaza. This siege is a cash cow for Israeli producers too.

I gaze over at the sprawling city of tarps, visible from everywhere we walk. Egypt is so close, we can almost smell it. I ask Farrah when she last crossed the border. She finds this question very funny.

'I live so near! – but I have not been to Egypt for, I don't know, maybe twenty years. And there is no chance now.'

Farrah barely moves from this area, but she asks if she can visit me in Gaza City. We agree to go to the al-Deira Hotel terrace and spend an afternoon drinking coffee overlooking the sea. She's heard of the hotel, but never been there. Gaza City centre, with its fancy hotels, its history museum, its cultural centres and its late night cafés where men and women can sit together, is like a different land.

We eventually return to her house, to find Shadi drinking tea with her father, round his small smouldering twig fire. Farrah takes me into the family living room. She shows me great cracks warping the walls from top to bottom. Some are so wide, I can almost fit my hand inside. The cracks have made the walls tilt like drunks propping each other up.

'The Israelis use very strong bombs to destroy the tunnels; our home trembles every time,' she says. 'You see, the walls are collapsing. Every house around here is like this.'

Like they are all being shaken to death.

By now it is late afternoon, and Shadi says we should leave soon: night-time can be dangerous in al-Salam district. But then J'meeah arrives, and we find ourselves persuaded to stay a while and drink sweet mint tea. When dusk settles, Farrah lights lamps and even though it's cool, we stay outside, among the cushions and the bloody cats. Shadi and I end up lingering for another while, as J'meeah tells us stories of when she used to be a camel driver, back in the days when this area had no tunnels and no *How-How* ... just Bedouin tents and endless groves of almond and olive trees, their thirsty, tenacious roots pressing into the eastern Sinai.

Muhammad and all the things he might have done

Noor and I are still visiting families across the Strip. We venture to places I haven't yet seen in Gaza, quiet villages tucked away inside the middle areas of the Strip, around Deir al-Balah and Nuseirat, where the war did not rage so violently, but people were still killed and homes destroyed. Because nowhere was safe. We listen to testimonies almost every working day, and by the time the weekend comes we are both physically and mentally exhausted.

One Saturday I return to my old haunt, Hammam al-Samara, to spend the afternoon steaming and bathing quietly. Abu Abdullah, the keeper of the *hammam*, is still there and as he welcomes me back, his moustache still twitches like a little silver fish. With quiet pride, he tells me that the old Turkish bathhouse somehow withstood the war without much damage.

I take my things into the changing area and undress, already enjoying the damp heat. Over the last fifteen months I have been here many times; this *hammam* has become a sanctuary of sorts, a place where I can retreat when I need some space from the maelstrom of Gaza. Today there are half a dozen other women inside the steam chamber. We greet each other, make friendly small talk and enthuse about spending the afternoon like this. But we say nothing about the war, as though there is some unspoken agreement between us not to discuss anything dark while we relax inside these thick, warm walls. I lie on my towel and chat to a young woman called Jehan, who tells me she's a lawyer. Like me, she comes here to retreat from the cold realities of life in Gaza. I suddenly recall seeing her here several times before.

'Ah – I know: you're the one who always smokes in the changing room!' I exclaim. She gives me a wink and we both laugh.

We lie side by side swathed in clouds of steam, as water pumps through the old pipes. After some time, another woman joins us in the steam chamber. She settles down, introduces herself and begins to tell me about her house being destroyed during the war. But Jehan immediately cuts her off.

'*Habibti – khalas*! Stop speaking about the war! Talk of politics or war is for outside. We have come here just to relax.'

The woman falls silent, then moves away. I lie back on my towel and gaze up at the shoal of tiny portholes that refract small circular rainbows, feeling deeply relaxed for the first time since I came back. I am weary down to my bones.

I spend hours in the *hammam*, finally emerging in the late afternoon, scrubbed and glowing. I feel a hell of a lot better. I wander back into the main sitting area, to pay Abu Abdullah.

'How long are you staying in Gaza?' he asks.

'I have to leave in a few weeks,' I tell him. My three-month visa will expire at the beginning of April. I have very mixed feelings about going, but in my guts I do sense that it's almost time for me to live outside Gaza again, before I burn myself out.

'Have you seen any of the other *hammams* in the Middle East?' he asks.

'No – I haven't.'

'This is one of the oldest in the whole region,' he says.

'The house the Mamluks built!' I joke.

Abu Abdullah nods and smiles. All of his gestures are leisurely. He points to a carving on the wall above, with a lengthy, intricate inscription embedded in the stone.

'This is from the Mamluk period,' he says, and again I hear that quiet pride in his voice.

The Mamluks were slave soldiers, traded across the lands of the Turks and raised as vicious fighters. Led by the ferocious and flame-haired Sultan Baybars, they swarmed over Egypt in the thirteenth century. Baybars's defeat of the Mongols has been described as one of the most important battles in world history as he literally stopped the hordes in their tracks. He then set about wiping out the remaining Crusader kingdoms across the Middle East. Mamluk viceroys were appointed to major coastal cities, including Gaza, bringing peace and stability. In Gaza City, beefy Mamluk builders constructed Hammam al-Samara around this period, in the old quarter of the city near the ancient Orthodox church. It was fitted with a labyrinth of steam chambers, marble basins for ablutions, and this shoal of tiny portholes that allowed enough natural light to enter the chamber for women to disrobe and bathe in the nude without being spied upon by leering men.

The city itself was also beautified. The thirteenth-century Syrian scholar and geographer, al-Dimashqi, lyrically described Gaza as 'a city so rich in trees it looks like a cloth of brocade spread out across the land'.[52] But no empire lasts for ever, and three centuries later a new regional power rose to the fore. The Ottomans emerged from one of the Turkish principalities and captured Constantinople in 1453. Their leader, Selim I (nicknamed 'Selim the Grim'), marched into Syria, capturing Gaza en route to the more important regional prize of Egypt – where he took the title, 'Caliph of Islam'. Selim's

empire stretched across the Muslim world, and Gaza was sucked
into the Ottoman province of Syria.

෯෴

When I emerge from the steps of the *hammam*, the street feels cold
and lonely. I am expected at Saida's house for supper and decide
to walk there – it is only about fifteen minutes away. I cross the
busy street beside Souq al-Zawiya. Avoiding the crowds as best I
can, I stroll down a narrow hill passing by a school and come to
a roundabout where a single tree stands almost defiant, spanning
the width of the small roundabout. This is the local landmark of
Sidra – legend has it that a famous and beloved sheikh was buried
beneath this tree long ago, and for that reason alone this tree can
never be cut down.

Walking along Jaffa Street, I soon reach the red gate that marks
the courtyard where Saida and her family live, behind a local
pottery workshop. The courtyard smells of paint and varnish, but
the workshop lights are out. I enter Saida's building, climb the dark
stairs and knock on the front door of her home. Maha comes to
the door.

'*Marhaba*. My sister is not here; she is downstairs, visiting
Muhammad.'

'Ah – do you think it would be OK if I went downstairs to say
hello to him?'

I have never actually met her cousin Muhammad. Maha shrugs
her narrow shoulders.

'*Leeysh-la*? (Why not?)'

I go back down one flight of stairs and knock on the door to
my left. The girl who opens it resembles Maha – after all, they're
cousins. This is the home of Saida's father's brother and his family,

including Muhammad, the young man whose legs were sliced off during the war.

'Is Saida here?' I ask.

'Yes,' she says. 'Come inside.'

She leads me through the dim apartment to a back bedroom, where Saida is sitting with her cousin. He is lying in bed, a blanket pulled up to his waist, concealing the stumps of his legs. On the wall above the bed is a large poster of Hamas. Saida is sitting on the other side of the narrow room.

'*Habibti*!' She stands to greet me and we kiss each other. I have not seen her so much these last few weeks, we have both been so distracted by work. I've missed her, and am looking forward to spending the evening with her and Hind and Maha. I don't have much time left, and want to spend as much of it with them as I can.

'This is my cousin Muhammad,' she introduces me to the young man lying in bed. I step forward to shake his hand, but he shakes his head, placing his hand over his heart. Ah, he is one of the pious young men who don't shake hands with women.

'I'm so sorry about what happened to you,' I say, sitting down beside Saida.

Muhammad looks at me; he is a slender young man, 19 years old, with a thin face and an indoor complexion. He surprises me with an almost bashful smile.

'*Shukran. Inshallah*, the doctors will be able to help me.'

God willing, I think to myself. Thousands of Gazans have been maimed and injured in this war and the chances of them receiving the specialist medical treatment they need are minimal. Israel continues to restrict patients' access to hospitals outside Gaza.

'Muhammad was studying in university before the war,' says Saida.

When she first told me what had happened to her cousin, she cried, but now she's dry-eyed though her voice is flat with dismay. We always think these tragedies are going to happen to someone else.

'What were you studying?' I ask Muhammad.

'Physical education. I was training to be a sports teacher.'

There is a small pause, and then the three of us, all at the same moment, begin to laugh.

the *mathaf*

Across the Strip, especially in the north and in Gaza City, where the war was at its most brutal, people are stoically rebuilding their homes and their lives. Visiting all these different communities makes me appreciate more keenly how people on the edges of Gaza, the farmers and the Bedouin – and those in the cramped refugee camps – live so apart from the rest. I feel like I'm peeling through layers of small different worlds that co-exist inside Gaza, while still musing on the past and its imprints on the present. Most of the people I meet through my work are just trying to survive day by day; my amateur inquiries into Gaza's ancient history are of little interest to them, especially now. I need to leave Gaza very soon, but before I go, I want to talk to someone who *is* passionate about history and find out what it means to them.

And this is how I come to be sitting with Jawdat al-Khoudari, the owner of the only *mathaf* (museum) in Gaza, one afternoon in early spring, trying to gauge his opinion on history. But this meeting is not going to plan at all.

'Why am I interested in history?' Jawdat looks at me and blinks slowly like an ox. 'Why are you wearing green and white today? It is about personal preferences, nothing more.'

'But you've spent years excavating and restoring Gaza artifacts – why *is* history such a passion for you?' I ask.

Another pause, then: 'You know, I decided a while ago that I was not going to talk to any more foreigners. You ask too many questions.'

'So why did you agree to meet me today?'

'I made a mistake,' he says politely.

Jawdat is slow and ponderous, with a Gazan accent as thick as his waistline. He is an engineer with his own construction company, and the best-known historian-cum-archaeologist in the Strip. He's been preserving local history here since the mid-1980s, when he began collecting stones from old buildings which were being demolished to make space for new ones. He began excavating artifacts too and buying them from other construction crews. Over the years he has unearthed hordes of ancient treasures – pottery from 3,500 BC, Roman columns, Egyptian masks, Hellenistic wine jars and early Islamic tiles. Eventually he built this *mathaf*, overlooking the sea just north of Gaza City, to house some of his best finds.[53] The *mathaf* opened in the autumn of last year, complete with an outdoor café where a stream trickles between the wooden tables – and an indoor restaurant, where sections of wooden sleepers from the old Gaza railway track have been recycled into columns and beams.

Jawdat and I are sitting in the *mathaf* restaurant now, drinking cappuccinos. It is a big, elegant space filled with plants and natural light. After weeks of visiting smashed-up homes and grieving families, it feels restful, and totally surreal. I'm trying to talk to Jawdat about his work and his love of history – but having invited me here today, he doesn't really seem to want to tell me anything.

'Are you still excavating Gazan artifacts?' I ask him, lighting another cigarette. He gives me another long, searching look ... and says nothing. I try again:

'Look – why is Gaza's history so important? Why does it matter so much anyway?'

I am trying to provoke a reaction from him, but I'm asking myself this same question. Gaza is one of the oldest stories in the world. But its histories have been neglected and destroyed, treated as though they are almost worthless. So are these remains only meaningful for academics, collectors and curious writers?

But now Jawdat is staring at me like I have just sworn filthily at him.

'Are you trying to make me nervous? Look at us, our situation – what's the basis of our conflict with Israel?'

'The history of who this land belongs to ...?'

He leans forward, his big hands extended towards me.

'The whole story of Gaza is history – and history matters because Israel has claimed history as its own, to prove its case. Our history is evidence of our roots here on this land. Just look around you. I am telling you now: if you don't know the history, then you don't know anything of this place.'

This is the most that he has said since we sat down. Now I fall silent because I want him to continue speaking. Jawdat is taking his time. I can hear him thinking.

'Yes, the Jews have claimed the history of this land as theirs,' he says without looking at me. 'But listen to me ... they are just the new occupiers. I ask you something: in 200 years, how will the history books record Israel's occupation of us?' He holds a thick thumb and index finger just a few centimetres apart. 'It will take up this much space in the history books. One sentence. Like nothing.'

'Because all Gaza's history has been occupation?'

'Exactly. And our history is the evidence of the great civilisation of Gaza. I have found coins, you know, dating from 450 to 430 BC. We were minting our own silver coins back then.[54] And I tell you now, if Israel wants to settle this conflict by bringing archaeologists to find out who this land belongs to historically, then I will say to them, "*Itfadalouh* – Please, come and see for yourselves!'"

Zionists claim that Jews have always been present in historic Palestine. But for successive centuries there was no Jewish population in Gaza. The only direct Israelite rule of Gaza in antiquity was the Hasmonean dynasty, in 145 BC, which lasted for just over a century (even then, the Gaza Jews were probably a minority of the local population). A Jewish community did settle in Rafah in the ninth and tenth centuries, and again in the twelfth century – when a community of Samaritans was also based in Rafah. Most of the Jews, however, left Gaza after Napoleon's brief 1799 conquest of the Strip, which also ignited European interest in the region. Zionist Jews began to immigrate to Palestine from the late nineteenth century, often fleeing persecution. By the start of the British Mandate in 1918, however, Jews made up just 5 per cent of the population of Palestine.

'Do you think Gazans really know their own history?' I ask Jawdat.

'Listen to me,' he says, more vehemently this time. 'The people here, they said this December 2008 war was the most terrible ever in Gaza. But' – he looks me straight in the eye – 'this was *nothing*! You think about all the wars before – like the First World War and the thousands of people who died here then and the mass destruction of buildings. This war was nothing.'

I know what he means – compared to previous Gaza wars, this one was bloody and quick. But still shattering.

imagining A. Love

Almost three months after I returned to Gaza, some people tell me they believe it is time to move on from the war, while others say Gaza will never get over what the war ripped out of them. I am also a different person from the woman who arrived here almost a year and a half ago. Life has been so full-on, so vivid and intense, and though I feel exhausted, I wouldn't have it any other way. But my time here is nearly over, for now. My interviews are complete and I have just finished my report for the Centre. The director has made it clear that I'm welcome to stay and continue working with them. I have lots of friends here, and though I don't have a lover any more, I would find another. But then I remember Wafa', the lovely *muhajaba* with attitude, saying to me over a coffee one afternoon, 'Louisa, you told me you wanted to leave Gaza while you still love it, so I think you should go now.'

I know that she's dead right. I know I will come back here again, but for a while I need to be outside this siege.

At the Centre, it is a ritual to hold a tea party when a member of staff leaves. This being Gaza, there will be goodbye speeches and I will be expected to say something too. I spend the morning of the tea party fretting about what I'll say and pestering Shadi about how to pronounce this and that in Arabic, so that I can get it just right. After a while he looks at me and shakes his grey head.

'*Habibti*, why are you worrying so much? Just say the words you want to – you know we will all understand what you mean.'

That afternoon, when my colleagues have all gathered around the conference table in the upstairs library and we've drunk our tea and coffee and eaten slices of creamy, lurid, pink-and-yellow gateaux, the deputy director clears his throat. Everyone falls quiet as he speaks in his grave, precise English. He thanks me for my work at the Centre and makes a joke about my passion for spending as much time as possible outside the office. My colleagues' laughter ripples across the room. When he has finished, there is a brief silence, then I clear my throat and start to speak. I forget everything I prepared in advance and just say how much I've enjoyed working with such great people. But my Arabic is suddenly choked because tears are streaking down my face, and when I look around, Noor and Joumana and several other colleagues are crying too. I laugh and cry at the same time, realising that it really doesn't matter what I say right now. And suddenly I find the words to crack a few bad jokes about how the best thing that's happened to me has been working and smoking with Shadi and everyone starts laughing as Joumana hands me tissues for my wet cheeks and neck.

'*Aye*, Louisa, we will miss you!' she says as we sit there amid the tea and coffee dregs and creamy cake crusts, laughing and crying. And I think that if *Ustaz* Mounir was here today, he would be just a little bit proud of me.

For fifteen months my life has been mainly confined to 25 by 6 miles, but I still haven't seen all of Gaza, not at all. There is one more place in particular I really need to visit before I leave, to help me unravel another layer of the Gaza story. I ask Saida if she can come with me, but she's busy at work. I also know that she's keeping her distance because I am extracting myself from Gaza and she has to stay here. So I take a taxi alone to a place called Zuweida, in the middle area of the Strip, a few miles south of Gaza City.

I ask the driver to take the sea road, past the wide open beaches where huddles of fishermen tend to their boats and mend their nets, singing softly as they work. They sing of the sea, I drink in the sea. From the open window of the car, the salty air is warm, waves laced in foam splashing up the beach, the Mediterranean shimmering, a vast diaphanous blue. I will miss this beautiful place so much.

The driver turns left and heads inland, veering off the main road and onto a narrow lane streaked with sand. We're in a quiet place, an area set well back from the sea, not far from Salah al-Din Road. There are just a few old white houses with flaking paint shaded by gnarled olive groves. A place you could easily miss, even if you were looking for it.

The driver pulls over in front of a white gate and I clamber out of the car. The air is quiet. I can hear birds clearly, even distinguish between their songs. Traffic is still buzzing, but the city feels far away. The white gate is latched, but opens easily, and I step through it onto a fresh green lawn. It's perfectly mown, wrapped like felt around well-tended acacia trees, with plants and flowers perfectly spaced apart. It smells and tastes different here, the dusty salt air of Gaza softened by the moist greenery all around me. I can hear bees buzzing. It feels almost familiar: there is nothing to distinguish this from a well-tended English park garden, except for the long, straight rows of white gravestones.

In 1917 Britain had three wartime objectives relating to Palestine: to maintain its maritime supremacy; to preserve the balance of power in Europe; and to maintain security within Egypt, India and the Persian Gulf to its own advantage. The British government decided this latter objective would be best achieved by capturing Jerusalem, defeating the Ottoman forces in Mesopotamia and the Arabian peninsula and driving them out of the region, then dividing it between British- and French-administered territories. But first, the British had to conquer Gaza, an Ottoman stronghold, from where, like so many foreign belligerents before them, the Turks dominated the ancient Mediterranean coastal route from Syria to Egypt.

For the Egyptian Expeditionary Force (or EEF – though it was under British military command), the 1917 battles for Gaza were, in the words of one young British soldier, 'a nightmare of interminable marching, thirst and tiredness'. Gaza and the surrounding area were ideal defensive territory for the Turks. The Mediterranean Sea, sandy hills, and the rise of the city surrounded by hollows of orchards with impenetrable thickets of prickly pears, were formidable natural barriers. The Ottomans had also built trenches. During the first battle for Gaza, on 26 March, the EEF suffered 4,000 casualties, compared to the Ottomans' 2,500. A Turkish aircraft apparently dropped a message bragging: 'You beat us at communiqués, but we beat you at Gaza!'

The second battle, three weeks later, was also a bloody disaster for the young, pale-skinned British soldiers, who were exhausted by the heat, crying out for water and fighting on sand. The Turks enjoyed the advantage of holding fertile northern Gaza, while the Allies occupied the eastern edge of the Sinai. As they advanced north towards Gaza, the EEF were also laying down railway tracks to transport military goods, and vital water supplies.

On 1 November, during the third battle for Gaza, the EEF under General Edmund Allenby pounded the Strip from air, land and sea. The Ottoman forces were finally overwhelmed and beaten into retreat. The EEF encountered scant resistance around Gaza City and when they entered, found it empty and smashed: 'Here and there a dark face peeped stealthily from a doorway, but apart from the troops hurrying through, [Gaza] was a place of desolation.'[55]

Some 13,000 EEF soldiers were killed in the three battles for Gaza, most of them young men, far from the reach of their families, whose descendants cannot tend to their graves and leave flowers or sweet-smelling herbs, or even just sit here quietly in the Gaza spring sunshine. The cemetery seems completely deserted, the silence is serene.

I wander slowly up one line of graves, and down another, stooping to examine the engravings and names of a few of the men buried here:

Lieutenant S.J. Rowland, of the Royal Welsh Fusiliers, died on 2 November 1917

Private H. McLean, of the King's Own Scottish Borderers, killed on 20 April 1917, age 27

Private R. Cochrane, of the Royal Welsh Fusiliers, killed on 16 July, age 19

Lance Corporal A. Love, of the Highland Light Infantry, killed on 8 August

'A. Love' – what a name! I stoop in front of Love's grave, where small bright flowers are growing. What was he like, this young Scottish man? I wonder whether he had just left home, wherever his home was. I wonder too, how old he was, and whether he had ever drunk whisky, smoked a cigarette or made love before he died here in the pounding midsummer heat of Gaza. I wonder what his Christian name was and whether he really understood what he was doing here, the true scale of this war. What was it like for him, arriving here in the Middle East, the fierce Gaza sun on his pale Scottish skin, the sea breeze ruffling his hair and maybe the shadow of a moustache brushing across his upper lip? Was he excited to be on the Eastern Front, amid the dark-skinned Arabs? Did he miss a girlfriend or his mum? Maybe he was terrified and didn't want to be here at all.

The carnage of the First World War, as Jawdat al-Khoudari pointed out to me, dwarfed all subsequent battles in Gaza's recent history. But this cemetery doesn't feel morbid, just a reflective space where I could happily linger all day, thinking about all kinds of beginnings and endings. I sit down on the grass; it feels soft and almost warm. In a strange way it is the perfect place to be, before I say goodbye.

After a while, I gather myself together, consciously pushing my thoughts into the present as I meander back across the springy grass towards the waiting taxi. Then I notice someone – a man dressed like a gardener and carrying a hoe – walking towards me.

'*Marhaba*,' he says.

Muhammad Awaja is the keeper of this cemetery in Zuweida. He has wind-roughened skin and a sense of quiet about him, like a man who spends most of his time working outside, with his hands in the earth.

'Would you like to drink coffee?' he asks.

'Yes, please.'

Muhammad leads me to one side of the cemetery and offers me a stool beneath the shade of an olive tree, one of the old kind, its broad trunk supporting a brim of branches. His small house is just nearby, nestled beside a corner of the cemetery. As we are talking his wife brings us coffee, then sits down with us too. Her name is Widad.

'There are 734 men buried here,' says Muhammad. 'I know every one of them. Five hundred and ninety-three are British, many from Scotlanda. There are also Indians, Algerians, British Jews and seven Unknowns.'[56]

He has worked and lived here since 1983. The Commonwealth War Graves Commission pays his salary and Muhammad says that he and his family have no desire to leave. Neither do I. But the taxi driver is waiting, so when I've finished my coffee, I reluctantly stand to go.

'Can you sign the visitors book?' he asks.

I say it would be a pleasure and he goes to fetch it.

It is a large hardback book with a satisfying weight. When I open it, I see there have been just fifteen entries since November 1999, when an Israeli from Tel Aviv with an illegible name wrote in English: 'Very nicely kept. Very impressive.' I add my name to the meagre list, thanking Muhammad for the work he does here.

'Why have you stayed here for so long?' I ask.

I know the house and salary must both be incentives but even so he's clearly devoted to this place.

Muhammad thinks about that for a long, sunny moment. Then says simply: '*Ihtiram*'. Respect.

❦

I left Gaza at the beginning of April 2009. The Israeli immigration police officer who had told me to leave the Strip within a month was waiting for me at Erez. He detained me for hours, repeated that he would not allow me back inside Gaza, then permitted me to enter Israel just in time to catch my plane to London at Ben Gurion airport. He gave me a one-day Israeli visa, to make sure I got on the plane. But he neither frightened nor intimidated me; I had already won my own battle.

At the airport, I was thoroughly searched, as I expected to be. The officer conducting the search asked me why I had been in Gaza.

'Weren't you frightened of being inside that place?' she asked.

'Only when your military were bombing Gaza.'

'But *they* want to kill us.'

'That's what people in Gaza say about *you*.'

'We don't want to kill them – but sometimes we have to,' she said.

I flew to London, spent a few weeks back in Scotland and then moved to southern Spain for the summer, where I walked in the mountains, thought about Gaza a lot and began to write this book.

At the end of the summer I returned to Edinburgh, and rented a small flat beside the sea at Portobello. By this time Niveen was also living in the UK, with her daughter, and hoping her son could join them. She was happy to be in Britain, but in spite of everything, she missed Gaza. She told me the Smoothie had made it to Sweden – of course – and was doing very well for himself.

Another year passed, as it does, and then out of the blue I received a call from Shadi – to say that he had finally managed to cross into Egypt and would be spending a few weeks in Ireland as the guest of an Irish human rights group. I met up with him in a crowded downtown Dublin bar a week later. Shadi was shining. We drank a lot of beer, stood out on the street and smoked masses of cigarettes, and listened to raucous live music. By the time the bars closed, I was coming back to Gaza, this time via Egypt.

PART FIVE

Here on the slopes of hills, facing the dusk and the
     cannon of time
Close to the gardens of broken shadows,
We do what prisoners do,
And what the jobless do:
We cultivate hope. [...]

From 'Under Siege' by Mahmoud Darwish

the same but now different

September 2010

The bus from Cairo to al-Arish, near the southern Gaza border, is full. Pilgrims are returning from Mecca. The man in the ticket office says that I have to take a different bus, to a city called Ismailiya – some 125 miles from my intended destination – and change there instead. At Ismailiya bus station two young students, both called Muhammad, befriend me and we share a rattling public taxi to al-Arish. The Muhammads get out first, refuse to let me pay my share and tell the taxi driver to look after me. At al-Arish bus station, it takes less than five minutes to find a taxi driver who agrees to take me to the Rafah border crossing – and completely rips me off. I don't really care. After eighteen months away, I am almost back inside Gaza.

'Why you going to Gaza?' asks Amer, the taxi driver, as he takes one hand off the steering wheel to light the cigarette clamped between his dry lips. We're bombing along the highway towards Rafah, surrounded by bleached desert. Amer has strung trinkets from his driving mirror and they swing wildly as my seat smacks the suspension.

'I used to live in Gaza, I'm just going back to see my old friends.'

He nods but makes no comment. The fifth or sixth makeshift checkpoint looms into view. Another posse of bored Egyptian officers who want to gather round and inspect my passport. After a

couple of minutes they wave us on. As Amer pulls away, the bald
tires skid, immersing us in a cloud of gritty dust.

'Is it busy at the Rafah crossing?' I ask him.

He offers me a grin through broken, stained teeth.

'Not really. Not like a real border – it's ... you know, half-open.'

I have no idea what to expect. But when we pull up outside the
Rafah crossing, it all looks very quiet. A few Bedouin taxi drivers
are loitering near the entrance, touting for trade. About a dozen
people have sought the only available shade, a small tatty café with
an overhanging tarp. Their bags and suitcases lie strewn around a
tree stump. They must be Gazans: no one else would be here.

Amer hoicks my suitcase out of the boot and dumps it on the
ground. He's in a hurry now. I pay him, then stand for a moment
next to the imprint of his taxi tyres, weary, thirsty, dazed. I arrived in
Cairo at midnight last night. Now it is almost midday and the sun is
pulsing dry white heat. I need water and shade. I hand my passport
to an Egyptian officer at the entrance gate to the Rafah crossing, ex-
pecting to wait at least a few hours. But my name is called even before I've made my way to the café. The officer makes one swift phone
call and waves me through into the main terminal building.

The Rafah crossing departure hall is huge and almost empty. Just a
handful of people are perched on rows of nailed-down plastic seats,
the kind you find in fast-food restaurants. A uniformed Egyptian
behind a glass screen beckons me forward, takes my passport and
politely asks me to wait. I sit down and start rolling a cigarette. The
first drag makes me feel quite light-headed. As I smoke, I watch the
Egyptian behind the screen frowning as he picks up passports and
puts them down again until they are spread around him like spilt
blue ink. Gazans walk up to the screen to speak to him. I hear them
asking: *Ya Allah* – when will they finally be allowed to cross?

A woman plonks herself down beside me with a heavy sigh.

'Five hours, I've been here,' she says. 'They are so rude, these Egyptians; all they say is wait, wait ... and I've got my kids with me.'

She points at her three kids, skidding across the floor, which is strewn with sweet wrappers, empty plastic cups and mushy cigarette dog-ends.

'Where do you live?' I ask her.

'The UAE. This is the first time I have visited my family in six years, you know – I just want to spend one month with them.' She shakes her head, heaves herself back out of the plastic chair and goes in pursuit of her kids.

After an hour, I walk up to the screen. The same man is there, still picking up passports. He looks up.

'I am sorry – five minutes, please.'

After another hour, I go up to him again.

'Please: another five minutes,' he says.

In these two and half hours, a mere handful of people have been processed. Half a dozen uniformed officers have appeared behind the same screen, but have completely ignored us all. Most of the Gazans are now slumped in their seats. I'd forgotten how much of their lives is spent waiting.

Eventually, my name is called. The same officer, his frown now a crevasse between overgrown grey eyebrows, hands me my stamped passport.

'Very sorry for delay.'

The woman with her three kids has just crossed. I follow them down a dim corridor, towards Gaza. Half-way down the corridor is another Egyptian passport control that seems to serve no purpose whatsoever. The officer flicks through my passport without looking, because he's too busy staring at my breasts. Silently, I hold out my hand for my passport. He licks his lips.

'You fuck,' I hiss under my breath.

At the end of the corridor, I peer through tinted glass on my left. In a hall on the other side of the crossing, hundreds of people are surging towards a glass screen, waving their documents like a flutter of small flags. These must be Gazans who are trying to leave.

Outside the departure hall, a bus is waiting to escort us to the Gazan side of the crossing operated by Hamas. We pay to board it. As he wrestles a bulging suitcase towards the bus, an elderly Gazan tells me that he and his wife have been waiting here since dawn. They are as round-shouldered as each other.

'We were detained at Cairo airport, herded onto a bus and driven straight down to this crossing, just like animals,' he says. 'Then we sit here waiting more than six hours. Do we not deserve more dignity than this, entering our own country?'

Gazans have their own special detention cell at Cairo airport. They are usually 'deported' from the airport by being bundled onto a bus and driven straight to the Rafah Gate. This is the price extracted from them for the privilege of being allowed outside the Strip.

The bus trundles over the border into Gaza, past a posse of Egyptian soldiers lounging on top of a battered tank slouched beneath the shade of a tree. At the Gaza terminal, there are more bum-numbing moulded plastic chairs. But the Hamas officers are far more efficient: most of the Gazans clear passport control within moments. I cannot see any other foreigners here, so I'm not surprised to be the last one sitting. A small man in plain clothes walks over and sits beside me. He says he needs to ask me some questions. He asks why I'm here. I used to live here, I tell him, and have returned to write some freelance articles for a Scottish newspaper.

'Where are you staying?' he asks.

'With friends.'

'But where?'

'In the city centre.'

I am renting an apartment from my old landlord Abu Ali again, but don't want to mention his name in case Hamas spooks appear at his gate.

This tactic always worked with Israeli officers. But the Hamas officer waves over another man, a bulky specimen with a spiky moustache and a bovine stare. Bulky says to the small guy: 'We need information from her.' Then he stands over me to make sure I realise he means business.

Another Hamas officer searches my bags and ignores my two bottles of whisky. More officers with thick beards and hard eyes join in, arguing among themselves about what to do with me. Nervous and claustrophobic, I start raising my voice. 'Why can't you just let me into Gaza?' They stare me down – and it dawns on me that they can send me straight back to Egypt. I don't like these men, but the information they want is basic. I am just making things hard for myself. Now I want to back down. But there is no point negotiating with Bulky. I look towards the small man who first questioned me.

'Please, can we find a way to resolve this?' I ask him quietly.

He confers with his colleagues. Two Hamas security officers will drive me to my apartment and speak to my landlord. For my own security.

It's late afternoon when we finally leave the Rafah crossing compound, accelerating north towards Gaza City. Gaza looks the same. The same pitted roads, battered cars, flat green fields and rows of palm trees. The same raw grey concrete houses, the knackered knock-kneed donkeys ... the same, but different. I can feel it already.

As I speed towards Gaza City with my two minders, I feel disembodied, as though I'm not really here myself, but watching footage of somebody else arriving. When the Hamas jeep pulls up outside Abu Ali's building, a plain-clothes Hamas officer is already waiting for me at the gate. He repeats the security mantra and I acknowledge his words with a small nod, without asking how he got here before me. Abu Ali opens the gate, looks from me to the officer standing beside me – and his expression instantly rearranges itself into a compliant smile. I stand back as he and the officer confer, and then shake hands, without breaking their smiles. A few minutes later, as the Hamas officer and the minders are leaving, Abu Ali looks at me, one eyebrow raised in question.

'I am so sorry,' I say, mortified at the trouble I've brought to his gate.

'Don't worry, this is Gaza. Welcome back!'

The first person I call is Saida. '*Habibti!*' Her voice sings down the phone. She demands that I come straight over to her house.

'Leave everything. Just get a taxi here, so that we can see you.'

'Just give me half an hour, *habibti,*' I say.

I slump on the couch, smoke one cigarette, then another. These last few months, I have been near-obsessed with getting back inside Gaza. Now that I am actually here, I'm tired and unsteady, unsure of how I feel. The first time I came to Gaza, almost three years ago, I remember standing on the al-Deira Hotel terrace, smelling the petrol-blue Mediterranean and wrapped in the same un-feelings. I go to the bathroom to wash my face – the tap water is still tepid, salty – then call a Lebanon Taxi. I'm in that exhausted but restless state of jet lag, my nerves jangling.

When the driver arrives, I don't recognise him. He heads east across the city, towards al-Tuffah where Saida lives, as I stare out of the streaked windows. The traffic is heavy with shiny four-wheel drives and dozens of dinky little tuk-tuks, roaring up and down the streets and farting blue fumes. I wonder whether they come from the tunnels, or Israel, or both. The taxi driver has a tired, sullen look about him and ignores me when I tell him I used to live here. I ask how things are now. His shrug is a tired, sullen gesture.

'Nothing changes. Too many taxis ... nowhere to go.'

When I open the gate into the courtyard in front of Saida's house, the old potter is still squatting in his workshop, glazing vases and bowls. He looks up and casts me a smile.

'*Marhaba*, we haven't seen you for a long time.'

The familiarity is welcoming; but the green Hamas flags hanging from the gate are not. Saida's family are not Hamas.

I clamber back up the familiar raw concrete steps, appreciating the breeze from the window frames that still have no glass. Saida must have heard me – she is standing at the top of the stairs.

'You came back, *habibti*! Really, I did not think you would.'

Her arms are already around me.

'I told you I was coming back!'

'Yes – but I didn't think they would let you in!'

We embrace, laughing, and when she lets me go, Saida keeps smiling. But she looks thinner and tired.

'My work is too demanding,' she complains, almost cheerfully. 'But what else do we have here? You know Gaza ...'

Her sister, Maha, is in the living room, hunched over a desk, studying. She kisses me and pinches my arse. She turned 18 while I was away, has ripened into a real beauty and is going to study engineering at university in Gaza. I pinch her arse back and she squeals. As the three of us are bantering, I hear their mother, Hind, hollering for me from her bedroom. I find her sprawled on her double bed and give her a full body hug.

'*Ahlan wa sahlan!*' she exclaims. 'I cooked dinner for you, Leeza!'

When we emerge from the bedroom, her husband, Nadim, stands poised in the kitchen doorway with his son, Muhammad. Nadim acknowledges me with a nod and a twinkling smile; I can tell he's glad to see me. But Muhammad looks a bit cowed, as though he has shrunk inside himself. I ask Nadim if he is still playing football.

'Every weekend,' he says, 'thanks to God.'

Compared to the rest of the family, he looks fit and fresh. He excuses himself to go and pray.

Hind pushes me into the kitchen, where we crowd around the table for supper. As she stuffs herself, she laments the fact that she's still fat. Saida rolls her eyes. It almost feels like I have never been away.

Hind wants to know if I have seen her daughter, Alla'. I explain that I haven't been back to the West Bank since I left Gaza eighteen months ago – and because I've just come through the Rafah crossing, there is no way I can now travel to the West Bank via Israel. As I entered Gaza via the Rafah crossing, I would have to exit via Rafah too: I cannot enter or leave Israel via the Erez crossing in northern Gaza. Hind tells me that Alla' has applied for a permit to come back to Gaza for a few days with her two children.

'Maybe they will be allowed to come soon – while you are here, Leeza. I have not seen them for seven years now.'

Tears are shining in her eyes.

Later that evening, inside Saida's bedroom, as we are drinking coffee and eating soft dates, Saida says to me, '*Ummi* thinks that my sister, Alla', will be coming to visit us very soon. *Ummi*, she doesn't really understand about the permits – but if my sister and her kids cannot come, she will be so upset.'

'Do you think the Israelis will give her a permit?' I hear the doubt in my own voice.

Saida throws her shoulders up slowly, then lets them drop – ah, the Gaza shrug!

I remember Hind weeping after telephone calls to her children and grandchildren over in the West Bank; I remember Saida and Maha singing Arabic songs to their brother in Chicago on Skype – all of them determined to stay in touch, despite not knowing if they will ever sit in the same room together again. Even now that Rafah is 'open', many Gazans in diaspora won't risk coming back for fear of being imprisoned here once again.

'And what about you – how are things?' I ask Saida.

She presses her lips together for a moment, then says, 'I tell you the truth, things are harder, you know. Because nothing ever changes, not in a good way. I work hard at my job at the human rights centre – to have some purpose here – and so I guess in some ways I *am* lucky; but the problem is that we don't have much fun now. You know, when Hamas stopped us women from smoking shisha, then my friends decided to stay at home, so they can relax in peace.'

Hamas recently announced that women are prohibited from smoking water pipes in public, on the pretext of the risk to their health. Unmarried couples are now forbidden from sitting together in some cafés and restaurants, and mixed couples walking on the street are being stopped by the police on suspicion of being unmarried.

'So what do you do in the evenings now?'

'Stay at home!' she laughs, rather sadly. 'Go to work and come home, visit my relatives, speak with my parents. I keep myself busy, but there's nothing new, *habibti* ...'

Her voice is the same: calm and contained. Stoic. But she doesn't look happy. She wants a good man by her side, but says she despairs of finding him here.

We talk for a long time, about love and life and our families and our dreams. Saida asks how long I will stay this time. About six weeks, I say. Then I have work back in Scotland. Later, recalling the green Hamas flags outside, I ask her who put them up.

'You remember my cousin Muhammad, the one who lost both his legs in the war? After a long time he managed to get out of Gaza: he went to a hospital in Malaysia and got new legs there. When he came back from Malaysia with his new legs, we had a big party for him. Many of his *shabab* friends came and they put up the flags – because they are all Hamas now.'

Saida asks me to stay the night. But though I'm more than tired, I want to go back to my own silent apartment, and my unpacked luggage, and sleep. I call a taxi.

'It's good to see you, *habibti*,' she says, squeezing my hand.

I love her, and this family. I know I can always retreat here if being back in Gaza feels difficult, and that's all I need right now.

It's been a hell of a day – and somehow it is still only 9.30 in the evening. I ask the taxi driver to drop me half-way down Umar al-Mukhtar Street, in the city centre. The shops will be open, I can walk the ten minutes back to my apartment and get a breath of cool evening air before I collapse into bed.

The street is quieter than I expected. I'm used to the city centre buzzing at night. The street lamps are dead, but the shops lit up, casting light onto the uneven pavement. I buy coffee and milk from a small store. When I leave the store and wander down the street, some people give me stares that make me feel vaguely uneasy because they are not friendly at all. Am I not supposed to be here alone on the street, at this time of night? There are a few other women around, walking in couples, all of them wearing *hijabs* and *jilbabs*. I've never had this sense of almost hostile disapproval here in Gaza before – people meeting my eyes with a frown or a scowl, a few aggressive sneers.

I reach the turn-off for my street. Two Hamas police officers are sitting on chairs pushed against a wall.

'Is she a foreigner?' I hear one say to the other.

'Must be. No *hijab*.'

I'm really not in the mood to talk to them, or anyone. But as I walk past, one of them calls out, 'Hey – are you a foreigner?'

'Yes.' I wonder what's coming next.

'Where you from?'

'Scotland.'

'Where?'

'Scotland. You know: north of London.'

'Scota-Land ...' The officer who called to me shakes his head. His mate giggles and nudges him to carry on.

'I went to Saudi once,' he says.

I walk a few steps towards them, to see them more clearly. They are both young and bearded.

'How was Saudi?' I say.

'Wonderful – so beautiful! What do you think about Gaza?'

'I like Gaza a lot. I used to live here.'

'You don't live here now?'

'No. I live in Scotland – I am just visiting for a few weeks.'

'Ah ... what about the Jews? What you think about them?'

'I think the Israeli occupation is destroying Gaza. What do you think?'

'The Jews want to kill us all! They attack us every day, people are always frightened. In the war, my house was destroyed. You've seen the helicopters and the F-16s – you never know when they're going to come back again. So we have to protect our people ...' He goes on about how 'the Jews are going to come back and finish off Gaza – God alone knows when. But they will.'

I am shattered and just want my bed now – but can't resist asking if he thinks Hamas can still protect people in Gaza.

'Look – you see these streets,' he says. 'We make new laws and now there is security on these streets – no *fawdah* [chaos] like before. But we are trapped. The Jews are strangling us. They have the power. I just want to get out of here. Where do I want to go? Anywhere – just out of this prison.'

the cage

I sleep late. After eventually dragging myself out of bed, I take a tepid shower and wander outside. I need to buy provisions. My first stop is the Metro Supermarket at the bottom of my street. When I step inside the supermarket, my eyes bulge at the sight of the shelves stuffed with brand-name goods, everything from nappies to Coca-Cola, bars of European chocolate to plastic bottles of ketchup – genuine Heinz – in a dozen varieties.

'What's going on here?' I say to the man behind the till.

'*Marhaba* – where have you been? It's very different here now, eh?'

'Where does all this stuff come from – the tunnels or from Israel?'

'Israel. They are letting many things in, the situation is better now. Gaza like New York!' he says in triumphant English.

I buy a week's worth of provisions and the prices are like New York too.

I thought only a handful of people knew I was back. But my phone keeps ringing and I keep bumping into old friends on the street. Laden with provisions, I eventually head back to the apartment to eat and rest, and to call Shadi. But before I have a chance, he calls me.

'Six thousand, six hundred and sixty-six welcomes back to Gaza!'

'Where are you?'

'Outside your door!' he cackles.

Cigarette between his stained fingers, he greets me with his lopsided grin. I'm utterly delighted to see him. I have a present for him, of course – a bottle of his favourite – and a carton of red Gauloises.

'Come on, we are going out,' he says.

We head off in the-best-in-the-West.

'I cannot believe this wreck is still on the road,' I exclaim.

'Even the best-in-the-West has been missing you!'

He takes me to a new place, an open-air café with terraces of tables and chairs set in the garden on a fresh green lawn. It's called the Galleria.

'You know, my friend owns this café, but I am like the boss here,' he brags as we sit down. 'I come here every night; this is where all the artists meet, the activists and the internationalists too.'

We spend the evening drinking lemon and mint juice, smoking and catching up. The last time I saw Shadi was in a rowdy downtown Dublin bar. In this radical change of scene he's still the same Shadi, still restless as the sea. His *jawaal* never stops ringing. I tease him about his grey hair, which is now longer and tangled, and looks quite wild. He is smiling, but looks unhealthy, and for the first time he talks about leaving Gaza.

'You know my brother lives in Norway and now there are many Gazans over there. Maybe I will take the family to live there next year, if we have the chance.'

I cannot imagine Gaza without Shadi.

Other people come over to say hello and some of them join us. Many of the Gazans that I know are political animals; they tell me they feel their communities are lost, shattered into fragments by these years of siege, the internal political conflict between Hamas and Fatah and the Israeli occupation that has become the status quo.

'We need new civil society leaders to guide us,' says one man, who has been a human rights lawyer for many years. 'Our society, it's all broken. Our collective interests have been taken over by self-interest. We are – I am sorry to say it – broken and selfish, focused on personal power; each man out for himself. This political situation is destroying Gaza – all of Palestine. We have to find another way to move forward together.'

But Hamas has been closing local civil society organisations across the Strip, except for those it directly supports.

There is still a contingent of international activists living in Gaza, including the Free Gaza movement. Some are here tonight, including Vittorio, the swarthy, pipe-smoking Italian who roared at the Israeli navy when we went out to sea with the fishermen. Vittorio was arrested by the Israeli navy while out at sea with some local fishermen at the end of last year, and deported. But just a few months later, he was back inside the Strip. He joins us too, tapping his pipe on the table, and tells me, his voice growling from rough tobacco, that he's planning to leave Gaza soon for a break in Italy. But Vittorio never will leave Gaza: a few months from now, he will be kidnapped, taken to an empty Gaza City apartment – and strangled with a telephone cord by Gazan men who will demand the release of Salafists in Hamas jails, and who want to humiliate Hamas by showing them there is still *fawdah* on the streets. Many Gazans, including Shadi, will weep and grieve, shamed by his murder.

Another of the activists asks if I want to go and pick olives with them in Beit Hanoun as the harvest is just beginning. They are

leaving early tomorrow morning. I really don't feel like getting up
at the crack of dawn, but manage to heave myself out of bed and go
to meet them. They've hired a minibus and we trundle up to Beit
Hanoun, where Samir, who runs the local community initiative, is
waiting for us.

'Louisa, welcome back to Gaza!'

Samir looks the same, too – those intense burning eyes; that
serious smile. He has organised the olive picking, of course, and
arranged another entourage of local press.

A group of us walk out of Beit Hanoun, along a track leading
towards the Israeli border. I realise we are heading in the direction
of the row of white cottages where the Swailams used to live. As
the border looms, I can see the local landscape has changed: groves
of spindly orange and olive trees have been planted, their leaves
refract the light. There is a small nursery of saplings waiting to be
planted. This land is being refarmed, regenerated, regrown. The
last time I walked here, more than a year and a half ago, this whole
area seemed to have been stripped bare, but now it looks like the
farmers are slowly returning.

I wonder what the Swailam family are doing. All I know is that
old Abu Jamal died during the war, apparently of old age, and that
the rest of the Swailams are living in Beit Hanoun town and have
never returned to their land.

I see a man with a sun-weathered face sitting beneath the shade
of an awning at the side of his field; he looks at peace.

When we reach the trees where the olives are being harvested, a
small crowd of local farmers have gathered and spread black nets
around the base of their trees to catch the warm, dusty olives as
they fall.

'Things seem to be a bit better here,' I say to Samir.

'The situation is still difficult,' he says, 'but some of the farmers have come back, so we are here to support them.'

He never says that the situation is good, just varying shades of difficult.

'What about the Swailams – have you seen them?'

I can see the rubble of the Swailams' row of white cottages from this grove of trees. But there's no sign of life, or growth, on their land.

'Their houses, and their well, it was all destroyed during the war. They don't farm here any more,' he says.

The grove where we're working is near the edge of no-man's-land. I look over towards the Erez crossing: the tunnel with the torn tarp roof has been replaced by a cage that stretches across no-man's-land, connecting the two sides of the crossing.

We work for a while, then most of us slump under the shade of the trees to rest. Except for the farmers and their sons, who keep working away in the sun-pulsing heat. These are tenacious men who have returned to their destroyed fields to replant them, over and again. Theirs is such a quiet, powerful act; not like the Gazan fighters still sometimes flinging their impotent rockets towards Israel, then scuttling back home. Empires and occupiers may come and go, but ordinary people's love for, and connection to, their land has the deepest roots of all.

I have to leave the olive harvest around midday because I'm meeting a friend back in Gaza City. Wiping my sweaty, dirty hands on my trousers, I wave to Samir, the farmers and the activists and stroll back towards the road. As I pass the sun-weathered farmer still sitting at the side of his field, he hails me and asks if I would like a glass of water. I sit in the shade beside him and he hands me a cup filled from his well.

'We are trying to replant our garden,' he says. 'God willing, we will have orchards here again.'

He used to be a Fatah bigwig, he says, but these days he has retired from useless politics and prefers to tend his fields in peace.

'I stay away from Hamas and their spies; they don't come up here.'

Locals murmur that Hamas is recruiting local spies. Last night I heard people in the Galleria joking that there are two kinds of *zanana* inside Gaza these days: the unmanned aerial drones in the sky, and local Hamas informants with their ears to the ground.

I ask if the farmer knows anything about the Swailams. They have haunted me at times since I left Gaza and I can't imagine how they are surviving now. The old Fatah chief gives me the Gaza shrug.

'Only Jamal Swailam sometimes comes up here, I never see the rest of them.'

We sit and smoke a cigarette together and look out over the fields. I've always appreciated Gazan farmers' brevity of words. Just as I am thinking that it really is time to leave, a man cycles past slowly on a bicycle that looks much too small for him because he is overweight, almost bloated. But as the old chief raises his hand in greeting, I realise who this is.

'Jamal!'

I charge towards him. Jamal dismounts from his bicycle. We shake hands.

'How are you?' I demand.

He stands silently, shielding his eyes from the sun. Then says, 'We lost everything in the war ... Now we live in the town. There is no money, the Israelis destroyed our house, our land, our well. We have no water so we cannot grow anything now.'

I look at his bloated face and can't think of anything to say.

Jamal dips his hand into the basket on the front of his bicycle and pulls out a small, hard guava. He presses it into my hand.

After meeting Jamal, I call my old friend Tariq, who still works for the UN. I ask if he knows anyone who can help Jamal gain access to his land and maybe rebuild the well. I know the UN has assisted some of the neighbouring farmers. Tariq says he'll see what he can do. If the UN cannot help, then maybe, he says, the International Committee of the Red Cross (ICRC) can.

Two days later Tariq calls me back.

'*Habibti*, I'm sorry but the ICRC couldn't even go onto his land. It's too dangerous. He is too close to the border, they cannot help him.'

I remember the tired, defeated look in Jamal's eyes.

'Doesn't the UN here have a local job creation scheme?'

'Yes,' Tariq says with some uncertainty.

'Do you think they can find some paid work for him?'

'OK, look, I'll see what I can do,' he says.

He calls me back the next afternoon.

'*Habibti*, I asked about work for Jamal. That job-creation scheme: the only available work they have is as a road sweeper earning $8 a day.'

'Nothing else?'

'No, *habibti*, I'm sorry. There is still no other work.'

Abu Nidal goes first class to Cairo

It is good to be back inside Gaza, seeing my friends, and my colleagues from the Centre. But it is different this time in so many ways, especially the sad, flat atmosphere and the festering resentment against Hamas – who are still keeping tabs on me. Whenever I go up to Beit Hanoun or down to Rafah, my friends receive unwelcome phone calls from Hamas security, demanding to know who I've been visiting. (One afternoon I realise I'm being followed; but the plain-clothed spook behind me is such an obvious tail, I find it quite funny. Eventually bored with my meandering, he cuts across my path and asks a few inane questions about what I am doing in Gaza, etc. Then he scarpers.)

Hamas is tightening restrictions on women's lives, torturing political opponents, harassing youth workers, local human rights activists and independent journalists – anyone who does not obediently tow their political line – and morphing into the paranoid Islamic bully that most of the outside world always said it was. I barely hear anyone say a good word about them. People criticise them in hushed voices. 'Of course I like Hamas!' one of the al-Deira waiters tells me when I ask him how things are going. Then, dropping his voice, he mutters, at a volume only I can hear: 'Now we are frightened of them, you know.' Gaza, for me, has become a more sombre and resigned place. I miss the friendly *fawdah* that used to permeate these streets.

Amid the sadness washing around me, I'm also seeing Gaza

with new eyes, now that I know something of its history. I hone in on fragments and details that I was completely blind to when I first arrived here, almost three years ago. A small example: one morning I am in the old quarter of the city, just about to enter Souq al-Zawiya to buy fruit and veg (then over to neighbouring Souq al-Bastat, for a new stash of glittering, see-through lingerie). Waiting to cross the busy street into al-Zawiya, I glance up, admiring the buildings opposite – they are some of the oldest still standing in Gaza. The building directly across the street from me has 'The Municipality of Gaza' engraved in English, high across its façade. I've walked along this street so many times, but never even noticed these words before. I cross the street and stand gazing up at it. A Hamas policeman slouched on a chair at the entrance to the building is texting on his *jawaal*. And watching me ...

'It's in English,' I say to him, pointing upwards and stating the bleeding obvious.

'Yes – from when you British occupiers were here,' he retorts, going back to his text.

After buying my fruit and vegetables, and before browsing for lingerie, I go in search of another fragment of local history. There used to be a train station here in the old quarter, and someone has told me you can still see a few metres' remnants of the original track. I wander round and ask a few locals if they know where the old train track is. But no one seems to know. After an hour, I am parched with thirst but none the wiser.

The track remnant I'm looking for was part of a line laid by Egyptian and British forces in early 1917 to transport weapons, supplies and men between north-eastern Egypt and Gaza, bolstering their campaign against the Ottoman Turkish forces in Palestine. The Ottomans were holding the Palestinian border

against the British and Egyptians advancing north – and had
been relying on camel caravans to transport military supplies from
Constantinople. So Jamal Pasha, one of the three Young Turk
rulers of the Ottoman Empire (and known among local Arabs
as *al-Safah*, the Blood-Shedder), enlisted a German engineer to
construct a rail track linking the existing northern Jerusalem–
Jaffa railway – the first in Palestine – to the southern Negev
desert. Heinrich August Meissner obliged as the Germans and the
Ottoman Turks were allies. The new railway had two branch lines:
one reached Beersheba in the Negev, the other extended to Beit
Hanoun in northern Gaza.

British rule in Palestine started immediately after their victory in the third battle for Gaza. But the League of Nations did
not formally mandate the British to replace the Ottomans as the
'peacetime administrator of Gaza' until April 1920. By then, the
British had extended their railway line for deliveries of post-war
supplies into southern Palestine – accompanied by fresh water
piped all the way from the River Nile to Gaza. By the spring of
1920, Palestine Railways was offering passengers: 'Rapid and comfortable travelling facilities to all parts of Palestine [...] equipped
with modern Passenger Coaches, Sleeping and Dining Cars, Day
and Night Saloons, Luxurious Tourist Trains specially arranged.'
You could catch the train from Haifa in northern Palestine to El-
Qantara ('the Bridge') on the eastern bank of the Suez Canal, from
there take a ferry across the canal and hop aboard a train bound for
Cairo. By 1942, you could take the train from Cairo to Gaza, continue northwards to Haifa, then make your way via the city of Acre
to Beirut, then Aleppo in Syria, and on to the Baghdad Railway
that terminated at Basra.

This train journey between Gaza and Cairo intrigues me because it is unimaginable now – even though it used to be part of the local scenery. Trains are one of life's great pleasures; but this journey has been extinguished as Gaza slowly spins backwards in time. I want to meet somebody who caught the train from Gaza to Cairo, so I ask my friends if they know anyone who used to hop aboard.

Gaza is littered with stumbling blocks, but finding ordinary people with extraordinary stories is not one of them. Two days later, I am sitting in a pale drawing-room on the southern edge of Gaza City. The windows are open wide, the sea air cooling and freshening the room a little. I'm in the company of an elderly Bedouin, Sheikh Al-Whaidi. He sits upright in his armchair, his loose-skinned left hand resting on a smooth walking cane and his thin voice wavering slightly as he recalls the old days, when he used to catch the train to Cairo every month.

Imagine that it is early springtime in 1963. Sheikh Al-Whaidi (almost fifty years younger and known then as Abu Nidal) is the financial director of the *Palestine News*. He lives in Gaza City with his family, but has regular business in Cairo. Abu Nidal always takes the train and always travels first class. A first-class ticket costs 3 Egyptian pounds and 60 piastres (then the equivalent of US$10) compared to just 1 Egyptian pound for a second-class ticket. But the first-class carriages are air-conditioned, with big black leather seats and smooth wood panelling. In second class you just get wooden seats, no air conditioning – and a face full of sand from the open windows.

There is one train a day from Gaza to Cairo, says Abu Nidal. It leaves at 6 AM from the station at al-Tuffah, on the eastern side of the city. This is the only station big enough for trains to turn around, so it has become the main Gaza rail hub, handling both freight and passenger trains. The other Gaza City station, at Shaja'iya, in the old quarter, the one that I was looking for, is just for passengers.

It is a long journey to Cairo, more than 340 miles, about twelve hours by train. It's much quicker by car, but this road is notorious for accidents as drivers pelt across the eastern Sinai. The train is slower but safer.

Abu Nidal arrives at al-Tuffah station early, buys his first-class ticket and puts his overnight bag on the top rack above his comfy leather seat. The train sets off just after six in the morning. The guards and staff are all Egyptian. They wear uniforms and peaked caps. There is a small canteen serving drinks and snacks on the train and plenty of passengers on board: businessmen like Abu Nidal in dark suits, Gazan families visiting friends or relatives in Egypt, or just taking a day trip. Gazan students, too, on their way back to Alexandria University – the young men in trousers and open-neck shirts, the women in blouses and loose trousers or knee-length skirts, their dark hair pinned up or flowing loose around their shoulders. Oh yes, women dress like this in Gaza in 1963. It is another of those precious times when everything feels possible.

The train trundles south, following the route of Salah al-Din Road, occasionally curving from one side of the road to the other. It stops to pick up passengers at Deir al-Balah in the middle area of Gaza, then in Khan Younis. All the way to Rafah, the track is lined with groves of orange and lemon trees and Abu Nidal enjoys the sight of ripening vines, too, like the *dunams* of rich, dark grape vines that grow behind his house in Al-Sheikh Ejleen, on the southern edge of Gaza City.

The train picks up passengers in Rafah, too. But the moment it crosses the border and leaves Gaza, the land is transformed into an arid desertscape of sand dunes, camels, black Bedouin tents and scrubby, buckled-by-the-wind trees with deep, thirsty roots.

Because it is 1963, and Egypt is still 'administering' Gaza (what a benign word for a military occupation!), there is no passport check until the train reaches El-Qantara. Gazans travel on Palestinian documents issued by the Egyptian government; a privilege from their serial invader. Now the track skirts a shallow desert lake known as 'al-Bedawiya' because so many Bedouin camp here between Gaza and al-Arish, with their scrawny goats and barefoot, tangle-haired children. Abu Nidal is from the al-Tarabin Bedouin tribe, but he is a wealthy, urban Bedouin and didn't grow up in the traditional woollen black Bedouin tent, or *beit shar*.

A few miles past the lake, Abu Nidal looks up from his newspaper. He can feel the train braking and knows that he will soon catch a glimpse of blue, bright as lapis lazuli, as the track dips towards the Mediterranean coastline at al-Arish. This local resort is popular with both Egyptians and Gazans because of its beautiful long sweep of beach, decked with seaside chalets and restaurants. After picking up passengers at al-Arish, the train curves inland again, then snakes southwards through the Sinai. Here, away from the sea, the land is dry and cruel and the people who live here are literally dirt poor. The Gazans pity them.

The city of El-Qantara sprawls across the east bank of the 164-kilometre-long Suez Canal, linking the Mediterranean and Red Seas (when the canal opened in 1869, there was no bridge). The train grinds to a halt at El-Qantara and Egyptian officials clamber aboard to check that the passengers' papers and travel documents are in order. But even for the Gazans, this is a mere formality. The passengers gather up their bags, and children, then disembark en masse, crowding onto a ferry that chugs them over the murky canal waters to the west bank. This is where the journey

often gets delayed, waiting for the ferry, or for the train that is supposed to meet the passengers on the west bank. But today Abu
Nidal and his fellow travellers are lucky. When the ferry docks,
their connecting train is waiting.

Once on board the second train, Abu Nidal stretches out in
his seat, newspaper crumpled in his lap, and dozes off to the steady
rhythm of the carriage.

It is another four or five hours before the train finally pulls into
Bab el-Hadid (Iron Gate) station in central Cairo. When they
arrive, dusk is descending but the early springtime air is still warm.
As Abu Nidal and the others clamber down onto the platform,
they are hit by the stench of body odour, hot food, rotting leftovers,
piss, rancid fumes and stale air.

Bab el-Hadid is a seething ant colony; there are passengers, guards,
deft pickpockets, touts, tourists, black Sudanese, some blotchy
white Europeans, even Russians (President Nasser is courting the
Soviets), Egyptian merchants, shouting pedlars, local prostitutes,
wily beggars, infested street children, Arab women adorned in gold,
bearded imams and Christian Copts. Abu Nidal threads his weary
way through this overwhelming crush. He has to be at the office
early tomorrow morning.

'Did you always enjoy the journey?' I ask.

'*Taba'n* (Absolutely)! You know, we always arrived with our
coats covered in dust and sand, even in first class! I enjoyed the
train, and Cairo too. But home is home. After a few days or a week,
I was always ready to come straight back to Gaza.'

I know what he means. Every morning now I feel the magnetic
pull north, towards the place I call home.

I've been sitting with Abu Nidal for a couple of hours now. Suddenly I need the bathroom. He points me in the general direction and I wander along the hallway, trying to find it. But this a big house with a lot of rooms. I come upon another, smaller, lounge, where a woman is lying on a couch, her eyes closed, breathing steadily. She must be Abu Nidal's wife. I turn to leave her in peace, but she senses my presence in the doorway, gives a little shudder and springs upright, her eyes startled open.

'I'm sorry, I didn't want to wake you – I'm just looking for the bathroom.'

'You are the writer who has come to talk with my husband?'

'Yes, he's been telling me about the train ...'

'Ahhhh, that train ... did he tell you that I took it too, a long time ago?'

'I thought maybe you had taken it together.'

'Oh no! I took the train to Cairo alone. In 1959.'

'Really? What were you doing in Egypt?'

'I was studying English at Alexandria University. Afterwards I completed my teacher training. At first I was an English teacher here in Gaza, then a headmistress for many years. But I'm afraid that, after all this time, I have forgotten my command of English somewhat.'

Her unhurried English is fluid and fluent. I haven't heard anyone say 'somewhat' for years. She pats the couch. I perch on the arm.

'What was it like, going to Cairo on the train?'

Her small dark eyes light up as though suddenly switched on full beam.

'It was really wonderful! In those days if you wanted, or indeed needed, to travel to Cairo, you just packed a small bag, walked to the station, bought your ticket and left. Even after my studies, when I was back home in Gaza, I would just say to my family, "let's go to Cairo tomorrow" ... and we could! Can you imagine?'

The Haifa–Cairo railway survived the 1967 Six-Day War between Israel and its Arab neighbours. Israel reoccupied Gaza and used the train line for almost another decade, to transport military goods and personnel to the Sinai, and Gazan labourers to work in Haifa and Tel Aviv. But the tracks suffered chronic neglect and were gradually abandoned. By the mid-1970s the railway line was a skeleton of its former self, a relic of another time, like Gaza itself these days. Who could have foreseen that eventually some of the wooden sleepers under the tracks would end up in Jawdat al-Khoudari's *mathaf*, or that only elderly people like Abu Nidal and his wife, Umm Nidal, would be able to tell the story of catching the train in Gaza? How do we ever know what's going to befall our country, our community or us?

Umm Nidal shows me the bathroom, then she comes to the drawing room with me afterwards. She and Abu Nidal have been married a very long time. Their children have grown up and left home, and they are enjoying their retirement as quietly as you can in Gaza. I sit listening to their memories of Gaza because it's a lovely way to spend a long, hot afternoon. None of us know that, in just a few weeks, Abu Nidal will die here quietly, at the grand age of 82. In my mind, he is still there, sitting upright, his left hand resting on his walking cane and his voice somewhat hoarse after all this talking, insisting that I come back on Saturday for a good Bedouin lunch.

chance of rain: zero per cent

I criss-cross Gaza, not by train, but by public taxi, spending hours gazing out of smeared car windows. I watch how the land and trees change across the Strip. In the far north, where the Swailams used to farm, the soil is rich and dense, and the fields lush and green. From the edge of Beit Hanoun until the beginning of Gaza City is mostly sprawling, ugly, concrete jungle, but threaded in between are the strawberry fields of Beit Lahiya, the ever-present glitter of the sea, and the quiet palm- and bougainvillea-lined streets of al-Rimal district where I am staying. South of Gaza City, the middle area of the Strip is also fertile, and wide avenues of palm trees – now laden with clumps of shining red *rutab* dates – lend an air of weathered calm to the towns of Nuseirat and Deir al-Balah.

There's also rich farmland in the area of Mawasi, which lies south of Nuseirat. Mawasi was one of the locations where Israeli settlers spent decades spawning vast greenhouses to grow fruit and salad vegetables before being dragged – in some cases, literally kicking and screaming – out of the Strip in August 2005, when the Israeli government finally withdrew its settlements from Gaza. Now that the settlers have gone, the Gazan farmers have resumed their harvests, selling guavas, figs and lemons in peace, though they still cannot export their produce because of the siege. The guava plantations are built on land that looks almost as rich, green and moist as Scotland. One afternoon, near Mawasi, I visit a new seaside hotel built from traditional bricks of baked mud. It has spacious, loft-style rooms, a garden decorated with voluptuous mud statues ... and a short tunnel leading from the hotel onto the beach: a wink to the local subterranean smugglers still working down at the border. It is a beautiful, audacious and optimistic set-up, though I'm the only customer. The Mawasi guava plantations lie inland.

But threaded in between them are tracts of empty coastline, with just a handful of lonely houses standing apart from each other as though they have no friends. Here at the beach front, the land is parched like sun-bleached bones, the soil crumbling into dust that sustains nothing. This is where Gaza kisses the Sinai desert.

The BBC weather forecast I read before leaving Scotland stated that the chance of rain in Gaza was 'zero per cent'. And there has been no rainfall since I came back. Everyone is complaining that the end-of-summer rains are overdue, the land is parched. I wonder whether the Sinai desert is stealthily encroaching north, like the foot soldiers of the British army before their battles for Gaza. If so, what will this do to the already dire quality of the water, which makes my guts ache and gives me the shits most mornings? Suddenly it feels important to know, so I arrange to meet Monther Shoblak.

Monther is director of the unimaginatively named Gaza Coastal Municipalities Water Utility, which has overall responsibility for water and sanitation services across the Strip.

'Welcome, my dear!' he croons as I enter his presidential-style office. He directs me to sit at the top of a gleaming conference table, set opposite his expensive-looking desk, where a hefty gold plaque is engraved with his name in Arabic and English. His shining black hair carefully swept back, Monther flashes me a rakish smile.

'Now, Louisa, what is it that I can tell you?'

'I want to know about the water situation in Gaza. The drinking water, that is.'

Monther leans slightly forward, his fingertips arched together, like a BBC correspondent.

'Here in Gaza, we are completely dependent on the coastal aquifer, which lies 40–150 metres underground. The aquifer has an annual recharge of about 80 million cubic metres. The problem is that in Gaza we're using 180 million cubic metres of fresh drinking water every year. And because there is no vacuum status in the aquifer, 95 per cent of our fresh water in the Gaza Strip has now been used up.'

He pauses to let this fact sink in.

'We also have serious problems with the water that is available, like problems with nitrate and chloride concentrations.'

He stands and crosses the room, to a set of framed wall maps.

'Look – the purple sections on this map, and the orange sections on this one – you see how they fit together? In areas of Gaza where you find a high concentration of nitrate, you also find low levels of chloride – and vice versa. High chloride levels can cause kidney problems – though these can also be due to the amount of salt in our diet. But nitrate absorbs oxygen and it can cause major health problems, including blue baby syndrome. Nitrate is a silent killer.'

Because of the chronic shortage of fresh drinking water in Gaza, he tells me, many locals buy drinking water from the myriad private companies who run dozens of small desalination operations and sell drinking water from trucks. They don't have the facilities to detect levels of nitrate, which has no odour, colour or taste. Some 80 per cent of private water sellers in Gaza are not licensed or regulated, so these companies are no solution to the drinking-water problem, he adds.

'Some of the water is also heavily contaminated with bacteria.

But we can resolve the nitrate problem if we can lay out a new sewage system for Gaza.'

The Gaza sewage system is, famously, a mess. There are just three sewage treatment plants in the entire Strip – each unable to cope with the volume of raw waste being pumped into it. Up in Beit Lahiya, the sewage treatment plant was originally built in a natural depression without a sea outlet. Consequently, untreated waste water flows directly from the plant into stinking cesspools built just above a local Bedouin village, Umm al-Nasser. On April Fool's Day 2007 one of the cesspools burst, creating a 2-metre-high wave that engulfed the village. Five local residents drowned in shit. It was the second sewage flood to hit Umm al-Nasser in eight months. A new waste water treatment plant is planned for northern Gaza, and when it is completed the cesspools can finally be sealed.

The Al-Sheikh Ejleen sewage plant, just south of Gaza City, lies close to Wadi Gaza, once an ancient settlement with clean water wells and a pristine natural wetland populated by migrating birds. Now it, too, is a series of stinking, foetid pools. The birds have fled and the sewage plant is spewing 20 million litres of raw and partially treated sewage straight into the Gaza Mediterranean every day, poisoning the coastline. But dozens of local fishermen still dock their boats on the beach opposite Wadi Gaza. Shoals of fish come to shore to gobble up the shit.

Monther acknowledges that there has been mismanagement of local sewage plants. But he reminds me that water treatment cycles are constantly being interrupted by Israel's continuing to restrict or deny essential operating materials and spare parts, and the frequent power cuts. Suddenly he seems a little deflated and we both fall silent. I remember the empty houses on tracts of wasteland in south-eastern Gaza, and the weather forecast predicting no rain.

'Is the rainfall decreasing here?' I ask him.

'Ten years ago we received up to 600 millimetres of rain per year in Gaza,' he says. 'But in 2007 the rainfall was around 400 millimetres, and for the last two years it has been just 250–300 millimetres.'

Most of the rain falls in northern Gaza, around Beit Lahiya and Beit Hanoun – one of the reasons that Beit Hanoun used to be the garden of Gaza. The south-east of the Strip, which is classified as semi-desert, receives the lowest rainfall, sometimes just 70 millimetres a year. In spite of the increasing drought, Gazans have not managed their water resources very well. Less than half the rainfall is harvested, yet harvesting rainwater is simple: it involves setting aside tracts of land, removing the top layers of mud and replacing them with sand, to create porous infiltration basins which help to recharge the depleted aquifer. In the past, this would have been useful. Now it's vital. But a lot more has been happening here.

'What we need is a strategic solution,' says Monther. 'And we don't have much time: by 2015 Gaza will be deprived of good-quality water.'

'You mean drinking water?'

'Yes, I do. In five years, the Gaza coastal aquifer will almost certainly be dry.'

'So what needs to happen now?'

'Either we have to build desalination plants or we will have to import our water.'

'Which do you think would be better?'

He tilts his head to one side and casts me a final smile, but it's not a happy one.

'Frankly, my dear, I really don't mind which. But we only have until 2015. That is our deadline.'

When I leave Monther's office, I go to meet Saida. When I see her, she beams and kisses me on both cheeks. We've arranged to have lunch at one of our old haunts, the Haifa Restaurant. I tell her about the meeting with Monther as we take a taxi from the city centre. She listens intently, as she always does. We ask the taxi driver to drop us off beside the beach just outside Gaza City. It's mid-afternoon, sunny and perfectly warm. We take our shoes off and stroll along the shore. We have plenty of time and a good lunch is waiting for us at the restaurant. We choose to forget about the water crisis and enjoy the moment.

Saida is in an unusual mood today; she gaily wedges her black heeled sandals into her bag and skips playfully along the beach. The tide is going out and she stops to draw on the wet sand with her fingers.

الحياة جميلة

Life is beautiful, she writes in a big, curling script. I've never seen her quite like this, apart from the evening we danced with her sister and her mother, more than two years ago. She looks almost radiant. In these last couple of weeks, something inside her has been released. We collect shells from the sand and shallows, exclaiming over their beauty, laughing at everything and nothing.

'You know, when we were little we used to tell the shells our secrets,' she says, running her finger along the whorl of a perfect white shell. '*Ummi* and my father would bring us to the beach, my brother Muhammad too, and we would pick up shells and take them home and whisper to them. And hide them to keep the secret safe.'

'Do you remember the secrets you told your shells?'

She laughs again, a lovely, uncontained laugh. But she does not tell me what they were. I know Saida very well by now: she's the kind of woman who tells her secrets to shells because they will never talk. But she *has* just told me why she's so light of heart. Three years after returning home to Gaza, Saida (whose name means Happy) thinks that maybe she *has* finally just found love.

We wander past rickety fishermen's huts, where they store their gear, and snooze in the shade. We watch young men with gleaming, salt-caked skin dunk themselves in the sea as they watch us too. A small fishing boat glides into shore, and as it lands the fisherman is joined by a man driving a donkey and cart along the beach. He hitches the boat to the cart, and the beast drags it along the sand towards one of the huts. Sunlight amuses itself on the waves. The soul-destroying situation inside Gaza grinds on, but this afternoon it seems that everything is bright. Including us.

'Will you come back here, *habibti*?' she asks me suddenly.

We are both standing barefoot in the shallows, the sun warming our faces.

'Back here to Gaza? Yes, of course I will.'

It has never occurred to me that I won't come back here; Gaza has seeped into me, like the sea.

'Come back soon,' says Saida. 'Meet me in Gaza. Because I cannot come to meet you.'

the Wadi of Pleasure

A few days before I leave Gaza once more, I take tea alone on the al-Deira terrace, then find myself slowly strolling towards the beach once more. I have an hour or so before I have to go and meet someone, and the beach is always a good place to dawdle. The fishermen are out at sea, children are swimming and two men are playing an energetic game of paddle in the shallows. I glance over without really looking at them, lost in my own thoughts.

'*Marhaba*, we thought you had left for good,' one of them says to me.

Startled out of my reverie, I glance up at him and only half-recognise his face. But when I look over at his partner, I am suddenly delighted because I never expected to see the bearded beach acrobat ever again. He's not wearing the stripey bathing costume I first saw him in, but modest shorts and a loose white T-shirt. He still has the thick grey beard though, and the look of vitality about him. The acrobat nods me a greeting, but does not say anything.

'How are you?' I ask, conscious that I'm grinning at him.

'I am fine – how are you?'

He is gazing at me from the side, without making direct eye contact, the way a cat sizes you up. I know this gaze: it means he is a pious man who doesn't look women outside his family in the eye, for fear of some impure thought entering his head.

'Are you still doing ...?' I stall because I don't know the word for 'acrobat' in Arabic.

'Acrobatics?' he says. 'Yes, sometimes I still do acrobatics.'

'Where did you learn?'

'On the beach.'

I can already feel our conversation coming to a close. I don't want to embarrass him. But there *is* one more thing that I want to know about him.

'Excuse me, but what's your job?'

'I am an accountant.'

A religious accountant from Gaza who performs acrobatics on the beach. You really couldn't make it up.

❦

This final story is not the last one that I heard in Gaza; it wasn't like that at all, of course. Whenever people told me their stories I wrote them down in my notebook, to be rearranged later in some kind of order. But this story belongs at the end. So for now let's assume that I heard it during my last couple of days in Gaza, as I was packing my bags and saying my goodbyes.

Abu Baha lives with his wife in a neat bungalow with a well-tended garden, just outside the centre of Gaza City. He is the uncle of one of my old colleagues from the Centre, and has agreed to tell me his story of fleeing from the Negev desert to Gaza in the summer of 1948, in the violent wake of the creation of the state of Israel.

When I arrive at his bungalow, I find a small elderly man, dressed in a well-cut beige safari suit. I greet him in Arabic and he replies in English as perfect as that of Umm Nidal.

'I was an English teacher for many years,' he says, by way of explanation, leading me into a lounge with low, soft-looking armchairs. We settle down. Abu Baha clears his throat and begins to speak.

'I am a Bedouin, my family is from the al-Tarabin tribe in the southern Negev. I was born in 1939, in a *beit shar,* a wool house: it's our traditional black Bedouin tent, always made of black wool because the sun is so strong it will spoil and fade any other colours. My birthplace, Wadi al-Baha, means 'the Wadi of Pleasure' because of the small yellow *baha* flowers that covered it in the springtime. Wadi al-Baha was 13 kilometres [8 miles] north of Gaza. I took my first steps there, just outside our *beit shar.* My father was Sheikh Hassan Jouma al-Farangi. He was a farmer, and my family grew wheat and barley and maize. We had a camp with two other Bedouin families and my father looked after all of us because he was the sheikh. Our tents faced east towards the sunrise; they were divided into a section for the men, and the women's section next to the kitchen.'

Abu Baha is smiling, relishing his own story. I'm smiling too. I feel like I have waited a long time to hear this story, and want to savour every detail.

'My mother was called Basma,' he continues. 'Her name means "Smile". At home we saw her smiling face, of course; but whenever she went outside my mother covered her face with a mask of gold, and she wore silver beads on her headscarf and down the front of her black dress. When I was very young we had blacks working with us, you know – men who had travelled with my father from the north of Africa. They lived with us as shepherds.'

The stories that I've heard about Gaza's Bedouin are knitting together, becoming clearer and closer. I sit back against the cushions, eyes wide open, and really listen.

'When I was 5 years old, I went to the local school. There were fifteen of us in one classroom, all of us boys. My father wanted me to go to school because the only thing that he read was the Holy Qur'an. Three years afterwards, I moved to the big school in Beersheba, 35 kilometres [22 miles] away. It was 1947. Our teachers at the school were Palestinians and we Bedouin boys boarded at the school. We learned all the subjects, and at night we dreamed of being genius enough to go and study in Jerusalem!

'My first year at Beersheba was when the troubles started between us [Palestinians] and the Jews. I remember that when we finished school for the summer [in June 1948], we didn't know how to get home safely. In the end, a local Palestinian official arranged for us to travel home under a British guard. We reached home safely under the guard, but that summer there were more problems between us and the Jews. My father brought weapons for our camp to defend ourselves against them. But their weapons were better than ours.'

The Zionists began to expel Palestinians from their homes even before the end of the British Mandate. At dawn on 9 April 1948, members of the Irgun and the Stern Gang (Jewish militias) entered the village of Deir Yassin. The Jewish mob flung hand grenades into the villagers' homes and shot indiscriminately, killing between 100 and 240 Palestinians, including entire families. A number of the village women were raped, then murdered, by them.

Just over a month later, on 15 May, the British Mandate ended and the state of Israel was born. The Jewish community erupted into celebrations; hundreds of thousands danced, cheered and kissed each other in the streets. By now, almost a quarter of a million Palestinians had been driven from their homes. After the end of the British Mandate, the Zionist campaign intensified; more Palestinian villages were attacked, occupied and destroyed, their inhabitants massacred. The Zionists swept across northern Palestine. Then, bolstered by their successes, they began to move south towards the Negev desert, where the Bedouin lived and herded their animals.

One afternoon in September 1948, the Bedouin of Wadi al-Baha had just finished cutting the wheat and barley and were harvesting their maize when they saw tanks approaching from the north-west. They were Israeli tanks. The Bedouin had already built a defensive trench around their camp and also around the stone house that Abu Baha's father had built for his family the year before and that they called the Villa.

'My father was not in the camp that day, he was away working.' Abu Baha is still smiling, but the tone of his voice has just changed, as though he's mentally sifting through something painful. 'The Israelis lined up all the men from our *ashira* against the wall of the Villa. "We will come back here tomorrow and if any of you are still here we will kill you all," they said. And I saw them kill a man that day: Sheikh Abdullah was just an old blind man riding past on his donkey and they shot and killed him. We saw them do it, and we had heard about the massacre at Deir Yassin, so we were all very frightened.

'When my father finally returned home, it was dusk. He sat down with the other men and they began to discuss where we should escape to, because we had to leave that very night. Some of the men said they were taking their families to Beersheba and others said that they were going to Gaza. My father decided that we would go to Gaza as well. So we packed up everything onto our camels, including my 10-day-old baby brother. We rode to Gaza that night and I always remember that it was a full moon.'

Abu Baha recalls the moonlit journey to Gaza by camel. 'We ate *sabar* (prickly pears) to sustain us and I remember that, on the way, we heard Palestinians calling out that Jews were waiting to ambush us in the next valley. So we took another road and we entered Gaza east of al-Bureij camp. Most of the Palestinians arrived in northern Gaza, but we entered from the east and we set up our tents there.'

In 1947 the District of Gaza, as it was then known, had between 60,000 and 80,000 inhabitants. By December 1948, the population had swelled by 200,000. Gaza was filled with camps of white refugee tents. Altogether, more than 750,000 Palestinians were expelled from their homes during the *Nakba*, or 'Catastrophe,' many still clutching the keys to their homes. At least 530 Palestinian villages had been destroyed.

When Israel and Egypt agreed a ceasefire in January 1949, they drew up the Armistice Line designating the new borders between Palestine, Egypt and Israel. Gaza changed shape, both demographically and physically. Its population had almost trebled, yet its land mass had shrunk by a third. It became a Strip.

A woman enters the lounge, carrying a tray of glasses. Abu Baha introduces her as his wife, Firyal. She sits beside him, her hands neatly folded in her lap. Meantime he is still in full flow.

'When we arrived in Gaza, we lived in our tent for a few months. But my father was bringing weapons to the Palestinian fighters and there was some trouble. We had to leave Gaza. We moved to the Sinai and for the next few years we lived in different Bedouin settlements. But there was also trouble between the Israelis and the Egyptians. Finally, in 1952, my father said, "*Khalas*, we are going back to Gaza."'

Abu Baha was 13 years old when his family returned to Gaza. I ask him what Gaza City looked like in 1952.

'Ah, *so* different! Just a few of the old districts like Zeitoun, where we lived, in the old quarter of the city. You could see all the way from the Saraya[57] to the Mediterranean Sea. There were just small roads with many sand dunes and little clusters of houses. We rented a house and a small piece of land. We lived on our land

most of the time, even though we had the stone house, because
a Bedouin always feels like he is a captive in the city. We planted
vegetables and we had fruit trees. In those days all our vegetables
came from Gaza, and we grew so many big sweet oranges that we
sold them all over the world.'

Four years later, in 1956, Israel invaded Gaza. Abu Baha was 17,
old enough to remember the event quite clearly, but he says little
about this brief first Israeli invasion.

'When the Israelis came into Gaza, we fled through the orange
groves to escape them. I remember they stole my father's car. But
they didn't stay in Gaza very long. After just a few months they left.'

In November 1956 the Israeli military rounded up Palestinians, men and boys, in the city of Rafah, herded them into a local
school and killed around 111 in one bloody day that elderly men
and women from in and around Rafah have never forgotten.[58] But
Abu Baha says nothing about this. Even in a place as small as Gaza,
people have extraordinarily different versions of the same history.

At the end of the 1950s, Abu Baha graduated from high school
and left Gaza to study geography at Alexandria University. Afterwards he returned to the Strip to teach.

'I was a geography teacher there for three years, and –' he gives
me a sudden playful look, his small eyes twinkling – 'I married one
of my students!'

Firyal and Abu Baha married in 1964. Afterwards he was
offered a teaching post in Doha. They moved to the Gulf and lived
there for almost thirty years.

When Israel ceded some administrative control of Gaza
(though not the Jewish settlements inside Gaza) to the Palestinian
Authority in 1994, Gazans living outside began to return to the

Strip – including Abu Baha, his wife and their children. He tells me that, on his return, one of the first things he did was to revisit his birthplace, the Wadi of Pleasure, which now lies inside the state of Israel.

Leaning forward in my seat, I ask Abu Baha what it was like, returning to his birthplace. I can see that he has anticipated the question.

'I will show you,' he says, rising to his feet.

In the hallway of his uncluttered home, half a dozen sepia photographs are mounted on the walls, each in a heavy gold frame. They are treasured old photographs of parents, families and large Bedouin gatherings. The women are wearing ornate headdresses fringed with small coins. In the middle is a photo of a man standing in wide, open countryside. Just a fringe of trees in the background and a flat mound of stones beside him, an empty space that looks as though it was once filled. Abu Baha stands to one side of the picture.

'That was Wadi al-Baha,' he says, 'the remains of it. I didn't stay long. Because there was nothing, nothing but these stones. You see them?'

I nod.

'That was the house my father built, the Villa.'

We stand in silence together, gazing into the photograph.

'Is it still painful, looking at it after all these years?' I ask him quietly.

When he doesn't answer, I turn to look at him. Abu Baha nods, still smiling.

'You know, I keep it here for my children, and their children, to see. So we never forget where we really come from.'

Epilogue

I left Gaza at the end of October 2010. Months later, at the beginning of the following spring, the Arab world erupted. From Tunisia to Yemen people poured through streets and into city squares clamouring for change. Within months stale repressive old dictatorships across the region seemed fragile, doomed even, as their own people took up against them. When the Egyptian President Mohammed Hosni Mubarak was forced out of office, the new government of Egypt committed itself to increasing Gazans' freedom of movement in and out of the Strip via the southern crossing at Rafah. And young people in Gaza poured into the streets too, shouting for their own revolution.

But the Arab Spring didn't come to Gaza. When I asked my Gazan friends why, their answers were all remarkably similar. The youth demonstrations had been quickly, violently quashed by Hamas, and many demonstrators beaten and cowed. 'Egypt is a big country, but we are very small and Hamas is too strong for us,' one of them e-mailed me. 'Now we are living under two occupations: Hamas and Israel.'

At the end of October 2012, I came back to Gaza again because I still missed my friends and old colleagues and wanted to see how they were faring. It was a brief visit of just two weeks. But it was enough time to see Saida, now married and holding her first baby, and to see Shadi, who gave me his usual effusive welcome. Shadi and his family have decided to stay in Gaza after all. 'We belong here, this place is part of us', he said, with his crooked, happy-sad smile.

My friends and colleagues were the same wonderful people, but Gaza looked so different, on the surface at least. I was taken aback by the smooth new tarmac roads stretching across the Strip, and the swathe of brightly lit new hotels, restaurants, cafés and supermarkets around the centre of Gaza City, including the gleaming new five-star ArcMed Al Mashtal Hotel (which had stood unfinished for years), with its sumptuous landscaped swimming pool.

Where has all this new money come from, I asked my friends. They told me about the 800 new local millionaires (most of whom own tunnels down in Rafah), and about the opportunities open to people with strong Hamas connections – while the gap between the minority rich and majority poor has become a gaping chasm, as the Israeli siege drags on. Then they described the rise of Hamas: how the movement has consolidated its power by tolerating no dissent, using Israel's continuing siege and Western international sanctions to justify its increasingly repressive regime. One of my friends calls this Hamas's 'policy of self-absolution'.

Having secured its political supremacy in Gaza, Hamas is now quite literally a force to be reckoned with. During my visit, violence between Israel and Hamas ratcheted up once again. When I left, on 12 November, I had a feeling in my stomach that something bad was going to happen. Twenty-four hours later, Israel assassinated the Hamas military commander Ahmed al-Jabari and began its latest military assault on Gaza.

Western sanctions against Hamas have served no purpose and have utterly failed to protect civilians inside Gaza. Hamas may respond to international dialogue, as the movement now seeks further international legitimacy. The continued isolation of Hamas by Western governments, however, will only strengthen the militants within the movement, not those who are prepared to seek change through dialogue. But these horrifying escalations of violence between Hamas and Israel, where the overwhelming majority of people killed are always Gazans, will continue for as long as Israel maintains its military occupation of Palestine, including its siege of Gaza, which is now in its seventh year.

Acknowledgements

I owe a huge debt of thanks to my colleagues and friends inside Gaza. First, a massive and heartfelt *shukran* to Raji Sourani and his team of indomitable human rights defenders in Gaza City, who continue to hold Israeli and Palestinian perpetrators of human rights abuses to account, whilst living under siege themselves. It was a privilege to work with you. Special thanks to Khalil, Hamdi, Mona, Jehan, Reem, and of course Salah!

A million thanks to my wonderful community of friends across Gaza, for their laughter, generosity and support: to Zekra and her family – who literally made me one of their own; to Khalil, Zahia and their family; to Tamer, Safah, Aitemad, the sublimely talented Soumaya El Sousi, Adham, Mohammed El Majdelawi, Dr Mona, Assma, Said Al Madhoun, Manwah and her family up in Beit Hanoun; and to Faiza and her parents, her sister Saida and their neighbours (especially J'meah) down in Rafah. Thanks to Donna for inviting me out to sea. Thanks to Saber Al Zaneen, who taught me about true resistance, and to his family. Thanks also to Miriam and Mohammed who always make me feel welcome, and to Sabri, for his wise instruction. Thank you to all the staff at café Mazaj, to Samir at the Al Deira hotel, to Mohammed the taxi driver for laughter and cigarettes, to Fathers Alexius and Andreas for their grace, and to Tariq Mukhimer, Louise, Darah and Sarah M.

Thank you to all the individuals and families in Gaza who shared their often very painful stories with me. Many thanks to

Andrea and Kathy, for their vital practical assistance. Over in the West Bank, thank you Raja, for guiding me to Palestine in the first place and being my good friend the whole time I was there. Thank you to Ashraf, Anne of Paris, Samer for my first Arabic words, Stuart Shepherd – and thank you Mesky, for being such an inspiring, joyful and kind friend.

Closer to home, I want to thank Bev Cohen and Lawrence Joffe for their wonderful editing expertise, my literary agent David Grossman for his wisdom and unfailing support, my publisher Lynn Gaspard, and my brilliant motley crew of friends: Rahul, Geraint, Gica, Jan, Nick Thorpe, Stephen, Heather, Adam Salmon, Tuesday, Peter, Myriam and Rhemie, Katie, Jo and Kyna, Siri, Pat, Rania and Chris, Mike Stewart, Helen, Carol and Sue B. Thanks to Karin for a summer in her perfect 'casita'. Extra special thanks to the 'A team', including Lorna Miller, Trish, Ruth, Anja, Cath and Amy Duncan, who each typed for me when my fingers literally failed. And thanks indeed to Ma and Richard for their love, support, and many desperately needed glasses of red wine.

Notes

1. After Hamas's takeover, Israel stated that it would allow only basic humanitarian supplies into Gaza. A list of 'duel use' items, including fertilisers and steel pipes, were banned on the pretext that they could be used in manufacturing weapons. Construction materials were also banned, plus tinned fruit, mineral water and numerous other items. At one point the list included pasta. Israel only published an itemised list of the banned goods in June 2010.

2. For those who want to know more, Palestinian Islamic Jihad (PIJ) was set up in the late 1970s, inspired by its namesake in Egypt. PIJ operated out of Gaza until 1987, when it was exiled to Lebanon. Its HQ is now in Damascus, but its forces' operations are in the West Bank and Gaza. PIJ has carried out dozens of suicide bombings in Israel, often targeting Israeli civilians.

3. Abu means 'father of', so Abu Ali means 'father of Ali'. Umm Ali means 'mother of Ali'.

4. The Gaza Strip needs around 240 megawatts (MW) of electricity per day, in winter, to maintain normal services. Functioning at full capacity, the Gaza power plant supplies 103 MW of electricity, supplying almost 700,000 people, nearly half the local population. The rest comes from Israel (100 MW) and from Egypt (17 MW). See pchrgaza.org

5. Fatah was founded in 1959 by diaspora Palestinian refugees, including Yasser Arafat, with the aim of liberating Palestine from Israeli occupation. The name Fatah is the reverse acronym of 'Palestine National Liberation Movement' in Arabic. 'Fatah' is also used in religious discourse to signify the early expansion of Islam, referring to the seventh-century Hudaybiyyah Treaty between Mecca and Medina, when many people converted to Islam, strengthening the new religion.

6. http://198.62.75.1/www1/ofm/mad/discussion/127discuss.html

7. Hamas was founded in Gaza in December 1987 by, among others, a nearly blind quadriplegic called Sheikh Ahmed Yassin. Israel tacitly supported Hamas at first, hoping it would undermine Fatah. But Yassin et al. rejected all negotiations with Israel and developed Hamas's military capabilities to carry out operations against Israel: 'Anything that would give the Israelis sleepless nights' (Zaki Chehab, *Inside Hamas*, New York: Nation Books, 2007, p. 22). When Yassin was assassinated by Israel in March 2004, this only galvanised Hamas and in January 2006, the movement won the Palestinian national elections, ousting Fatah. During the Hamas takeover of Gaza in June 2007, many, but not all, Fatah activists fled to the West Bank.

8. Al-Qassam is named after Izzedine al-Qassam, born in 1882 in Jabla, originally a

Phoenician settlement on Syria's Mediterranean coast. A Shari'a judge, he later created a militant movement of *jihadi* cells that attacked Jewish settlements, to prevent Jews immigrating to Palestine. Al-Qassam was killed in northern Palestine on 20 November 1935, during a battle with British police, and hailed as a Palestinian *shahid*, or 'martyr'.

9. According to the historian Gerald Butt, the land of Canaan 'truly came into existence' between 1800 and 1500 BC, and Gaza became its capital. Canaan was later absorbed into vast ancient Egypt. The Assyrians occupied Gaza about 730 BC, followed by the Babylonians. Their king, Nebuchadnezzar, so the story goes, built the luscious hanging gardens of Babylon some time around 600 BC for his homesick wife, Amytis, who was pining for the trees and fragrant blossoms of her homeland, Media – now part of Iran. The hanging gardens were apparently destroyed by earthquakes after 200 BC. But some cynical old men claimed they were never more than the poetic creation of a fabulist. Gerald Butt, *Life at the Crossroads: A History of Gaza*, Nicosia/London: Rimal Books, 1995, p. 27.

10. Gazans are permitted to visit the West Bank and Jerusalem, but have to obtain a permit from the Israeli authorities in order to do so: these permits are often denied, or issued for only a few days, or even hours. Palestinians from the West Bank and Jerusalem are not permitted to visit Gaza.

11. Palestinians use the Israeli shekel as their currency.

12. In 2007 there were approximately 650 permanent and temporary Israeli checkpoints across the West Bank and East Jerusalem, all manned by the IDF. (Source: Office for the Coordination of Humanitarian Affairs [OCHA].)

13. Every Gazan who wants to travel to the West Bank, Jerusalem or Israel has to secure a permit from the Israeli authorities to do so. This involves, first, applying to the Palestinian District Coordination Office (DCO) in Gaza, which assesses the application. If accepted, it is then passed to the Israeli DCO, which decides if the individual can pass through the Erez crossing. If so, the Israeli DCO in turn passes the application on to the Israeli Coordinator of Government Activities in the Territories (COGAT), a unit within the Israeli Ministry of Defence that coordinates civilian issues between Israel, international organisations and the Palestinian Authority. Permit applications from Gaza go to a unit within COGAT, called the Coordination and Liaison Administration of the Gaza Strip, headed by a colonel from the Israel Defense Forces (IDF). Gazans can receive permits to visit the West Bank for one day, or even just for a few hours. Unmarried Gazan men under 35 rarely receive permits. Gazans also need permits to visit, live, work or study in the West Bank.

14. See Gerald Butt, *Life at the Crossroads*, p. 87.

15. Martin A. Meyer, *A History of the City of Gaza*, New York: Columbia University Press, 1907, p. 121.

16. The PLO leader, Yasser Arafat, made this maxim famous back in 1995, when, at a speech celebrating the birth of his daughter, he said that anyone who did not accept Jerusalem as the capital of Palestine could 'drink from the sea of Gaza'.

17. Eight refugee camps were established in the Gaza Strip in the aftermath of the 1948 *Nakba* ('Catastrophe'), when around 700,000 Palestinians were expelled from their homes by the Zionists and fled to Gaza, the West Bank and

neighbouring Arab states like Jordan and Lebanon. Many Palestinians still keep the keys to their former homes. Jabalya is the largest refugee camp in the Gaza Strip. In total, UNRWA assists some 5 million registered Palestinian refugees across the region.

18. The city of Rafah was split between Egypt and Gaza in 1978, when Egypt and Israel signed the Camp David Peace Accord, and Israel withdrew from the Sinai Peninsula. The buffer zone between the two sides, which stretches for 8.6 miles, is known as the Philadelphia corridor and is currently controlled by Hamas.

19. When Hamas took over Gaza in June 2007, they sacked all police and security personnel employed by the Palestinian Authority (PA), the majority of whom were Fatah supporters. Thousands of ex-police and others remain out of work in Gaza, but still receive their salaries from the PA, which wants to keep them on side.

20. Batis was loyal to the Persians, who invaded and occupied Gaza around 525 BC as a prelude to marching on to their real goal, neighbouring ancient Egypt. Under their rule, Gaza became a citadel, a crossroads between Persian Asia and Persian Egypt, and continued to be a major regional trading hub.

21. In November 2005 the Access and Movement Agreement (AMA) was signed by Israel and the Palestinian Authority (PA) to 'facilitate the movement of people and goods within the Palestinian Territories'. The Rafah crossing opened that month and remained open until June 2006, monitored by international observers. However, exports from Gaza were not permitted, despite this having previously been agreed. From June 2006 Israel closed the Rafah crossing for 86 per cent of working days, citing security reasons. The crossing was sealed after the June 2007 Hamas takeover, when Hamas prevented PA officials from carrying out their designated AMA duties. (Source: Office for the Coordination of Humanitarian Affairs occupied Palestinian territory [OCHA-oPt], November 2006 report on AMA; and www.aljazeerah.info)

22. Intifada literally means 'to shake off'. In September 2000 former Israeli Prime Minister Ariel Sharon visited Jerusalem's Temple Mount, which is sacred to both Jews and Muslims. Many Palestinians considered this a deliberate provocation. When some threw stones at Jews worshipping at the Western Wall, the Israeli military retaliated, killing five Palestinians and triggering the second intifada, which spread from Jerusalem to Gaza and the West Bank. When a ceasefire was finally agreed in February 2005, at least 3,307 Palestinians had been killed, including 654 children, and 972 Israelis, including 117 children. (Source: crimesofwar.org)

23. Drones are aerial vehicles with no human crew on board. Some carry 'lethal payloads', or missiles. Among other drones, Israel uses the Hermes 450, nicknamed Zik, which takes video footage and stills images.

24. Israeli administrative detention (AD) is detention without charge or trial, authorised by administrative order as opposed to judicial decree. Under international law, AD is permitted under certain circumstances. However, according to some international and Israeli human rights groups, Israel's use of AD 'blatantly violates these restrictions' as it has 'administratively detained thousands of Palestinians for prolonged periods of time without prosecuting them, without informing them of

the charges against them, and without allowing them or their attorneys to study the evidence [against them]'. (Source: btselem.org)

25. According to the ICRC, Israel claims it has had no 'Coordination partner' in Gaza to facilitate the prison visits after the Hamas takeover. The ICRC states that Israel '[i]s entitled to take measures to ensure its security – but it is not entitled to prevent Palestinians from visiting their relatives in jail in Israel.' Under Article 49 of the Geneva Convention, 'Individual or mass forcible transfers as well as deportations of protected persons from occupied territory to the territory of the Occupying Power [...] are prohibited [...].' It is worth noting that Hamas denied the ICRC access to Israeli hostage Gilad Shalit.

26. *Dabke* means 'stamping of the feet' and this energetic line dancing is the most popular Arab folk dance in Palestine, Iraq, Jordan, Syria and Lebanon. It originated in the Levant, so the story goes, when stone houses were roofed with mud and straw, which had to be stamped on to make it compact. The roofers developed *dabke* dances and songs to make their work more fun.

27. Mumtaz Doghmush established the Army of Islam as his private militia in 2006. When his 'soldiers' kidnapped Alan Johnston in March 2007, Mumtaz ignored pleas from Doghmush clan elders to release the journalist, who was later freed by Hamas. The Army of Islam is influenced by, but not affiliated to, al-Qaeda. Since taking over Gaza, Hamas has brutally stamped on the power of the Gaza clans, including the Doghmush, who used to wield huge power across the Strip. Alan Johnston's kidnap may well have been an attempt by Mumtaz to reassert himself as a power figure in Gaza.

28. The Salafists are an extreme Islamic movement inspired by early Islam. The first three generations of Muslims, sometimes known as 'the Pious Predecessors', are the inspiration for their orthodox interpretation of Islamic law and practice. The Salafists are Sunni Muslims who believe that Islam has declined because pure Islamic teachings have been abandoned. A minority of them are violent *jihadis*.

29. The keffiyeh is a traditional Arab headdress, usually worn by men. Its distinct check weave has been described as the pattern of fishing nets. It was a trademark of Yasser Arafat, who was rarely seen without one.

30. In October 1956 Israel invaded Egypt, with the backing of Britain and France, which both wanted to topple President Nasser after he had nationalised the Suez Canal. Israel briefly occupied Gaza and the Egyptian Sinai peninsula until UN Emergency Forces replaced the Israelis in March 1957. Egypt regained control of Gaza and held it until the 1967 Six-Day War.

31. On 12 April 1984 four Gazans hijacked an Israeli 300 bus and drove it south of Gaza City, pursued by the Israeli military. An IDF unit then stormed the bus, killing two of the hijackers. The other two were captured alive, but killed in detention, apparently on the orders of the Israeli secret service, Shin Bet. (Source: http://www.haaretz.com/print-edition/news/newly-released-papers-reveal-how-shin-bet-tried-to-hide-bus-300-killings-1.386889)

32. Certain categories of Gazans are consistently denied permits to cross Erez, especially unmarried men under the age of 35, whom Israel considers the highest 'terrorist' risk group. In my own experience, local human rights workers are also frequently blacklisted.

33. The buffer zone was established in 1995 as part of the ongoing Israeli-Palestinian Interim Agreement ('Oslo 2'). Originally it was 50 metres wide, but when the second intifada kicked off, Israel unilaterally extended the zone to 150 metres, all of it inside Gaza. From mid-2008 Israel extended the buffer zone to 300 metres, severely restricting local Palestinian farmers' access to their own land.

34. A dunam is equal to about 900 square metres.

35. The Givati Brigade, formed in December 1947, played an active role in the 1948 establishment of the state of Israel. It now operates as part of the IDF Southern Command and its troops have been deployed inside Gaza during military operations. According to Palestinian historians, the brigade may have been involved in the 'ethnic cleansing' of Dimra village during Operation Yo'av. (Source: Palestineremembered.com/Gaza/Dimra/index.html)

36. Between September 2000 and June 2008, 580 Palestinian children were killed by the Israeli military. (Source: pchrgaza.org)

37. Hani Sha'ban Naim was killed on 7 February 2008 at Beit Hanoun Secondary Agricultural School. He was 41 years old. (Source: http://electronicintifada.net/content/seven-gazans-killed-day-israeli-air-shelling-attacks/3316)

38. Gerald Butt, *Life at the Crossroads*, p. 78.

39. They were both at it: Israeli and Gazan forces fired volleys of missiles towards each other during the countdown to the 6 AM *tahdiya* on 19 June 2008.

40. For information on the Free Gaza movement, see freegaza.org

41. The 1993 Oslo Accords were the first direct agreement between the government of Israel and the PLO. They were intended as a framework for future negotiations, during which 'final status issues' such as the status of Jerusalem and the right of return of Palestinian refugees would be settled. These issues, however, remain unresolved.

42. Sonic booms are shock waves caused by objects travelling faster than the speed of sound and can create enough pressure to blow out windows. Israel has frequently used sonic booms against the population of Gaza.

43. The small Israeli city of Sderot lies 1 kilometre from Beit Hanoun.

44. See Susan Beckerleg: http://www.assatashakur.org/forum/they-all-look-like-them/1135-origins-status-african-palestinians.html

45. Physicians for Human Rights – Israel, 'Holding Health to Ransom – GSS [Israel's General Security Service] Interrogation and Extortion of Palestinian Patients at Erez Crossing, August 2008. See phr.org.il

46. Extract from a review by Ibrahim Darwish of Gerald Butt's *Life at the Crossroads*, published in *Al Quds al Arabi*, Vol. 21, Issue 6211 (Monday 25 May 2009), p. 10.

47. Figures from the Palestinian Centre for Human Rights.

48. None of the buildings surrounding the 'Olaiwa home had been bombed and there was no evidence of fighting in the immediate vicinity. This indicates that the Israeli military either misfired a shell or else fired a shell at random that struck the apartment, killing Amal 'Olaiwa and her four children.

49. Rory McCarthy, *Guardian*, 19 January 2009. Estimates vary as to how many of the al-Samounis were killed: McCarthy, quoting the head of Gaza's Emergency Medical Services, reported forty-eight dead; the Palestinian Centre for Human Rights (PCHR) reported twenty-seven dead. (Source: http://www.pchrgaza.org/

portal/en/index.php?option=com_content&view=article&id=8023:5-january-2009-amal-al-samouni-&catid=144:new-reports); and the Israeli journalist Amira Hass, who spent almost four months inside Gaza after Operation Cast Lead, later reported twenty-nine had been killed. (Source: http://www.haaretz.com/death-in-the-samouni-compound-1.7284)

50. On 5 January 2009 three members of the Abdul-Dayem family were killed by Israeli flechettes (4-centimetre-long metal darts that pierce human bone); two other membersofthesamefamilylaterdiedoftheirinjuries.(Source:http://www.pchrgaza.org/portal/en/index.php?option=com_content&view=article&id=3802:war-crimes-against-children-&catid=47:special-reports&Itemid=191) On 6 January, twenty-one members of the al-Dayah family were killed inside their home in Zeitoun when an Israeli bomb destroyed the house. Radwan al-Dayah, who was critically injured in the attack, died in hospital. Israel later admitted the attack on the al-Dayah home had been a mistake. On 16 January, Muhammad Shurrab was in a car with his sons Kassab and Ibrahim when their vehicle was shot at by Israeli soldiers. Kassab was killed instantly. Ibrahim bled to death in front of his father as the Israeli soldiers prevented an ambulance from evacuating him, though the attack took place during a three-hour 'ceasefire' agreed by Israel for Gaza civilians to move around, buy supplies etc. (Source: http://english.ahram.org.eg/NewsContentPrint/2/0/52467/World/0/Israel-to-compensate-Gaza-family-over-war-deaths.aspx)

51. The tunnels in northern Gaza are not used for smuggling, but link houses together, creating passageways for fighters to move from one street to the next unobserved by the Israeli military.

52. Source: http://www.saudiaramcoworld.com/issue/199405/gaza-contested.crossroads.htm

53. The Palestinian Ministry of Tourism and Antiquities was set up in 1994, but has been very lax in preserving Gaza's ancient treasures.

54. These were imitation Greek coins: small, fine discs of silver, engraved with the image of the goddess Athena and her sacred owl, but minted in Gaza during the Persian era, though Persian coins never circulated in Gaza. Two of these silver coins are now on display at the British Museum in London.

55. Source: http://www.firstworldwar.com/diaries/sapperinpalestine.htm

56. There is another Commonwealth cemetery, in Gaza City, holding 3,050 graves of men who died during the First and Second World Wars. Like the cemetery in Zuweida, it is meticulously maintained. The Gaza City cemetery is tended by Ibrahim Jeradah (MBE), who has been the keeper of the cemetery for some fifty years.

57. The Saraya, in the centre of Gaza City, used to be the headquarters of the Israeli military in Gaza and is now the HQ of the Hamas police and intelligence services.

58. This massacre was first documented by the UN in 1956, and recently investigated by Joe Sacco in his graphic novel, *Footnotes in Gaza*, London: Jonathan Cape, 2009.